Inside
Prince Caspian

Inside
Prince Caspian

A Guide to Exploring
the Return to Narnia

Devin Brown

BakerBooks
Grand Rapids, Michigan

© 2008 by Devin Brown

Published by Baker Books
a division of Baker Publishing Group
P.O. Box 6287, Grand Rapids, MI 49516-6287
www.bakerbooks.com

Third printing, March 2008

Printed in the United States of America

Library of Congress Cataloging-in-Publication Data
Brown, Devin.
    Inside Prince Caspian : a guide to exploring the return to Narnia / Devin
Brown.
        p.   cm.
    Includes bibliographical references.
    ISBN 978-0-8010-6802-7 (pbk.)
    1. Lewis, C. S. (Clive Staples), 1898–1963. Prince Caspian. 2. Children's sto-
ries, English—History and criticism. 3. Christian fiction, English—History and
criticism. 4. Fantasy fiction, English—History and criticism. 5. Narnia (Imaginary place) I. Title.
PR6023.E926P76325 2008
823'.912—dc22   2007037055

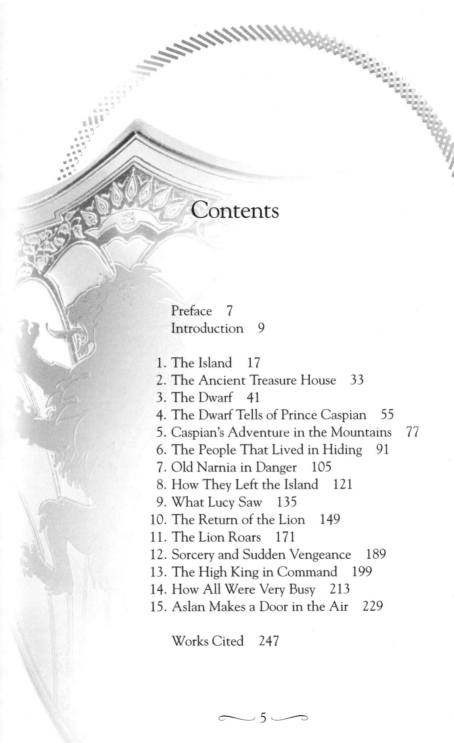

Contents

Preface

I would like to welcome those of you who read my earlier book, *Inside Narnia: A Guide to Exploring The Lion, the Witch and the Wardrobe*, and to say that in this second book I hope to provide the same sort of in-depth analysis, this time focusing on *Prince Caspian*. To new readers, I would also like to say welcome and to briefly explain my approach.

Even before Walden Media announced plans for the 2005 film adaptation of *The Lion, the Witch and the Wardrobe*, there were already a good number of books about C. S. Lewis and the Chronicles of Narnia. With the movie's release, this number has increased so much that I feel compelled to open with the same question I raised in the preface to *Inside Narnia*.

"Why another Lewis book?"

My answer is the same as before. First, unlike most books about Narnia, mine takes a *literary* rather than a purely *devotional* approach. This means that while I discuss the story's devotional aspects, I include many other elements as well. Second, in nearly all the works written about Narnia, each of the seven Chronicles is typically covered in just a single chapter. By devoting an entire work to *Prince Caspian*, as I did previously for *The Lion, the Witch and the Wardrobe*, I hope to provide the kind of detailed examination Lewis's writing merits and also to supply a good number of connections to Lewis's life and his other writings.

As before, I try to offer a sampling of the very best comments and opinions from other Lewis scholars—and there are many more of these to examine this time around. Also, I again include lots of connections to other works that influenced Lewis, especially those written by his friend and fellow Inkling J. R. R. Tolkien. Tolkien and Lewis read their stories aloud to each other, so they often shared many aspects in common, and these commonalities help us to better understand the work of both authors.

Inside Narnia and *Inside Prince Caspian* are intended to be commentaries on Lewis's stories, not substitutes for them. I assume that readers have finished *Prince Caspian* and so will not become irritated at any spoilers that appear. In order to help anyone who may want to switch back and forth between my book and Lewis's, each of my chapters has the same number and name as the corresponding chapter from *Prince Caspian*.

To make reading a little easier this time, when referencing material I indicate the source or author within the text, with the page number in parentheses following the material. For example: Paul Ford describes Old Narnia as an enchanted world where "courtesy, honor, and the spirit of adventure are the respected virtues, and in which hospitality is graciously offered" (316). By looking up the author or source in the bibliography (in this case, Paul Ford), readers can track down any material they would like to examine on their own. To keep citations to a minimum, when I have two or more quotes within the same paragraph from the same page of any source, I include the page number for only the first quotation.

My hope once again is to provide the kind of lively, in-depth discussion that Lewis fans both old and new—and even Lewis himself—would enjoy.

Finally, for their valuable suggestions and encouragement, I would like to thank Marvin Hinten, Jonathan Rogers, Stephen Yandell, and Karen Koehn.

Now on to *Prince Caspian*!

Introduction

Near the end of March 1949, C. S. Lewis put down his pen, leaned back in his chair, and gave a long sigh of contentment. He had completed the final handwritten manuscript of *The Lion, the Witch and the Wardrobe*.

Some people assume that after Lewis mailed off this first book about Narnia to his London publisher, Geoffrey Bles, he just sat around and waited until it was released in October of 1950, then, after reading the reviews, got out his pen and paper again and sat down to write *Prince Caspian* for publication a year later.

What actually happened was more complicated—and more amazing.

According to Lewis biographers Roger Lancelyn Green and Walter Hooper, after shutting the door on the wardrobe for the last time, Lewis immediately began working on a sequel but found it hard to create a second Narnia story. Three months after finishing the manuscript of *The Lion, the Witch and the Wardrobe*, Lewis had written the first two chapters of a new story about a boy named Digory who understands the speech of animals and trees. However, while building a raft with Polly, the girl next door, Digory cuts off a branch from an oak tree and loses his special powers. His godmother, a woman named Mrs. Lefay, mysteriously shows up, appears to understand what Digory has done, and seems inclined to help.

This is as far as Lewis had gotten in the story on June 14, 1949, when he met with Green and read aloud the opening chapters. It would be as far as he ever got.

Now referred to as the Lefay Fragment, this first attempt at a second Narnia book turned out to be a false start, and Lewis abandoned it shortly after reading it to Green. Later he would go on to tell a different story about Digory and Polly, one that would be published in 1955 as *The Magician's Nephew*, the sixth book in the series. There Mrs. Lefay is described as one of the last mortals with fairy blood and is introduced as the godmother not of Digory but of Digory's uncle. Years after Lewis's death, the Lefay Fragment was included by Walter Hooper in *Past Watchful Dragons* (56–72).

Realizing that he had come to a dead end with his first attempt at a sequel, Lewis promptly set off in a different direction, and this time his creative energies exploded. In an astounding eighteen-month period between the summer of 1949 and late winter of 1951, Lewis began and finished four of the most beloved and most successful children's works of all time. In order of creation, they were *Prince Caspian*, *The Voyage of the* Dawn Treader, *The Horse and His Boy*, and *The Silver Chair*.

On December 20, 1951, long before the Narnia series became a runaway classic, Lewis wrote to a friend, "I am going to be (if I live long enough) one of those men who *was* a famous writer in his forties and dies unknown" (*Letters of C.S. Lewis* 415). The former fame Lewis refers to is the international acclaim that followed *The Screwtape Letters*, published in 1942, and culminated on September 8, 1947, with Lewis's picture on the cover of *Time* magazine.

Lewis did not yet realize what he had accomplished in writing those first five Narnia books. When *Prince Caspian* was published on October 15, 1951, as the second installment in what would become a seven-volume set, Lewis could not foresee that one day he would be known around the world as the man who created the Chronicles of Narnia.

A Look Back at the First Film

Before moving on to explore *Prince Caspian*, I would like to offer some reflections of Walden's first Narnia movie since it has played such a large role in introducing a new audience to Lewis's stories.

In my opinion, the only thing better than seeing Andrew Adamson's film adaptation of *The Lion, the Witch and the Wardrobe* would be to read the original book version.

There are several things the movie actually does better than the book. While director Peter Jackson had to shrink Tolkien's huge trilogy down to movie length, director Andrew Adamson had a modest-sized book that allowed him to expand and extend some elements and, in this way, improve them. Three examples of this kind of improvement are particularly noteworthy.

First, while Lewis's narrator simply *tells* us that this story is about something that happened when four children "were sent away from London during the war because of the air-raids" (3), the movie *shows* us the bombing and the sense of powerlessness it created. When the children arrive in Narnia, they discover not only that they can help but that they are the only ones who can make a difference in the outcome of the war there. Thus Narnia becomes not merely an enchanting escape for the four refugees but a place where their actions have a real impact. Furthermore, with the addition of Adamson's London scenes, the fantasy world of Narnia has a direct parallel to the real world since Narnia also is overshadowed by a tyrant whose endless desire to dominate must be stopped. In the film, Peter sees young men who are not much older than he is leaving London to fight. Soon he himself must rise to a similar challenge.

Second, after Lucy arrives at the lamp-post, we read in the book that she heard "a pitter patter of feet coming toward her," and then that "a very strange person stepped out from among the trees into the light of the lamp-post" (9). In the film, this "pitter patter" is extended into several wonderful moments of suspense that mix mystery, marvel, and even a little fear. When Mr. Tumnus finally pops out, we share Lucy's astonishment to a much greater extent than we do in the book.

Third, the scene in which Mr. Beaver first speaks in the film is also extended in a marvelous way, and once again we share the children's surprise and awe—as we are meant to. Peter calls to the Beaver as he would a non-talking beaver in our world, trying to get him to come to him, and this makes the moment when Mr. Beaver finally talks even more striking than in Lewis's original.

In these three ways the film is able to improve upon the book.

In other ways the movie does not quite live up to its source. It does not fully capture the emotional highs and lows of the original, and this is unfortunate. Nor is it able to evoke the profound feeling of awe associated with Aslan.

On the walk to the Stone Table, Lewis depicts Aslan as being both sadder and more vulnerable than he appears in the movie. The narrator tells us, "Both the girls cried bitterly (though they hardly knew why) and clung to the Lion and kissed his mane and his nose and his paws and his great, sad eyes" (150). There is not much crying in the film, nor is it ever this intense. After the execution, Lewis has his narrator step in again to say, "I hope no one who reads this book has been quite as miserable as Susan and Lucy were that night; but if you have been—if you've been up all night and cried till you have no more tears left in you—you will know that there comes in the end a sort of quietness" (158). Adamson's adaptation never reaches this low, and perhaps because of this, it also fails to evoke as great a feeling of joy when Aslan returns to life.

Perhaps one reason the movie is not able to live up to its source in this area has to do with the lack of the story's narrator, who not only adds and explains but also uses poetic and metaphoric language to heighten the emotional intensity. When Aslan's name is mentioned for the first time in the book, the narrator breaks in to comment:

> Perhaps it has sometimes happened to you in a dream that someone says something which you don't understand but in the dream it feels as if it had some enormous meaning—either a terrifying one which turns the whole dream into a nightmare or else a lovely meaning too lovely to put into words, which makes the dream so beautiful

that you remember it all your life and are always wishing you could get into that dream again. It was like that now. (67–68)

The narrator goes on to describe the children's reaction to Aslan's name, typically in simile or metaphor, which adds to the emotional power. All the film can do here is show the somewhat vague reactions on the children's faces.

When Peter, Susan, and Lucy finally meet Aslan, the narrator plays a similar role. It is at this point in the story that we get the famous line, "People who have not been in Narnia sometimes think that *a thing cannot be good and terrible at the same time*" (126, emphasis added). When Aslan roars after his resurrection at the Stone Table, the narrator tells us that "his face became so terrible" that Susan and Lucy "did not dare to look at it" (164). Without recourse to the narrator, Adamson's Aslan, while commendable, is not quite as good as Lewis's and is nowhere near as terrible. It is not that the film Aslan is cuddly—when he roars, he really roars—but his terrible side is not as apparent as it needs to be. It is significant that the film omits the dialogue in which Peter, Susan, and Mr. Beaver argue over who should go up to Aslan first. This dispute would not make sense in the film.

Narnia expert Paul Ford has pointed out the occurrence of "simultaneous awe and delight" that Lewis conveys in the Chronicles, a unique experience Ford labels as numinous (319). While there is sufficient delight associated with the movie Aslan, he fails to generate the same level of awe found in the novel, and for book lovers, this is a significant loss.

Having covered the film's two major lackings, I would now like to turn to four minor ones, items that show a lack of attention to the text. First, the Witch's dwarf should not have eaten the last piece of Turkish Delight, for certainly he knows it is only magic food and, more importantly, that it will lead only to further craving. Second, Edmund needed to clearly apologize to each of his siblings after his talk with Aslan, as he does in the book. Lewis sees apologies—real ones with no excuses—as vital to any forgiveness. Third, Adamson has the wounded Edmund lying alone on the battlefield, but Lewis puts Mrs. Beaver at his side, showing the full reconciliation that has occurred since Edmund's betrayal. Finally, the sense of mystery surrounding the hunting of the White Stag is missing in the film. Lewis makes a point to tell us that the White Stag has the ability to grant wishes, hinting that the four children have a deep but unspoken longing to return to their home and parents at the story's end.

I would still offer my congratulations on a film that in some ways measures up to the book—particularly in the settings of Narnia in winter and the Professor's house—and even improves on Lewis's creation from time to time. To be more fully successful, the filming style on the next Narnia story needs to make better use of the imagination. We should not be shown everything so clearly. The second film needs to find the cinematic equivalent of metaphor, to make better use of sounds and images that suggest but do not fully reveal.

I would also like to say thanks to Andrew Adamson and Walden Media. They have introduced this wonderful story to a large audience who would not have known of it otherwise, and because of the film, many of them will certainly want to read the book. I liked the movie version of *The Lion, the Witch and the Wardrobe* very much and am looking forward to the rest of the films with great anticipation. In *Prince Caspian*, when the children meet Aslan, the narrator tells us, "They felt as glad as anyone can who feels afraid, and as afraid as anyone can who feels glad" (153). This kind of awe, this profound mixture of feelings, will be a high standard for the next film to aim for.

Are They Allegories? What About the Order?

Because of their relevance to *Prince Caspian*, two general statements about the Chronicles of Narnia might be helpful here.

First, most people who have studied the Chronicles closely agree that they are not allegories, that there is not a one-to-one correspondence between the stories and the characters or events in the Bible. Thus Peter is not an allegory for the apostle Peter, Edmund is not supposed to be Judas, and Aslan is more properly considered a Christ-figure than an allegory for Christ.

In addition, many Lewis scholars would argue that the Chronicles should be read in the original order of publication rather than in the revised chronological order, a change that was made after Lewis's death. This would make *The Lion, the Witch and the Wardrobe* first and *Prince Caspian* second, rather than second and fourth as suggested by the numbers on the spines of the chronologically ordered books. By reading the books in order of publication—therefore holding *The Magician's Nephew* until later—readers know only what the four children know and thus are able to share their wonder and delight. Recently a group calling itself the 2456317 Club was created to promote reading the Chronicles in the published order. The club name is based on how the volumes of the chronological edition must be rearranged to get the original order.

The movie adaptations are, at least so far, being released in the original order. This may suggest that the films' creators prefer the order of publication. Alternatively they may have chosen to make *The Lion, the Witch and the Wardrobe* first simply because it was the best known of the seven stories.

And now on to chapter one!

1

The Island

The Dedication

"To Mary Clare Havard."

Technically speaking, these are the first words from Lewis in *Prince Caspian*. So who was Mary Clare Havard, and why would Lewis dedicate a book to her?

Lewis dedicated *The Lion, the Witch and the Wardrobe* to Lucy Barfield. He then added a now-famous paragraph about how she would be too old to read fairy tales when the book was finally published but would possibly start reading them again when she was older. Both Lucy's and Mary Clare's fathers were members of the Inklings, Lewis's writing and discussion group. Humphrey Havard, Mary Clare's father, was also Lewis's physician. The two had met when Dr. Havard was making a house call to treat Lewis for influenza.

Although Mary Clare was about the same age as Lucy, Lewis felt no need to put in a disclaimer about her being too old for fairy tales. The year before, Lewis had asked Mary Clare to read and respond to the typescript of *The Lion, the Witch and the Wardrobe*, and he already knew that she liked this type of story. Many years later, Mary Clare married and had four children of her own. In a letter included in Walter Hooper's *C. S. Lewis: A Companion and Guide*, she notes that her children were all "brought up on the Narnia books" (759). They must have experienced a unique sensation on seeing that *Prince Caspian* had been dedicated to their mother when she was young.

Mary Clare's children could also have found their grandfather memorialized in one of Lewis's books. When Ransom returns home in the second chapter of *Perelandra*, the doctor requested to be present is named Humphrey.

The Story Behind the Title

According to biographers Green and Hooper, Lewis never kept the early drafts of his stories. Once a book appeared in print, he discarded even the final manuscript. Lewis's practice is unfortunate for two reasons.

First, there is something magical about a page of words that have come directly from an author's pen or typewriter. Seeing a manuscript of a well-loved book—better yet, actually holding it and touching it—can take the reader back in time and provide a real connection with the author. This is not to say that certain printed books do not also have the ability to evoke intense feelings, but holding a page of a manuscript that was also held by a favorite author is the next best thing to meeting him or her. Perhaps it is a way of meeting.

While many of the letters Lewis typed or penned still exist, all of the original typed or handwritten pages from his books are gone, except for a couple of plot ideas and early fragments preserved by chance in one of Lewis's notebooks.

Second, without any of the early versions of Lewis's stories, we are not able to see the changes he made between his first draft and the final one—and these changes would not be mere curiosities. Some of them certainly would shed light on Lewis's intentions, on what he was trying to do or say through certain passages, and on what themes and other aspects he was trying to bring out more clearly.

We do know that a number of changes occurred regarding the title of the work that eventually came to be known as *Prince Caspian*. If readers glance at the title page on their way to chapter one, they will notice that Lewis gave a double title to this second Chronicle, the only time he did so in the Narnia series. The full name of the book, *Prince Caspian: The Return to Narnia*, was not Lewis's first title. He originally called the story *Drawn into Narnia*, a name that Green and Hooper note was "changed on the advice of the publisher who thought it would be difficult to say" (309). Lewis's second suggestion, *A Horn in Narnia*, was also rejected by the publisher, who argued that *Prince Caspian* would be more memorable. Lewis insisted on keeping the subtitle *The Return to Narnia* to reflect his original emphasis.

Before we move off the title page, which in most editions is the only place where the subtitle is displayed, several points are worth making. First, the two-part title reflects the fact that this time Lewis will begin by telling two different stories, two separate strands that will eventually be woven together: the story of young Prince Caspian's struggle to free Narnia from a tyrant and gain his rightful throne, and the story of Peter, Susan, Edmund, and Lucy's return for another adventure.

Second, readers may notice Lewis's use of the definite article in *The Return to Narnia*. By calling this second story *the* return, Lewis seems to be saying this would be the only return to Narnia, which, as seen later, is not the case. When Lewis wrote *The Lion, the Witch and the Wardrobe*, he did not think there would be a second book; similarly, when he wrote *Prince Caspian*, he did not think there would be a third Narnia story—at least not in certain terms. This fact is made clear in his *Letters to Children*, in which Lewis states, "When I wrote *The Lion, the Witch and the Wardrobe* I did not know I was going to write any more. Then I wrote *Prince Caspian* as a sequel and still didn't think there would be any more, and when I had done *The Voyage of the Dawn Treader* I felt quite sure it would be the last" (68). Readers may wonder if Lewis's recollection here is an oversimplification, because near the end of *Prince Caspian*, Peter will state that although he and Susan are not going to come back to Narnia, he is "pretty sure" that Aslan intends for Edmund and Lucy to get back "some day" (221).

Third, Lewis's subtitle can hold a second meaning besides simply the return of the four Pevensie children. When the story opens, the land that Peter, Susan, Edmund, and Lucy go back to is not the Narnia the children left behind at the end of *The Lion, the Witch and the Wardrobe*. The kingdom must be set right; it must itself return to being Narnia—Narnia as it was intended to be. This second meaning of *return* is highlighted by Douglas Gresham, Lewis's stepson, in his introduction to the wonderful radio theater version of the story produced by Focus on the Family. Gresham explains the intentions of his stepfather (whom he refers to as Jack):

> A theme of return became a key part of the story. Jack didn't look at a return in [merely] the obvious physical sense but went deeper to consider a restoration, a restoration of those things that are true—true life, true leadership, and mostly true faith. *Prince Caspian* tackles that idea, and broader themes of the battle between good and evil, spiritual obedience and discernment, and ultimately joy—a festive joy when what was wrong has been put right again.

In his well-known work *Companion to Narnia*, Paul Ford notes a parallel between the restoration found in *Prince Caspian* and the chapter "The Scouring of the Shire" from *The Return of the King*, in which Tolkien's hobbits must also return the land, in their case the Shire, to its proper state (18). In one of his letters, Lewis himself made the point that *Prince Caspian* is about "the restoration of the true religion after a corruption" (*The Collected Letters* 1245). In chapter ten of *Prince Caspian*, Aslan will tell Lucy, "Now all Narnia will be renewed" (143).

It is clear that *The Return to Narnia* is a subtitle rich with meaning.

Prince Caspian is equally rich in its illustrations by Pauline Baynes, which for many readers are as cherished as the story itself. The full story of how the young illustrator came to work with Lewis on the seven-volume project and what Lewis thought of the drawings she provided is told in my book *Inside Narnia: A Guide to Exploring The Lion, the Witch and the Wardrobe*.

The Opening

Lewis begins *Prince Caspian* with a phrase identical to the one at the start of *The Lion, the Witch and the Wardrobe*: "Once there were four children whose names were Peter, Susan, Edmund and Lucy" (3). Certainly an author as inventive as Lewis could have found a more original opening if he had wanted to. Almost as if to illustrate this fact, Lewis will begin *The Voyage of the* Dawn Treader, the third volume in the series, with a sentence that is famously original: "There was a boy called Eustace Clarence Scrubb, and he almost deserved it" (3).

So why choose such a commonly used opening as "Once there were four children . . ."? Here in his first five words, Lewis is setting out to evoke the timeless feeling of a fairy-tale opening, to write his own "once upon a time" story with a similar universal, almost mythic, formula. In addition, by using a similar opening for his second book, Lewis may be welcoming back readers who had come to love *The Lion, the Witch and the Wardrobe*.

Next, in a single paragraph, Lewis sums up the events from the first story, explaining how the four children had previously entered Narnia and lived there for years as kings and queens, before returning from an adventure that seemed to take no time at all. Lewis concludes with the statement "no one noticed that they had ever been away" (3). The use of "no one" here seems to refer to Mrs. Macready and perhaps the visitors who are mentioned as still talking out in the hallway at the end of *The Lion, the Witch and the Wardrobe*. Throughout the Chronicles, Lewis will focus on the growth and maturity for which the adventures in Narnia serve as a catalyst. So while no one noticed that the children had been gone, readers must assume that anyone close to the four young people would have noticed a change in them, particularly in Edmund. In chapter ten of *Prince Caspian*, Aslan himself will comment on how Lucy has grown since their first adventure.

A Year Later

Readers are told that all this had happened "a year ago" (3), a phrase that must mean "*about* a year ago" because in *The Lion, the Witch and the Wardrobe*, Edmund tells the White Witch, "I'm at school—at least I was—it's the holidays now" (33). As *Prince Caspian* opens, the holidays are all but over. It is the very last day of the summer break, making it around fourteen months since the first adventure, and the children are waiting on a platform for the trains that will take them to boarding school, in Lucy's case for the first time.

Lewis will choose to have *The Voyage of the* Dawn Treader take place during summer vacation as well. Why choose the same starting time for all three stories? Missing school was not a problem, for in every case the children return to England only a moment after leaving. Perhaps Lewis wanted to give a cyclic feeling to these first three stories, with each book taking place around a year later. Perhaps since the children attend single-gender boarding schools, the holidays provide a convenient time when they are all together. In *The Silver Chair*, Eustace and Jill will leave together for Narnia during the term, which will be atypical. However, they attend an unusual school, Experiment House, which Lewis points out is coeducational.

Jonathan Rogers has made the following observation about the opening setting of *Prince Caspian*: "Four children sit in a sleepy little train station waiting for the trains that will take them back to school. What could be more mundane and unremarkable?" (25). Lewis's point here is that adventures can and often do begin in the most unlikely places. In *The Voyage of the* Dawn Treader, the adventure will begin while Edmund and Lucy are just sitting on a bed.

One further note may be made about Lewis's decision to have the children travel to Narnia from a train platform. Included in the advice the Professor gave the children at the end of *The Lion, the Witch and the Wardrobe* was the promise that their return to Narnia would be unforeseen: "It'll happen when you're not looking for it" (188). One of the biggest lessons Peter must learn in *Prince Caspian* is not to be limited by his preconceptions. In chapter eight, when Trumpkin explains that it was Susan's horn that dragged them off the train platform, Peter will declare he "can hardly believe it" (101) because he had expected that they would be the ones doing the calling. It could also be added that Peter was expecting that they would be traveling to boarding school, not to Narnia, from the train platform.

As Doris Myers has noted, this second Chronicle "deals with a later stage of childhood" (134), a time where the world becomes more complex, and this will become a key point in understanding Lewis's second Narnia tale. The children are chronologically one year older; however, their first adventure has matured them more than the one year alone would have done. From the information in Lewis's "Outline of Narnian History," included in Walter Hooper's reference work *C. S. Lewis: A Companion and Guide* (422), the four children in *Prince Caspian* are now fourteen, thirteen, eleven, and nine.

The children's greater maturity is seen right away as they feel a strange tugging from an invisible force. Instead of panicking, Edmund calls for them to "all catch hands" so they will stay together (5). Readers may be too swept up in the story at this point to notice that Lewis has Edmund take the lead and issue orders here, rather than Peter as might be expected since he is not just the oldest but also the high king. For as hierarchical as some critics find Narnia to be, leadership will actually be far more shared than absolute. In *The Lion, the Witch and the Wardrobe*, Edmund also appeared to act on his own initiative when he decided to go after the Witch's wand, and later when he declared his intention to pursue the White Stag, he again did so without seeking permission from Peter.

Although all four children feel the tugging, Edmund is the first to recognize it as magic. At the start of *The Voyage of the* Dawn Treader, Lewis will give Edmund a similar role and will add an intriguing comment. When Eustace rushes toward an enchanted picture, readers are told that "Edmund, *who knew something about magic*, sprang after him, warning him . . . not to be a fool" (10, emphasis added). Perhaps in both books Lewis wants readers to recall that of all the children, it is Edmund who, through his encounters with the White Witch and his healing by Lucy's cordial, has had the most direct contact with magic and so might know the feeling associated with it better than his siblings. As he states here in *Prince Caspian*, "This is magic—I can tell by the feeling" (5).

Readers who listen carefully to the Focus on the Family Radio Theatre adaptation of *Prince Caspian* will notice an interesting change made in this first scene. There the lines of dialogue that identify the strange force as magic and urge the others to catch hands are said by Peter, not Edmund, thus undoing whatever point Lewis may have intended to convey.

Paul Ford uses the order of the dialogue given here to suggest that it is Lucy who first feels the tug, followed by Edmund, Peter, and Susan respectively. This order can be seen as an indicator of what Ford labels their "relative childlike receptivity to the call into Narnia" (331). This same order will be repeated and become highly significant in chapter eleven, as Aslan is visible first to Lucy, then to Edmund, next to Peter, and finally to Susan.

Never at Home

As he began the story of the Pevensies' second journey to Narnia, Lewis faced the same problem he had encountered a decade earlier in writing the second volume of his space trilogy: how to avoid making the sequel too repetitious. In *Perelandra* Ransom leaves Earth as he did the first time, but Lewis sends him to Venus instead of Mars, journeying in a white casketlike object rather than a spaceship. In *Prince Caspian*, the same four children again are taken out of England, but now they are transported simply by a sudden jerk on a train platform rather than going through a wardrobe. Instead of traveling to the forest near the lamp-post as they did the first time, they now appear in the woods outside of Cair Paravel, their old castle, which now is in ruins.

One similarity that will run throughout all the Chronicles might go unnoticed and so is worth pointing out: when the children travel from England to Narnia, they almost never leave from their home. In *The Lion, the Witch and the Wardrobe*, the four children had been sent away to the Professor's and so depart from there. Here in *Prince Caspian*, they vanish from a train station. In *The Voyage of the* Dawn Treader, Lucy and Edmund will be staying with relatives when they are pulled into Narnia. In *The Silver Chair*, Eustace and Jill will enter Narnia while at school. Digory and Polly will leave from Digory's uncle's house in *The Magician's Nephew*. Finally, in *The Last Battle*, all those who travel from England to Narnia will be riding on trains or again waiting on a platform. Even Shasta, who makes a journey from Calormen to Narnia in *The Horse and His Boy*, does not leave from his own home, which we later learn is in Archenland, but from the home of his surrogate father.

Why would Lewis have his protagonists—with the minor exception of Eustace, whose home seems anything but homey in *The Voyage of the* Dawn Treader—never leave from home? As Alan Jacobs has noted, all of Lewis's children are "somehow disjointed, partly or wholly uprooted" (10). By never depicting the children at home, Lewis is able to evoke a longing for home, for a true home. In an essay titled "The Weight of Glory," Lewis claims that we all have a desire for "our own far off country" (29). In *The Last Battle*, he has Jewel the Unicorn express this longing: "I have come home at last! This is my real country! I belong here" (196).

Good Enough

When the children arrive in what they later learn is Narnia, something is missing. On the first journey, when the four children came out from the wardrobe into Narnia, there was a mysterious sense of enchantment woven into the land. Yes, Narnia was under the control of the White Witch, and she had made it always winter and never Christmas. But somehow, despite this, there was an immediate sense of wonder and awe evoked by the snowy woods and mysterious lamp-post. In *Prince Caspian*, the woods that the children must work their way through hold no enchantment— they are just woods. Later, readers will be told that the Telmarines "are afraid of the woods" and imagine they are "full of ghosts" (55). But there is nothing in these woods to cause fear. There is no sense of any kind of spirits inhabiting them—good or evil. As Colin Manlove has noted, "We are in a more everyday world now" (139).

Because there is no special feeling, Lucy has to ask Peter, "Do you think we can possibly have got back to Narnia?" (5). His answer speaks clearly about the magical quality that has been lost or repressed. Peter responds, "It might be anywhere," a comment that could never have been said about the Narnia of the first book.

In *The Lion, the Witch and the Wardrobe*, Lewis used a formula in creating Narnia that was similar to the one followed by Tolkien in creating Middle-earth: strange but not too strange, familiar but not too familiar. Here at the start of *Prince Caspian*, Lewis intentionally makes Narnia totally familiar, with the kind of overgrown woods that could be found anywhere. The strangeness found in the first story—the strangeness of the evil Witch, the talking animals, and even the very landscape itself—has been lost or, as readers learn later, silenced or pushed underground.

Lucy's question highlights a valid objection to Lewis's first two titles for the book—*Drawn into Narnia* and *A Horn in Narnia*— and actually provides an argument for hiding *The Return to Narnia* on the title page. Displaying any of these titles in large print on the cover would prevent readers from walking alongside the four children because we would know more than they do at this point, a condition Lewis typically avoids.

Tolkien had a similar problem when his publishers chose *The Return of the King* as the title for the final volume of *The Lord of the Rings*. Tolkien's complaint was that it eliminated some of the suspense, because readers would know in advance that Aragorn is going to be successful in reestablishing his rule. In the same way, readers who note Lewis's second title know before the children do that they are back in Narnia.

As Colin Manlove has noted, an element of confusion runs throughout *Prince Caspian* (139), and this is another difference from *The Lion, the Witch and the Wardrobe*. This confusion first manifests itself here in the children's inability to determine if they are in Narnia or not. It will recur as the children are unable to understand why Cair Paravel is in ruins and again when they find it difficult to get their bearings on their way to Aslan's How. Most importantly, this element of confusion will be associated with Aslan's appearances to Lucy. What exactly she and the other children are supposed to do at each point in their adventure is something they must to some extent figure out on their own. This confusion, along with the ambiguity that accompanies it, gives *Prince Caspian* a greater complexity than *The Lion, the Witch and the Wardrobe*. And this complexity makes the land of Narnia more realistic this time, more like the world we live in. As Manlove rightly argues, "The ambiguities of the world as we have experienced them are more native to it than they were in the last book" (140).

Now, as the children climb out of the thicket and reach the sea, Peter mildly declares that this unknown place they have gotten to is "good enough" (6), an ambivalent comment that could never have been made about the earlier Narnia. Edmund agrees to this limited appraisal, pointing out that it is better than "being in a stuffy train on the way back to Latin and French and Algebra!" The happiness the children experience while splashing in the shallows, looking for crabs and shrimp, is genuine, but it is the ordinary kind of happiness experienced by children who can go wading instead of having to return to school.

This ordinariness, this lack of enchantment, is appropriate. King Miraz, the tyrant who holds power over Narnia, is not a wizard. He is not a magical creature like the White Witch. Instead, he is merely a two-bit dictator, the descendant of lowlife pirates, and not particularly bright or imaginative—the same kind of self-seeking autocrat found in minor institutions and backwater organizations of every world. Like his kind everywhere, after he usurps the crown, he does away with his opposition through hunting "accidents," trumped-up charges, and hopeless quests. He will pretend to be fond of his nephew only until he has an heir of his own. Unlike the Witch, who is killed by Aslan at the end of a dramatic battle scene, Miraz will meet his end, very appropriately, by being stabbed in the back by one of his own henchmen after tripping on a "tussock" (194). The repression Miraz imposes on Narnia, while harsh, is as dull and joyless as he is, and so here Lewis gives the landscape a mundane feel, not a magical one. Later the children will find ripe apples, marking the end of summer in Narnia. By making it the same season in both countries, and even the same time of day, Lewis removes yet one more aspect that had made Narnia so special and so different from our world in the first book, where summer became winter and Lucy's day visit became night.

In *The Lion, the Witch and the Wardrobe*, there was a silence in Narnia that was filled with awe. Edmund experienced this eerie silence when he entered the Witch's castle: "There was nothing stirring; not the slightest sound anywhere" (92). There was an opposite kind of awe-filled silence associated with Aslan. In *The Voyage of the* Dawn Treader, the crew will be engulfed in wonder and silence after they leave Ramandu and sail on the Last Sea. By contrast, in *Prince Caspian*, the silence that greets the children on their arrival and the silence they walk in as they search for fresh water is not one that is filled with awe; it is the silence of a land whose life has been stifled, of a land put to sleep and waiting for someone to wake it. If the land of Narnia the children entered the first time was a place where it was always winter and never Christmas, now it is a place with summer but without May Day or the Fourth of July.

What About Those Sandwiches?

Although the four children have grown and matured since the first book, in some ways they must be and must remain the same.

Susan—always the cautious and practical one in *The Lion, the Witch and the Wardrobe*—now brings the frolicking group back to reality, noting, "We shall want something to eat before long" (6). On the next page, she insists that Edmund and Lucy wear their shoes while exploring. In chapter three, when Edmund suggests they will have to swim the thirty or forty yards separating them from the mainland, Susan—although she is the strongest swimmer among them—will express concern about "currents" (31). Susan's chronic worrying is something with which her siblings are well acquainted. In chapter nine, attempting to put a somewhat better face on his older sister's fears, Edmund will tell Trumpkin, "Don't take any notice of her. She always is a wet blanket" (119).

After they find a stream and have a drink, Edmund, who fell victim to the Witch's Turkish Delight in the first book, is still the one most concerned about food and wants to eat the sandwiches right away rather than wait. In *The Lion, the Witch and the Wardrobe*, Lewis depicted Edmund talking "with his mouth full of Turkish Delight" (37). Near the end of this chapter, Edmund will be described similarly as speaking "with his mouth full of apple" (12), a comment that also perhaps says something about Edmund's age and gender. After Lucy recognizes they are in the ruins of something "like the great hall" they had once feasted in, Edmund will respond, "But unfortunately without the feast" (16). After a supper of apples, Edmund will be the one described as longing for "a good thick slice of bread and margarine" (18).

Since both girls' lunches were left behind on the platform, the children have only two meals to share among four. Peter has his sandwiches because they were stuffed in the pocket of his coat, which he was holding. Edmund does not have his coat, so exactly how and why he happens to have his lunch is left unexplained—possibly he was holding it in his hands.

Because the children met the Beavers early in *The Lion, the Witch and the Wardrobe*, food never became a serious problem in the first story. Here in *Prince Caspian*, Lewis must provide for them in a different way, through circumstances that seem realistic. Readers can easily accept the fact that the group happens to have some of the sandwiches their mother had made. This somewhat diminished meal becomes their lunch. As supper draws near, the four arrive at the ruins of an old castle, where there just happens to be an apple orchard. In the next chapter, Lewis will introduce an element of providence in connection with the orchard. There Peter will remember Lilygloves, the chief mole who helped plant the trees, saying, "Believe me, your Majesty, you'll be glad of these fruit trees one day" (21), a comment that suggests a sense of supernatural care because it comes true in an unexpected way a thousand years later.

This same element of providence will continue as the boys seem almost miraculously well prepared for having been plucked off a train platform. First, Peter will happen to have matches in his pocket so they can light a campfire. Second, both Edmund and Peter will have pocket knives that allow them to cut back the ivy from the door to the treasure chamber. Third, Edmund will happen to have his new electric torch, or flashlight, which provides the light they need to retrieve the gifts. Finally, Peter will have a pocket compass that will help them hold their direction.

Perhaps boys in Lewis's day carried these kinds of things in their pockets to a greater extent than their modern-day counterparts. Perhaps their first trip to Narnia trained Peter and Edmund to be better prepared for adventure when it comes. Alternatively, perhaps Lewis wants readers to think there is a force greater than mere chance at work in all these seeming coincidences.

Chapter one ends with Peter, Susan, Edmund, and Lucy leaving the thick, spiritless forest and arriving at a mysterious opening where there are no trees, "only level grass and daisies, and ivy, and gray walls" (14). This strange place is further described as "a bright, secret, quiet place, and rather sad," a depiction that leaves readers sharing the same sense of wonder as the four children.

What neither the children nor the readers know at this point is that at the exact moment the children felt the irresistible tug on the platform, someone in a far distant land, a young man in dire need, was putting a special horn to his lips, a magical horn that promised to summon strange help of some kind.

Discussion Questions

In an essay titled "The Weight of Glory," Lewis writes:

Do you think I am trying to weave a spell? Perhaps I am; but remember your fairy tales. Spells are used for breaking enchantments as well as for inducing them. And you and I have need of the strongest spell that can be found to wake us from the evil enchantment of worldliness which has been laid upon us for nearly a hundred years. (31)

When the children arrived in Narnia in the first book, the land was under the evil spell of the White Witch. The Narnia we find at the start of *Prince Caspian* has had Miraz's spell of secular materialism imposed on it, somewhat like modern Western civilization. The once-magical land has now become disenchanted, and the four children have been summoned to help break the spell and return Narnia to its former state.

1. To what extent is Lewis correct in claiming that our world is under the spell of worldliness? Where or at what times do we see it?
2. If the Narnia stories can be seen as attempts to wake us from this spell of worldliness, what specific aspects might they rekindle in us? For example, you might look at our sense of adventure, our faith, our appreciation for and wonder at the natural world, our longing to be connected to something bigger than ourselves, and so on.

2

The Ancient
Treasure House

This Wasn't a Garden

Chapter two opens with Susan being the first to realize that the open, level space they have come to was once the courtyard of a now-ruined castle.

As a writer, Lewis gave himself a complicated task by choosing to have the four children become skilled young adults during the first book, then to have them go back to being children when they return to England, and now to have them reacquire their adult skills as they revisit Narnia as children. Toward the end of chapter one, Lucy demonstrated a childish lack of awareness by thinking hermits and knights-errant eat roots of trees. Here at the start of chapter two, Susan and Peter are clearly still older and wiser than their siblings. But as time passes and the air of Narnia has a chance to work, the children's former abilities quickly return, leveling out much of the age difference.

Peter is quick to see that Susan is right, and he points out the outlines of what was the castle's great hall. At his mention of the people who lived in the castle long ago, the enchantment of Narnia begins to come alive in a small way, giving Lucy "a queer feeling," a sensation also experienced by Peter, so much so that readers are told he turns and looks "hard" at her (15). Although the children have returned to a land that has lost much of its supernatural element, there remains a small ember of Narnia's magic that has not been extinguished. Here on the first page of the second chapter, there is a tiny quickening, a small flicker of something unexplained. Still this first glimmer is not light—not yet. Peter's curiosity and his confusion continue to grow, and he can only question aloud, "I wonder where we are and what it all means?"

Susan is stumped by a "terrace kind of thing" at the far end of what was once the hall (16). Again a brief spark ignites, and Peter becomes "strangely excited." He points out that this must be the dais where the high table used to be, the place where the king and the nobles would have sat. This observation causes the children to begin thinking of their own castle and of the days when they were kings and queens, reveries that are interrupted by Edmund's practical concerns about supper and the lengthening shadows.

After a failed cooking attempt, the children resign themselves to a supper of raw apples, but as the narrator points out, "The spirit of adventure was rising in them all, and no one really wanted to be back at school" (18). Lewis's use of *no one* is significant here, for as readers may remember, on the first trip to Narnia, Susan expressed interest in returning home several times near the start. Even though Susan displays more fortitude this time around, her fears and her concerns about comfort will continue to plague her, as will be seen later in the chapter and throughout much of the story.

If Edmund was the first to realize intuitively that it was magic pulling them on the platform, it is Peter who uses logic here to conclude that the ruined castle they are in is their very own Cair Paravel. The difference between the boys' types of thinking will be significant later, when Peter will refuse to believe in Lucy's claim to have seen Aslan because it does not make sense to him, while Edmund will be more open to the possibility.

Lucy, the most spiritually sensitive of the four, confesses she has felt there was "some wonderful mystery hanging over this place" (20). Peter then carefully constructs a four-point argument to support his claim. His fourth point is to remind his siblings of the apple orchard the moles planted outside the north gate of Cair Paravel on "the very day before the ambassadors came from the King of Calormen" (21). Here Lewis is careful to provide a link with *The Horse and His Boy*, where he will have Susan sob, "Oh, if only I had never left Cair Paravel. Our last happy day was before those ambassadors came from Calormen. The Moles were planting an orchard for us" (71).

Edmund points out a problem with Peter's conclusion: the passage of time in England and Narnia do not match up, a discrepancy that is unresolved until the next chapter, in which Edmund himself offers an explanation. Here, readers do not know more than the children; however, they may remember more than the children do. In *The Lion, the Witch and the Wardrobe*, the Professor told Peter and Susan, "I should not be at all surprised to find that the other world had a separate time of its own" (49). And so readers may outpace the children in figuring out that many years of Narnia time must have passed during the one year in England.

There is another clue readers may remember but the four children seem to have forgotten here. In his last words to the children in *The Lion, the Witch and the Wardrobe*, the Professor gave them instructions about future journeys to Narnia, telling them, "It'll happen when you're not looking for it" (188). Certainly the children were not looking for a return to Narnia while waiting on the train platform, and so the Professor's prediction has proven true.

Lucy already seems older than she did that morning when they first arrived. She is the first to come up with a way to verify Peter's theory, suggesting that if it is correct, the door to the treasure chamber should be behind them. Two pages later, she will recall how many steps there should be. When the hidden door is exactly where predicted, Susan proposes that they let further exploration wait until the morning, a comment reminiscent of her over-cautiousness at the end of the first book, where she urged, "By my counsel we shall lightly return to our horses and follow this White Stag no further" (186). In both books, Susan's siblings confront her fearfulness. Here Lucy reproaches her older sister's hesitancy to explore further with "Susan! How can you?" (22). On the following page, when Susan resists going down into the chamber to explore, Peter will have to remind her to start acting like the queen that she is.

Treasure and Accidents

Down in the treasure chamber, the children hunt through riches buried beneath dust so thick that it is hard to know they are treasures. Lucy, Susan, and Peter retrieve their Christmas gifts in the reverse order they were given in chapter ten of the first book, which allows the discovery of Peter's sword and shield, and his return to his status as high king, to serve as the chapter's climax.

The narrator breaks in to explain that Edmund was not with the others when the gifts were given and therefore has no gift, and then further points out, "This was his own fault" (26). A writer with more indulgent sensibilities than Lewis would never have let Edmund go through life without a special Christmas gift—what would happen to his self-esteem? Throughout the Chronicles, Lewis is very firm about choice, free will, and responsibility. Here in the second volume, Lewis wants to make sure readers remember that Edmund *chose* to leave his siblings and *chose* to betray them to the White Witch, and for this reason he was not with them when Father Christmas appeared. It is true that Edmund repented of his mistakes and apologized. He then did everything he could to make up for his error, even nearly sacrificing his life to destroy the Witch's wand during the battle. However, Edmund still will go through the rest of the Chronicles without a gift, and here in *Prince Caspian*, he will not even be outfitted with an ordinary sword until chapter eight.

During the centuries the children were gone, the glass bottle holding Lucy's cordial has been replaced by one made of diamond,

a material that by both its cost and its toughness displays the pre-
ciousness of the elixir. Readers are told that more than half remains
of the magical cordial that can "heal *almost* every wound and every
illness" (27, emphasis added), a qualification not made in the first
book, where Lucy was told, "If you or any of your friends is hurt,
a few drops of this will restore them" (109). Perhaps at this point
in *Prince Caspian*, Lewis had already imagined the incident in the
novel's final chapter where Lucy will help to heal Reepicheep's
wounds but will not be able to restore his tail, a situation that opens
the door for Aslan to comment on the mouse's excessive concern
with his honor. Perhaps Lewis came back to this chapter and added
this qualification of "almost" after he wrote that scene where Aslan
rewards Reepicheep. In *The Voyage of the* Dawn Treader, Eustace's
pain caused by the armband will be soothed by the cordial, but again
Lucy's gift will not be all-powerful. It will take Aslan to reverse the
spell that has made Eustace a dragon.

As they hunt through the treasure chamber, Susan finds her
bow and arrows magically preserved, but the enchanted horn that
will always bring help is nowhere to be seen, and this causes her
to remember she had taken it on the hunt for the White Stag, a
detail not mentioned in *The Lion, the Witch and the Wardrobe*. Why
would Susan have brought one of her precious gifts on the trip
when presumably Peter's and Lucy's gifts, as well as Susan's bow
and arrows, were left behind? Because the children valued the gifts
"more than their whole kingdom" (26), it seems likely they would
not typically have brought them out from their storage spots in
the treasure chamber. In fact, in *The Horse and His Boy*, Lucy will
explain to Thornbut, who has sprained his ankle, "If I had but my
cordial with me, I could soon mend this. But the High King has
so strictly charged me not to carry it commonly to the wars and to
keep it only for great extremities!" (179).

Readers perhaps may assume Susan's fearfulness caused her to
want to carry her horn during even a relatively safe excursion like
hunting the White Stag. Since her sister and brothers need to be
told this information, it is likely Susan brought the horn along
without telling them, another detail that speaks clearly about her

character. Susan concludes that the horn must have gotten lost as they "blundered" through the underbrush and back through the wardrobe (27).

Edmund whistles, and then someone—perhaps Edmund, but perhaps the narrator—concludes the missing horn to be "a shattering loss" (27). It is significant that Lewis leaves vague exactly whose conclusion this is, for as will be seen later, the horn has not been lost; in fact, quite the opposite—it is the gifts in the treasure chamber that have been "lost" to Narnia until the children's return. Susan's horn, precisely because she took it on the trip and then accidentally dropped it somewhere, was in a position to be recovered by Doctor Cornelius, as readers discover in chapter five. Rather than a shattering loss, Susan's misplacing the horn becomes an amazing stroke of good fortune. Or, as Colin Manlove calls it, this was "an accident with a purpose" (137).

In *The Silver Chair*, one of the important lessons Jill and Eustace will learn is, as Puddleglum states, "There are no accidents" (154). Here what *seems* to have been an accident with Susan's horn will providentially make it possible for Caspian to call for help hundreds of years later. This seeming accident thus will lead to the saving of Narnia. A similar incident will occur in chapter five. Doctor Cornelius will tell Caspian that he has been looking all his life for traces of the Old Narnians but has never found them. In the next chapter, when Caspian hits his head on a tree after his horse bolts, the prince literally falls into the hands of the Old Narnians, another seeming accident with a powerful aura of providence surrounding it.

When Lewis began writing *Prince Caspian*, he had two largely "unused" elements from *The Lion, the Witch and the Wardrobe* to draw on: Susan's horn and her bow and arrows. Yes, Susan did blow her horn when the wolf attacked her, and it did bring Peter, who killed the wolf in what was his first combat. But in this instance, the horn was not functioning in an enchanted way—an ordinary horn could have been used and Peter would have heard it. In Father Christmas's promise to Susan that help would come *wherever* she was, Lewis set up greater expectations than were fulfilled in the first story. Here in *Prince Caspian*, the narrator makes it clear this is "an enchanted horn" (27), further setting the stage for it to play a major role. Susan's bow and arrows—which are featured prominently in the film but were never used in the book version of *The Lion, the Witch and the Wardrobe*—will also be put to use this time around.

As the trip to the treasure chamber comes to a close, Peter draws his sword. His voice takes on "a new tone" as he declares, "It is my sword Rhindon; with it I killed the Wolf" (29). The sword's name is another detail not mentioned in the first Narnia story, and it will not have enough significance to be mentioned again in this story or in any of the others.

So what might have been Lewis's intention for this brief scene in which Peter speaks about his sword? One possible answer lies behind the sword's unique, nonmagical nature. When Father Christmas presented his gifts in *The Lion, the Witch and the Wardrobe*, he made it clear that the cordial, the horn, and the bow all contained extra powers within them. In presenting Peter's sword and shield, Father Christmas merely pointed out that they were "tools not toys" (108). Any success Peter has with them in battle is due to his own courage and resolve. As he draws Rhindon in the treasure chamber, rather than picking up just any sword as Edmund must, he is reminded of the first time he drew that very blade in battle and of his first victory when the odds were stacked against him. Here in *Prince Caspian*, Peter's gift from Father Christmas is indeed a treasure, and readers will perhaps see it as magical in its own way. This new tone in Peter's voice is the sound of confidence in his abilities.

The chapter ends as the day ends. Peter, Susan, Edmund, and Lucy fall asleep close to the fire, already on their way to becoming very different characters from the four children who were drawn off the train platform early that morning.

While the chapter closes on a positive note, readers may feel more apprehension than the four children seem to at this point. If this is Narnia, what has happened to the marvelous assortment of creatures so present during the first visit? What kind of a change in government would lead to not only abandoning Cair Paravel, the ancient seat of power, but allowing it to fall into such ruin and decay? Finally, what catastrophic events would have caused the children's priceless gifts to have been left behind to gather dust in the treasure chamber?

Discussion Questions

In *Perelandra* the protagonist, Ransom, is called to the planet Venus to battle an evil force that appears in the form of a scientist named Weston. In the dark of night, as he faces his fears, a Voice speaks to him, saying, "It is not for nothing that you are named Ransom" (125). Ransom, who is a linguist, knows that his name comes from an old derivation of *Ranolf's son*, and that it is only an accident that the two words sound alike. But suddenly he comes to the realization that "the whole distinction between things accident and things designed" was "purely terrestrial" (125). Similarly, here in *Prince Caspian*, the children look upon Susan's mislaying her horn as an accident and a terrible loss.

1. Discuss how what actually happened to Susan's horn is the opposite of "a shattering loss" and so has a feel not of an accident but of providence.
2. Does this incident have an application to the real world? Are there times when what we think was the worst thing that could have happened becomes the best thing that could have happened? Are there times when an incident takes on a feeling of being not an accident but part of a larger plan?

3

The Dwarf

Not Much Nice about Narnia?

Imagine it. The sun is coming up. It is day two of the adventure. The four Pevensie children are waking up on their first morning back in Narnia. But rather than excitement, a negative tone is interjected here by Lewis's narrator, who tells readers:

> The worst of sleeping out of doors is that you wake up so dreadfully early. And when you wake you have to get up because the ground is so hard that you are uncomfortable. And it makes matters worse if there is nothing but apples for breakfast and you have had nothing but apples for supper the night before. When Lucy had said—truly enough—that it was a glorious morning, there did not seem to be anything else nice to be said. (30)

This description is meant to contrast directly with Caspian's positive experience of living in the wild in chapter seven. There the narrator will state, "To sleep under the stars, to drink nothing but well water and to live chiefly on nuts and wild fruit, was a strange experience for Caspian. . . . But he had never enjoyed himself more. Never had sleep been more refreshing nor food tasted more savory" (84). The difference is that the four Pevensies are living in a land that has lost its enchantment, while Caspian, for the first time in his life, will be living in a world filled with it.

If one part of the children's quest is to help Caspian ascend his rightful throne, an equally important second part is that they must assist in returning the land to its rightful condition. Lewis wants readers to see a real disparity between the secular, materialistic New Narnia and what the narrator and other characters refer to as the Old Narnia, with its talking animals and its living spirits in trees and wells. The opening of chapter seven is intended to both mirror and contrast with the opening of chapter three here, and so to highlight what is missing in Narnia.

In a review essay titled "The Hobbit," Lewis maintains that there is a very special kind of book that admits us to a unique world of its own—a world that "seems to have been going on before we stumbled into it but which, once found by the right reader, becomes indispensable to him" (81). Lewis goes on to explain, "You cannot anticipate it before you go there, as you cannot forget it once you have gone." While Lewis had the world of The Hobbit specifically in mind when he wrote this, his description could be said to fit Narnia as well—not the disenchanted, dispensable, and forgettable overgrown woods we find at the start of Prince Caspian, but Narnia as it was meant to be.

After each adventure, the children express an intense longing to remain in Narnia or to be allowed to return. Now, although the four children have returned to Narnia, Lewis tells us that except for the weather, they find little for which to be grateful. The world they have returned to is not Narnia, not Narnia as they remember it.

Prizes for Swimming

Determined to leave what has now become an island, Peter, Susan, Edmund, and Lucy hike back to the narrow channel that separates them from the mainland. Here on the first page of chapter three, readers find the third mention of this channel. In chapter two, Peter thought it to be a man-made feature, something someone had dug. Perhaps the Telmarines, in their fear and hatred of Old Narnia, did construct a channel to cut off what was left of Cair Paravel from the rest of the country, but the narrator never explicitly states this. Alternatively, Lewis may have had in mind a natural process similar to the one that separates England from the European continent, a geological development that, along with the castle ruins, is suggestive of the passage of a long period of time since the children left. The same sort of geological process will be brought up in chapter nine when the children and Trumpkin reach the Rush River, which over time has carved a deep gorge.

In the first chapter, this channel was described as about thirty or forty yards wide. Now in chapter three, as the children stare at the water cutting them off from the rest of the country, Peter realizes that Edmund and Lucy will not be able to swim this distance, at least not yet. A few hours later, the magic of the Narnian air will have caused Edmund's former sword-fighting skills to come back to him, as seen in the fencing match with Trumpkin. By the time we reach chapter ten, Lucy will be "only one-third of a little girl going to boarding school for the first time, and two-thirds of Queen Lucy of Narnia" (132). But at this point in the story, the four children are in some ways still the same as when they left England the day before. Their maturation will be an ongoing process.

The narrator parenthetically inserts the fact that Susan has won "prizes for swimming at school" (30). Whether the children are regaining abilities developed during their previous years in Narnia or using skills acquired through practice in England, beginning in *Prince Caspian* Lewis will make a move toward protagonists with more realistic talents, a choice that will make the rest of the

Chronicles somewhat more serious and less escapist than the first novel. In a significant departure from Lewis's original, Andrew Adamson chose to include a scene in the first film that shows Susan practicing her archery and Peter and Edmund working on their sword fighting.

In an essay titled "On Three Ways of Writing for Children," Lewis describes what he calls a Boy's Book or Girl's Book in which the "immensely popular and successful schoolboy or schoolgirl" is able to perform incredible tasks, such as discover the spy's plot or ride the horse that "none of the cowboys can manage" (38). Lewis points out the deceptive nature of these school stories in which young people "have adventures and successes which are possible, in the sense that they do not break the laws of nature, but almost infinitely improbable," and claims that these works are far more likely than fairy tales to raise "false expectations" (37). As the Chronicles progress, Lewis will more and more avoid giving his main characters amazing abilities they seem to possess without any effort.

In the final battle scene in *The Lion, the Witch and the Wardrobe*, Peter, without any training, was described as fighting the White Witch with a sword that flashed so quickly it looked like three swords. By contrast, here in *Prince Caspian*, it is clear that Susan has developed her swimming and archery skills through regular practice back home. On the next page Peter explains that the skills from the children's last visit were acquired because they reigned for years and years and "learned to do things" (31). In the dramatic combat with Miraz in chapter fourteen, the battle skills Peter will display are a product of his years as high king and so are more credible than his fighting prowess in the battle scene in the first novel. In *The Silver Chair*, Jill will be skilled in horsemanship because she "went to a riding school in the holdiays" (192). Similarly, in *The Last Battle*, Eustace's and Jill's skills with a bow and arrow are also a result of normal hard work, as Eustace will explain to Tirian, "We've both been practicing archery ever since we got back" (65).

Susan the Gentle Saves the Day

Next, in what Doris Myers has rightly called "the last expression of guileless childhood" in the story (134), Lucy exclaims, "How excited they'll be to see us" (32), just as a boat comes into sight. The two soldiers guiding the boat are about to drown a dwarf, who is tied up and struggling. Suddenly an arrow strikes the helmet of one of the soldiers, causing him and his partner to jump overboard and flee back to the opposite shore. Here at the second urgent moment in the novel, Lewis has Susan take action on her own, a reminder of the earlier scene when Edmund, not Peter, took the lead on the platform.

In real life, no one turns into a leader overnight. Becoming a leader is a difficult and gradual process, one that both Lewis and Tolkien took great interest in and sought to portray realistically. Thus both Peter and Aragorn will struggle on their way to assuming leadership, sometimes doing nothing, sometimes doing the wrong thing. When Peter finally meets Aslan in chapter eleven, the young high king will exclaim, "I'm so sorry. I've been leading them wrong ever since we started" (153), a statement that Aslan does not refute. Similarly in *The Two Towers*, Tolkien has Aragorn declare, "All that I have done today has gone amiss" (404).

In the Focus on the Family Radio Theatre adaptation of this scene, the writers gave Peter a line of dialogue not in Lewis's original as the boat comes into view: "They're going to drown that poor dwarf. We have to do something." Perhaps the line was added to give listeners a clearer idea of what was taking place. Unfortunately it obscures Lewis's point about the early failures to act, which are part of every leader's process of maturation.

While it is likely that Queen Susan used her gift from Father Christmas during the fifteen years she and her siblings ruled Narnia, this is the first time readers have seen Susan shoot the bow she was given in *The Lion, the Witch and the Wardrobe*. Although in the first novel Father Christmas told Susan this was a special bow that would "not easily miss" (108), as noted earlier, in *Prince Caspian* Lewis suggests that it is Susan's archery skills and not the bow's properties that allow her to rescue Trumpkin here and then beat the dwarf in the shooting match in chapter eight.

It is worth pointing out that there is no assertion anywhere that Susan is a particularly talented bugler—anyone who blows her magic horn is promised help of some kind. Similarly, nowhere will readers find a statement saying that the healing arts are something that Lucy, though sensitive, is especially good at. Thus Lucy's healing cordial is also a gift that could be used with success by anyone, as is indicated when King Caspian takes it with him in *The Voyage of the Dawn Treader*. Although Lucy will use her cordial to mend Trumpkin's minor shoulder wound later in the story, Lewis will choose to have the contributions she and Susan make on this adventure derive more from their own qualities and talents rather than from a magical object they happen to possess.

In *The Lion, the Witch and the Wardrobe*, readers are told that during her reign as queen, Susan became known as Susan the Gentle. Perhaps it is her deep reluctance to see anyone hurt that causes Susan to respond with such extraordinary swiftness in this scene, before any of her siblings even realize what is about to happen to Trumpkin. Her gentleness is certainly evident in the fact that she spares the life of the soldiers in the boat, as she explains, "I wasn't shooting to kill, you know" (35). Almost paradoxically this same gentleness will manifest itself not in swiftness but in hesitation in a parallel scene later in the story, when Susan is unable to shoot the bear who is charging them for fear it is a talking bear. To make this point, Lewis will have the narrator step in to remind readers, "She hated killing things" (121). Susan's gentleness will surface again in chapter eight when, after besting Trumpkin in a shooting match, she will try to comfort him by suggesting, "I think there was a tiny breath of wind as you shot" (108). Likewise, after Edmund persists on referring to Trumpkin as Our Dear Little Friend, Susan will intervene, saying, "Oh, Edmund, don't keep *on* at him like that" (111).

Several additional points about Susan are worth making. First, although Susan the Gentle certainly has a gentle side, she can be and often is quite harsh with her siblings. In chapter nine, following a particularly contrite apology by Peter, she will complain, "I knew all along we'd get lost in these woods" (124). In chapter eleven she will snap at Peter and Lucy so sharply that Trumpkin must reprimand her, saying, "Obey the High King, your Majesty" (149). From the time the children leave Cair Paravel, Susan will be less a part of the group and less caught up in the spirit of adventure than the others.

A second point concerns Susan's role for the rest of the book. Her archery abilities will play an important part in convincing Trumpkin that they have been sent in response to the horn; afterward she will share in the rowing when they leave the island; and later she will suggest that Trumpkin join her in readying an arrow on their bows before the bear attack. But except for these relatively minor contributions, it can be argued that driving off Trumpkin's captors here will be Susan's last significant positive contribution not just in *Prince Caspian* but for the rest of the Chronicles.

Finally, after Trumpkin is untied and Edmund tells the dwarf that the two soldiers from the boat have fled to the mainland, Susan explains that she had intended to hit the soldier's helmet rather than to injure him. At this point, Lewis has the narrator break in with a rather telling comment: "She would not have liked anyone to think she could miss at such a short range" (36). Here readers can see the seeds of Susan's self-conceit and insecurity, elements that will make their presence known again in *The Last Battle*, where Susan's self-centeredness is shown by the fact that she will be reported to be interested only in things associated with her own popularity.

Providence in "Strange Chance"

Because Trumpkin's rescue is so dramatic and goes by so quickly, readers may fail to notice how providential it truly is. Had Trumpkin not been sentenced to a "grand execution" and sent down in "the full ceremonial way" to where the ghosts supposedly are (101), or if the children had come down to the channel a little earlier or a little later, Trumpkin's mission to meet the children at Cair Paravel would have ended in his death. His quest would have failed, and the children would never have gotten the message that Caspian was in need at Aslan's How.

The fact that these events do line up so perfectly may lead readers to conclude that Aslan must be behind all these seeming coincidences, as Shasta will note in *The Horse and His Boy* (208). Shasta comes to this conclusion after he learns that, in a scene reminiscent of the one here in *Prince Caspian*, the boat he was in just happened to come to the right place at the right time for him to be rescued.

Tolkien also uses unlikely coincidences—which occur with too much regularity to be mere chance—to point to an unnamed providence. Because of the similar positions Lewis and Tolkien shared on this issue, perhaps a somewhat lengthy look at providence in *The Lord of the Rings* may be helpful in showing how this same force is at work in *Prince Caspian*.

As David Mills suggests, in *The Lord of the Rings* we find "either a study in Providence or a horribly contrived plot" (23). He concludes that "the argument for the first is much stronger." To make sure readers get his point, Tolkien typically has some wise character come forward to suggest that these unlikely coincidences are *perhaps* more than just mere happenstance.

One of the earliest of these noncoincidences occurs in *The Fellowship of the Ring*. On the second night out from Hobbiton, Frodo, Sam, Merry, and Pippin hear hooves on the road behind them. Leaving the others hidden under the trees, Frodo creeps back to the lane where he sees a black shadow crawling toward him, and he suddenly feels an irresistible desire to put on the Ring. Things might have taken a disastrous turn, but *at that very moment* there comes "a sound like mingled song and laughter" (77). A troupe of wandering elves led by Gildor just happens to be walking by, and the Black Rider is scared off. In any story, the presence of unlikely coincidences such as this one, without the implication that they are not really coincidences at all, would cast an unfavorable light on the skills of the author.

As the company approaches, Frodo recognizes that they are High Elves and comments, "Few of that fairest folk are ever seen in the

Shire. . . . This is indeed a strange chance!" (78). Frodo's point seems to refer to the coincidence of meeting High Elves in the Shire, but readers also hear in his words a comment about the providential escape from the Black Rider. Indeed, later Gildor tells him, "In this meeting there may be more than chance" (83). Following Tolkien's pattern of keeping this providence unnamed, besides using a qualifying *may* here, Gildor also adds, "I fear to say too much" and offers nothing further.

Tolkien stages a similar scene two chapters later, when Merry and Pippin get caught by Old Man Willow and are about to be squeezed in two. Frodo, "without any clear idea of why," goes running up the path crying for help (116), and Tom Bombadil, who, like Gildor, just happens to be in the area, arrives in the nick of time to save them. At supper that night, Frodo raises a question that has been on readers' minds as well. He asks Tom, "Did you hear me calling, Master, or was it just chance that brought you at that moment?" Tom replies, "Just chance brought me then, if chance you call it. It was no plan of mine" (123). Although Tom had received news from Gildor's folk that the hobbits were abroad and thus was prepared for them, in his response "if chance you call it," we hear the implication that he does not call it chance, and his statement "it was no plan of mine" suggests that his providential arrival was in fact a plan of someone else who goes unnamed.

At the council of Elrond, Gandalf uses nearly identical words to describe the coincidence of driving Sauron from Mirkwood the very year that Bilbo came across the Ring. "A strange chance," Gandalf calls it, "if chance it was" (244). Similarly, Elrond tells the council members, "You have come and are here met, in this very nick of time, by chance as it may seem. Yet it is not so. Believe that it is so ordered" (236).

In chapter three of *Prince Caspian*, the children's arrival at the exact moment needed to save Trumpkin certainly shares this same aspect of being ordered. While perhaps seeming to be luck or coincidence, it is really the strange chance of providence. Lewis's point can be found in the hermit's words in *The Horse and His Boy* as he tells Aravis, "Daughter, I have now lived a hundred and nine winters in this world and have never yet met any such thing as Luck" (148). In this same book, Shasta reaches a similar conclusion. He first considers it lucky that he was able to find the mountain pass in the night, then states, "It wasn't luck at all really, it was *Him*" (168).

Like Tolkien, Lewis will not have his narrator directly reveal that events that seem like coincidences are not due to mere chance. This realization is something the readers, like the characters themselves, must come to see on their own.

The Dwarf At Once Takes Charge

Despite being just moments away from a terrible death by drowning and then being rescued by four strange-looking figures he believes may be ghosts, Trumpkin recovers extremely quickly. As the narrator points out, dwarfs are quite "capable" creatures (37), and Trumpkin, as readers discover, is no ordinary dwarf. Within a page after he is released from his bonds, we are told Trumpkin "at once took charge" (36), a comment that says as much about Peter at this point as it does about Trumpkin. Chapter thirteen will be called "The High King in Command," a title that suggests that at this earlier point in the story, Peter is not quite the high king and not quite in command.

As has been noted, from the instant they arrive in Narnia, the children gradually begin reacquiring the abilities they had developed on their previous visit. Later during the difficult journey to Aslan's How, the narrator will state, "Of course, if the children had attempted a journey like this a few days ago in England, they would have been worn out" (132). If the children are going to regain their former skills, then Lewis must show not only how they end up but also where they began. Thus the Peter we meet here in the early chapters of the book will not be the competent, decisive high king we find in the second half of the story, someone with years of successful military experience. Just as it was Edmund who took charge on the train platform and it was Susan's quick thinking that saved Trumpkin, now it is Trumpkin who straightaway realizes they must hide the boat. Peter, always the hardest on himself, responds, "I ought to have thought of that myself" (36).

Of course, we should not overlook the fact that it was Peter who figured out they were in the ruins of Cair Paravel. But despite the claim at the end of chapter two when Peter regained his sword that "the others all felt that he was really Peter the High King again" (29), Peter still has more growing and maturing to do. And this growth and maturation will come about realistically, resulting from the difficult decisions and hardships he will face along the way. As Peter Schakel has noted, the most important maturation in *Prince Caspian* "involves not the title character but those who are searching for him" (*Way* 54), and thus the children's efforts to reach Caspian "turn out to be not only a physical journey but also a journey of personal growth."

When Edmund mentions that they have firewood at the castle, Trumpkin responds, "Beards and bedsteads! So there really is a castle, after all?" (38). Here readers are treated to the first of what Paul Ford calls Trumpkin's "alliterative expletives" (439), expressions that typically have little or no literal meaning but are part of Lewis's characterization of the dwarf, in particular of his somewhat droll and folksy sense of humor. In chapter five when Caspian regains consciousness after his accident, he will wake to hear Trumpkin exclaim, "Horns and halibuts!" (66).

While usually only loosely connected in meaning—if at all—to the topic at hand, Trumpkin's expletives follow several strict phono-logical rules. First, the two words start with the same sound, although not necessarily the same letter—as demonstrated by "giants and junipers," the phrase Trumpkin will use after his shoulder is healed by Lucy's cordial (109). In addition, the second word always has more syllables than the first—as seen in "whistles and whirligigs" (69), "thimbles and thunderstorms" (98), "tubs and tortoiseshells" (124), and "bottles and battledores" (135). Finally, both words are plural, unless one of the words is a noncount noun that has no distinct plural form—as demonstrated by "soup and celery" (91) and "bilge and beanstalks" (148).

While all of Lewis's characters have a somewhat individual way of talking, Trumpkin's alliterative expletives give him an idiolect, a speech pattern clearly unique to him. In later Chronicles, Lewis will do more with idiolects as an element of characterization. In *The Silver Chair*, Puddleglum the Marsh-wiggle's characteristically dour disposition will come out in his distinct style of speaking. In *The Horse and His Boy*, the society-conscious and self-centered Lasaraleen will have a style of speech that particularly suits her, as seen when she will say to Aravis, "But, darling. . . . Positively ropes of pearls" (100).

As chapter three ends, it is Trumpkin who provides breakfast for the children rather than the other way around. In a scene reminiscent of the meal of fresh trout with the Beavers in *The Lion, the Witch and the Wardrobe*, Trumpkin serves up roasted pavenders. Then when the meal is finished, like Mr. Beaver, he lights up his pipe and prepares to tell his story.

Discussion Questions

Lewis's essay "On Three Ways of Writing for Children" was mentioned as part of the discussion in this chapter. There Lewis describes the Boy's Book or Girl's Book with its immensely successful schoolboy or schoolgirl who is able to perform incredible tasks with little or no preparation beforehand. Harry Potter and his magical abilities fit into this implausible category, and for the most part, so do his Quidditch skills. As has been noted, beginning with *Prince Caspian* but also to some extent in *The Lion, the Witch and the Wardrobe*, Lewis avoids creating this kind of protagonist.

What's so wrong with the Boy's or Girl's Book? (Think of the Hardy Boys or the Nancy Drew series, where the protagonists are barely old enough to drive a car but somehow are able to fly planes and sail submarines, and the adolescent heroes spend their free time catching international spies rather than scooping ice cream, babysitting, or mowing lawns.) In discussing this type of book, Lewis points out, "We run to it from the disappointments and humiliations of the real world: it sends us back to the real world undivinely discontented. For it is all flattery to the ego. The pleasure consists in picturing oneself the object of admiration" (38).

When we get back to our own lives in the real world, they seem less satisfying than ever. While we may dream of scoring the winning goal in the final moment of the championship game, this kind of dream may cause us to despise our real lives and the world we actually live in.

Lewis wrote that the dreams and longings a fairy tale awakens are quite different from those associated with the Boy's or Girl's Book. We do not find our world diminished because we have read fairy tales—in fact, quite the opposite. Lewis claims the reader of a fairy tale "does not despise real woods because he has read of enchanted woods: the reading makes all real woods a little enchanted" (38).

1. Are the dreams and longings aroused by the Narnia stories different from those that come from reading works like the Harry Potter or Nancy Drew and Hardy Boys books? If so, how? How does reading about the magic woods in Narnia somehow add enchantment to the woods we encounter in our world?

2. To what extent are Peter, Susan, Edmund, and Lucy more realistic than the protagonists in the typical Boy's or Girl's Book (or the typical Boy's or Girl's Movie)? If the Pevensie children are more realistic, might this have a beneficial effect on young readers? If so, how would you describe this positive effect?

4

The Dwarf Tells
of Prince Caspian

In Medias Res

In medias res is a Latin literary term that means "into the middle of things." It is used to describe a narrative that begins not at the start of the story but somewhere in the middle—usually at some high point in the action. The term comes from *Ars Poetica*, by the Roman poet Horace, and this quality of starting at the heart of the story is typical of classic epics such as *The Odyssey* and *The Aeneid*. Here in chapter four, we learn that the four Pevensie children have truly fallen *in medias res*, as they—and readers as well—have been drawn right into the middle of Caspian's story.

Donald Glover argues, "There is, in fact, little suspense while we listen to the recounting of the history of Prince Caspian" (144). But readers are more likely to agree with Lucy, who responds to Trumpkin's warning that it will be a long tale by saying, "All the better.

We love stories" (40). In fact, this section is as full of suspense and interest as its counterpart in *The Lord of the Rings* where Gandalf recounts, also in flashback, the long story of how he came to be imprisoned at Orthanc. Just as the events about Narnia's beginnings told in *The Magician's Nephew* are more interesting after reading the other books (so *that's* where the lamp-post came from!), Caspian's tale is more interesting because we have seen the children being dragged off the platform and now want to know what has called them and why they were summoned. Likewise, we have witnessed the dramatic arrival of Trumpkin and now want to know why he was about to be killed. Interestingly, George Lucas successfully employed a similar strategy of *in medias res* for the order in which he made his Star Wars films. He first developed his audience's curiosity about Yoda, Darth Vader, and Obi-Wan, and then in later episodes he went back in time and told their complete stories.

Anyone unconvinced of the rightness of Lewis's decision to tell Caspian's narrative through the four-chapter flashback that begins here should imagine reading chapter four as the book's *opening* chapter. The novel would then begin with the less-than-engaging sentence, "Prince Caspian lived in a great castle in the center of Narnia with his uncle, Miraz, the King of Narnia, and his aunt, who had red hair and was called Queen Prunaprismia" (41). Lewis has sparked our interest in the four-chapter narrative by telling us first that Trumpkin has come as a messenger of someone named Caspian, who is—or ought to be—king, and who currently reigns over a ragamuffin group of rebels calling themselves the Old Narnians, whoever they may be.

One of the first things the children learn about Prince Caspian is that his father and mother are dead. Lewis and Tolkien share a predilection for protagonists who are motherless or fatherless, either literally or figuratively. In *The Magician's Nephew*, readers will meet Digory Kirke, whose father has gone to India and whose mother is a house-bound invalid. In *The Horse and His Boy*, Shasta has no mother and has been long separated from his father. In *The Silver Chair*, Caspian's own son, Prince Rilian, will lose his mother and for ten years will live a fatherless existence after being taken prisoner by the Queen of Underland. After his release, Rilian will have only a few moments with his father before King Caspian dies, leaving his son to rule on his own.

The four Pevensie children never appear in the Chronicles with either of their parents, and this allows them a greater opportunity to grow and mature on their own. Andrew Adamson's decision to include Mrs. Pevensie in the London scenes from the first film is a departure from Lewis. Except for a two-sentence paragraph near the end of *The Last Battle*, Mr. and Mrs. Pevensie are not present in any of the seven stories, leaving the four children on their own. In *The Lion, the Witch and the Wardrobe*, Peter, Susan, Edmund, and Lucy are sent away to the Professor's. Here in *Prince Caspian*, they are alone on their way to boarding school. In *The Voyage of the* Dawn Treader, Edmund and Lucy will be left with relatives while their parents go to America.

In *The Lord of the Rings*, Bilbo, Frodo, and Aragorn are orphaned while young. In addition, Faramir, Boromir, Éowyn, Éomer, and Arwen have all lost their mothers. Paul Ford has noted that in Digory, Lewis gives readers "a picture very similar to one of Lewis himself at the same age" (171), a point that holds true for Lewis's other parentless young people and one that could also be made about Tolkien and his orphaned or partially orphaned protagonists. Both writers were young boys when their mothers died. Tolkien also lost his father, while Lewis's father became emotionally distant.

By way of compensation, Lewis will have Caspian acquire not only a wonderful tutor and mentor in the form of Doctor Cornelius but also, through marriage later, a spectacular father-in-law: a former star named Ramandu. Tolkien provides Aragorn a similar compensatory father-in-law in Elrond, the mighty elf-lord and ruler of Rivendell.

Queen Prunaprismia's Name and Literary Allusions

In Charles Dickens's novel *Little Dorrit*, we come across a scene in which Mr. Dorrit visits Mrs. General, the woman he has hired as a governess, in order to discuss his daughter Amy's progress. Amy is sent for and upon arriving addresses Mr. Dorrit as "Father." Mrs. General interrupts in her characteristically self-righteous and didactic mode, as Dickens records:

> "Papa is a preferable mode of address," observed Mrs. General. "Father is rather vulgar, my dear. The word Papa, besides, gives a pretty form to the lips. Papa, potatoes, poultry, prunes, and prism, are all very good words for the lips, especially prunes and prism. You will find it serviceable, in the formation of a demeanor, if you sometimes say to yourself in company—on entering a room, for instance—Papa, potatoes, poultry, prunes and prism, prunes and prism." (500)

And so readers of *Prince Caspian* might ask what connection, if any, we should make between Caspian's aunt Prunaprismia, mentioned here at the start of chapter four, and Mrs. General's silly comment about prunes and prisms.

First, it seems reasonable to say there may be no connection. The word *Prunaprismia* does not occur in *Little Dorrit*, only the words *prunes* and *prism*. Perhaps Lewis created the name not as an allusion to Dickens but simply because he liked the sound of the words. This is what he did previously with the names in *The Screwtape Letters*.

Readers had long speculated how Lewis came up with the unique names he assigns his devils—not just the main demons Screwtape and Wormwood, but also Glubose, Slumtrimpet, Slubgob, Toadpipe, and Triptweeze. In the preface to the 1961 edition of *The Screwtape Letters*, Lewis notes that curiosity about the names had led to "many explanations, all wrong" (xiii). His intention, he explains, was to make them negative merely by their sound and by associations with that sound. Thus Lewis speculates that *Scrooge, screw, thumbscrew, tapeworm,* and *red tape* all went into creating Screwtape's name, and *slob, slobber, slubber* (to perform in a slipshod manner), and *gob* played a role in Slubgob. *Wormwood*, besides having some negative sound associations, is also a word meaning something bitter.

So where does this leave us with *Prunaprismia*? To what extent might the words *prune* and *prism* have any specific associations to the name? We have no record of Lewis's feelings toward prisms, but we do know that Lewis disliked prunes. At the end of his essay "On Three Ways of Writing for Children," we find the following anecdote: "Once in a hotel dining-room I said rather too loudly, 'I loathe prunes.' 'So do I,' came an unexpected six-year-old voice from another table. Sympathy was instantaneous. Neither of us thought it funny. We both knew that prunes are far too nasty to be funny" (42). Perhaps Lewis is doing nothing more here than creating an odd, frumpy-sounding name with negative associations that will cause us to imagine an equally odd, frumpy, and negative character. For readers not familiar with the passage from Dickens, Queen Prunaprismia's name will function on this level.

Literary scholars use the term *allusion* in two senses. In the broad sense, an allusion may be said to be any reference to previous literary or historical material. In the narrow sense, allusion can be defined as a brief, unexplained reference to a figure, object, event, place, or action from literature or history that seeks to evoke a resonant emotional response from the associations already existing within a reader's mind.

In general, if we want to claim an author intended for something to be an allusion in the narrow sense, we need to argue three things. First, we must show that it is likely the author would have been familiar with the work or historical element in question. Second, we need to demonstrate that this work or historical element is sufficiently well known so that the readers would understand the allusion—otherwise we are left with merely the author's private association, his private joke. Third, and most significantly, we must make the case that the allusion evokes a response from its literary or historical associations that is consistent with the elements presented directly. An allusion gives us something a similar name without any connections would not.

It is hard to imagine anyone would disagree with the claim that the title of Ernest Hemingway's novel *For Whom the Bell Tolls* is an allusion to the well-known line from "Meditation 17" by John Donne, which states, "And therefore never send to know for whom the bell tolls; it tolls for thee." Similarly, a convincing case can be made that *Of Mice and Men*, the title of the novel by John Steinbeck, is an allusion to the equally well-known line from Robert Burns's "To a Mouse," which declares, "The best-laid schemes of mice and men / Gang aft agley [often go astray]."

Despite these two illustrations, the general rule is that it is better not to claim something is an allusion than to begin seeing allusions everywhere. For example, while Lewis does have a good number of allusions in the Chronicles, it is safe to say he did not choose Edmund's name so readers would be reminded of Edmond Dantes from *The Count of Monte Cristo*. Although some similarities could be drawn between the two characters, there are too many differences. Likewise, it would be hard to support the claim that Lewis chose Peter's name as an allusion to *Peter and the Wolf*.

So again, where does that leave us with Queen Prunaprismia? First, we do know that Lewis was quite familiar with *Little Dorrit*. In fact, he uses Mrs. Clennam, a character from the novel, to illustrate a point in his book of literary criticism, *English Literature in the Sixteenth Century*. Second, Lewis would have assumed that Dickens's "prunes and prism" was something most Narnia readers would have been aware of. The saying appears more than once in *Little Dorrit*, and, in fact, Amy goes on to practice saying "prunes and prism" so much that Dickens titles a later chapter of the novel "Mostly, Prunes and Prism." Finally, although we are told little about Queen Prunaprismia, she seems to be the kind of social climber who, like her husband, is all form and no substance, making her association with Mrs. General's advice appropriate. In fact, the case could be made that because Queen Prunaprismia is mentioned so briefly in *Prince Caspian*, Lewis's allusion to *Little Dorrit* provides an economical form of characterization.

Before leaving the topic of allusions, it could be argued that in his portrait of Caspian's nurse—who is introduced here at the start of chapter four and reappears again later—Lewis had in mind his own childhood nurse, Lizzie Endicott. In his portrait of Lizzie in his autobiography, *Surprised by Joy*, Lewis notes that "even the exacting memory of childhood can discover no flaw—nothing but kindness, gaiety, and good sense" (5). A description from Douglas Gresham's recent work *Jack's Life* makes the parallel with Caspian's nurse clearer. Gresham notes that as a boy, his stepfather was very fond of his nursemaid Lizzie, and she acquainted him with the traditional Irish folktales. According to Gresham, the young Lewis "listened in awe as she told him tales of the adventures of the faerie folk of long ago" (8). Here in chapter four we learn that Prince Caspian has been told the fairy tales of Old Narnia by his nurse, a fact that causes Miraz to become furious and order the nurse sent away. Like the Professor in *The Lion, the Witch and the Wardrobe*, who was partly based on Lewis's recollections of his former tutor William Kirkpatrick, the character of Caspian's nurse can be categorized as what Paul Ford calls an autobiographical allusion (105), a borrowing from personal life.

I Wish I Could Have Lived in the Old Days

Here in chapter four, we are introduced not only to the young Prince Caspian but also to his evil uncle, King Miraz, the self-proclaimed ruler of Narnia. In some ways, Miraz resembles the domination-seeking despot the four children encountered on their previous visit to Narnia—the White Witch. In some ways he is even worse, as Jonathan Rogers explains:

> This isn't the first time we've seen Narnia under a wicked ruler. But even the White Witch's hundred-year winter was a distinctly Narnian kind of tyranny—a tyranny by enchantment. The tyranny of Miraz is much more prosaic, enforced not by magic, but by murder and high taxes and repressive laws. All sense of wonder—everything worth wondering at—seems to have fled. (27)

In the next chapter, Doctor Cornelius will explain how Miraz assumed power under the title of lord protector following the death of his brother, Caspian's father (59). From his very first words here in chapter four, it is clear that Miraz has dropped any pretense of governing only until Caspian is older. Now, in an action characteristic of Miraz, he has completely reversed the truth of the real situation, portraying himself as the rightful ruler of Narnia and his nephew only as someone who might fill in if needed, as he tells Caspian: "You know that your aunt and I have no children, so it looks as if you might have to be King when I'm gone" (41–42).

Miraz then asks his nephew, "How shall you like that, eh?" (42), and Caspian's response—"I don't know"—bears examination.

First, it should be noted that here in chapter four of *Prince Caspian*, Caspian appears as a foil, or opposing parallel, to Edmund, who in chapter four of *The Lion, the Witch and the Wardrobe* heard a nearly identical statement from the White Witch. The self-designated Queen told Edmund, "I have no children of my own. I want a nice boy whom I could bring up as a Prince and who would be King of Narnia when I am gone" (38–39). Whereas Caspian is reluctant to accept Miraz's proposition here, Edmund was all too ready to assume power over Narnia and his siblings.

When Aslan himself will later offer Caspian the throne and ask if he feels himself "sufficient to take up the Kingship of Narnia" (206), Caspian will again express a similar hesitation, a reluctance Aslan will view as a sign of a good king. Lewis was greatly influenced by the works of Plato, and here in *Prince Caspian* Lewis reflects the claim made by Plato in Book VII of *The Republic*: "The truth is that the State in which the rulers are most reluctant to govern is always the best and most quietly governed, and the State in which they are most eager, the worst" (182). In a wonderful scene from the first film, Andrew Adamson drives the latter part of this point home by having Edmund eagerly try out the throne when he arrives at the Witch's castle. It is significant that in *The Magician's Nephew* when Aslan tells the future king Frank that he and his wife are to rule Narnia, the former cabby responds with a reluctance that resembles Caspian's, hence identifying himself as a good candidate for king: "Begging your pardon, sir, and thanking you very much I'm sure . . . but I ain't no sort of chap for a job like that" (151).

Second, although the prince answers his uncle's question here with an ambivalent "I don't know" (42), his reply seems toned down by fear—it could be argued that Caspian wants no part in being king but is afraid to say so. After looking at present-day Narnia with its lack of enchantment and its current sovereign with his lack of ethics,

Caspian may be thinking, *If Narnia is going to be the sad, repressive country it is, and if being king means being like you, I don't particularly want to rule.* Miraz, who is not overly perceptive, takes Caspian's words at face value and merely counters with, "Don't know, eh?" Miraz is also not particularly imaginative and so cannot conceive of anyone not sharing his selfish, materialistic values. In a response that tells readers everything they need to know about him, Miraz exclaims, "I should like to know what more anyone could wish for!" Here we are presented with Miraz's worldview in a nutshell. From his perspective, being king is the highest possible goal anyone could have, for as we learn, for Miraz it simply means being the boss over everyone and having every command obeyed. Two pages later, as irrefutable evidence that the Pevensies never existed, Miraz will argue, "How could there be two Kings at the same time?" (44), as though everyone knows that ruling means having absolute authority and never having to compromise.

One of the characteristics of the evil villains in both Narnia and Middle-earth is their inability to see or even to imagine any perspective but their own. Here Miraz cannot imagine the possibility that someone would not want to be king and have the power to impose his wishes on everyone else. Likewise in chapter five, Nikabrik will find it hard to believe that Caspian does not want to "go back to his own kind" and betray those who are different from him (67), because this is just what Nikabrik himself would do. In *The Two Towers*, Gandalf explains how Sauron suffers from this same limitation, telling Aragorn, "He does not yet perceive our purpose clearly. He supposes that we were all going to Minas Tirith; for that is what he would himself have done in our place. . . . That we should wish to cast him down and have *no* one in his place is not a thought that occurs to his mind" (485–86).

Despite what he says here to Caspian, Miraz does *not* want to know "what more anyone could wish for" (42). And when his nephew tries to tell him of his longing to live in the old days, the king silences him. He orders Caspian never to talk or even think about the stories of Old Narnia, and readers get a sense of the total control Miraz has sought to exert over anyone who defies him. Despite the fact that Miraz is a plodding, small-minded bully compared to the White Witch, both characters exhibit a similar reaction to any deviation from their wishes. In *The Lion, the Witch and the Wardrobe*, the Witch barred Edmund and the dwarf from even saying Aslan's name, declaring, "If either of you mentions that name again, he shall instantly be killed" (122).

Likewise here in *Prince Caspian*, Miraz orders, "Let's have no more of it" (44). To guarantee his command is carried out, he exiles Caspian's nurse. Later Doctor Cornelius will warn against speaking about Old Narnia, telling Caspian, "The King doesn't like it. If he found me telling you secrets, you'd be whipped and I should have my head cut off" (47).

In an appropriate contrast to the White Witch and King Miraz, who seek to silence their subjects, Aslan actually gives them the ability to speak. In fact, Aslan gives speech three times. The first time is at the creation of Narnia in *The Magician's Nephew*. The second occurs in *The Lion, the Witch and the Wardrobe* when he unfreezes the creatures the Witch had turned into statues for the collection in her castle. In a delightful passage from this scene where the statues are restored to life, we are told, "Instead of the deadly silence the whole place rang with the sound of happy roarings, brayings, yelpings, barkings, squealings, cooings, neighings, stampings, shouts, hurrahs, songs and laughter" (169). In *Prince Caspian*, Aslan gives speech yet again—this time to the silenced trees and streams as well as to all those who were forbidden by Miraz to speak their real thoughts.

In their attempt to completely dominate those around them, Miraz and the White Witch seek to repress ideas they themselves know to be true. As Doctor Cornelius will explain to Caspian, the stories of Old Narnia are facts Miraz knows but intends to keep unspoken. Similarly, in *The Lion, the Witch and the Wardrobe* when the Witch encounters the merrymakers who clearly have been visited by Father Christmas, she reacts by stating, "He has not been here! He cannot have been here! How dare you—but no. Say you have been lying and you shall even now be forgiven" (116).

When Miraz proclaims that the things Caspian has been told by his nurse are fairy tales, nonsense, and a "pack of lies" (43), he himself is the liar. Miraz knows that when his ancestor Caspian the Conqueror took power in Narnia, he did so by defeating and driving into hiding the very creatures the nurse had been describing. As Trumpkin has already explained to the children, the authorities themselves do not believe that ghosts inhabit the woods by the sea. They spread this falsehood so they can pretend that the people they execute or drown are victims of these ghosts. In chapter thirteen when Edmund delivers Peter's challenge to Miraz's camp, there will be no record of any astonishment at the presence of the giant and centaur who accompany him.

Caspian's longing to live in Old Narnia merits studying. The young prince expresses his wish to live in a time when the animals could talk, when "nice people" lived in the trees and streams, and when there were "lovely little Fauns" in all the woods (42). Back then, as Caspian tells his uncle, "everyone had a lovely time, and it was all because of Aslan" (43). In this list of particulars, Caspian reveals his longing for a land with a spiritual and ethical underpinning, a quality that has been driven out or driven underground in Miraz's Narnia.

In the essay "On Three Ways of Writing for Children," Lewis claims that while the Boy's or Girl's Book creates a desire in readers to see themselves as the popular and successful schoolboy or schoolgirl, the longings associated with a fairy tale take a different form. A child does not long for fairy land in the same way that he or she longs to be the class hero. Instead, Lewis says, "It would be much truer to say that fairy land arouses a longing for he knows not what. It stirs and troubles him (to his life-long enrichment) with the dim sense of something beyond his reach, and far from dulling or emptying the actual world, gives it a new dimension of depth" (38). The tales Caspian's nurse has told him have created exactly that kind of longing.

Jonathan Rogers notes that only later will Caspian come to the realization that "the myths he loves so much are fact," so at this point in the story, "they can only stir his longings, not fulfill them" (30). Yet these myths speak to him in a way that the dull world of Miraz's court intrigues never will.

In *The Silver Chair*, Lewis will include a similar scene where the Queen of Underland attempts to cast a spell that will make Jill, Eustace, Puddleglum, and Rilian believe that all the things they knew in Narnia were "but a tale, a children's story" (178). Puddleglum finally retorts, "Suppose this black pit of a kingdom of yours *is* the only world. Well, it strikes me as a pretty poor one. . . . We're babies making up a game, if you're right. But four babies playing a game can make a play-world which licks your real world hollow" (182). Similarly, even if Caspian's stories of Old Narnia should turn out to be "nonsense for babies," it could be argued that this made-up world is still far better than the one Miraz offers.

Caspian longs for a world that is more than the hollow, materialistic shell Miraz has produced, for a world with this "dimension of depth" Lewis describes in his essay. In the wish that he could have lived in the old days, Caspian also expresses a longing for a world with a clear moral order, instead of the world of moral expediency Miraz's conduct typifies. As Gilbert Meilaender rightfully points out, Old Narnia is a land of "courtesy and courage" (45), a place where "obedience to proper authority is a delight" and where "the fruits of such attitudes are obvious."

The fruits of Miraz's lack of morals will be obvious also. Given the opportunity, in chapter thirteen Miraz's ambitious counselor Glozelle will trick the king into accepting Peter's challenge to single combat. When this fails to do away with Miraz, Glozelle himself will stab the monarch in the back. By comparing Glozelle's actions with Trumpkin's, we can see how different the New and Old Narnians truly are. As Meilaender notes, even though Trumpkin doubts that blowing the horn will bring help, he is willing to undertake a hazardous journey to meet those whom others believe will come to help "if Caspian his king so commands" (45).

Paul Ford describes Old Narnia as an enchanted world where "courtesy, honor, and the spirit of adventure are the respected virtues, and in which hospitality is graciously offered" (316). Although Miraz is baffled by his nephew's yearning to live in the old Narnia and his ambivalence about reigning in the new one, readers can readily identify with Caspian.

He Was to Have a Tutor

In *The Return of the King*, Gandalf tells Pippin, "A traitor may betray himself and do good that he does not intend" (797). While Gandalf is speaking about Gollum, his words hold true for several of Tolkien's other characters, including Boromir and Saruman, as well as for the actions of Miraz here in *Prince Caspian*. By sending Caspian's nurse away, Miraz does good that he did not intend by opening the door for a new teacher, one who will have an even greater impact on the young prince. Gollum, hoping to have Frodo and Sam killed so he can obtain the Ring himself, guides them to Shelob's lair, a maze of tunnels that turns out to be the one way Frodo and Sam could enter Mordor. Miraz, hoping to do away with the silly stories he says are fit only for babies, replaces the nursemaid with a tutor who will offer Caspian precisely what he will need to grow into a very different kind of ruler than his uncle intends.

There is a Chinese proverb sometimes attributed to Confucius that states, "When the pupil is ready, the master will appear." Arthur had his Merlin, and Luke Skywalker his Obi-Wan Kenobi. Here in chapter four, Caspian's tutor and trusted counselor appears in the form of Doctor Cornelius just when the pupil is ready to take the next step in his development.

The character of Cornelius can be seen as another borrowing from the author's own life. When Lewis was a teenager, he was tutored by William Kirkpatrick, who became one of Lewis's most formative influences. While Doctor Cornelius will mirror Kirkpatrick in influence, it should be pointed out that the physical appearance of Caspian's short and round instructor will be nothing like that of Lewis's tall, white-whiskered tutor. Lewis used Kirkpatrick's looks with Professor Kirke, the children's host in *The Lion, the Witch and the Wardrobe* and Peter's tutor at the start of *The Voyage of the Dawn Treader*.

While Doctor Cornelius will be a model of the ideal tutor, one who puts his pupil's well-being ahead of his own, one of Lewis's earlier fictional creations was the exact opposite. Screwtape, the senior devil assigned to mentor the young Wormwood, seeks to dominate his pupil and, in the end, actually devours him. In the preface to the 1961 edition of *The Screwtape Letters*, Lewis describes this kind of domination, stating, "In human life we have seen the passion to dominate, almost to digest, one's fellow; to make his whole intellectual and emotional life merely an extension of one's own" (xi). While Cornelius does not take this stance toward Caspian, Miraz does. Fortunately, Caspian will escape from Miraz's clutches before his uncle has much chance to dominate him. In this sense, the fact that Caspian will have to flee the castle for his life can, like his nurse's banishment, be seen as a blessing in disguise.

Not surprisingly, except for his nurse's stories Caspian has been taught "nothing about the History of Narnia" (46), since any real knowledge about the past has been stifled by Miraz. Nor are readers surprised to learn that history immediately becomes the subject he likes best. Colin Manlove has described Caspian's overall education under his new tutor as the discovery that the world is more complex and more confusing than he supposed (139)—the universal lesson of coming-of-age stories. History teaches that there is more than the present, more than what we can see and experience right now.

Caspian's Astronomy Lesson

As Caspian and his tutor stand on the tower roof, readers are told, "Everything was so quiet that he could hear the sound of the waterfall at Beaversdam, a mile away" (49). Here in the mention of Beaversdam, we find Lewis's brief reminder not only of the children's first visit to Narnia but also of the providential help provided them—first through Mr. and Mrs. Beaver and then by Father Christmas, who promised Mr. Beaver, "When you get home you will find your dam finished and all the leaks stopped and a new sluice-gate fitted" (107–8). At this point in the story, readers have already seen that three of the gifts from Father Christmas have been magically preserved—Peter's sword, Susan's bow and arrows, and Lucy's cordial. So perhaps it is not unreasonable to speculate that the gift of Father Christmas's work on Mr. Beaver's dam has also lasted the millennium time span between the two books, and that the sound Caspian hears is water passing over this same dam.

Narnia is a world that, compared to ours, seems to have been given a second helping of life. Some of its animals have the gift of speech. The trees and streams have a spirit associated with them. And creatures from myths—dwarfs, fauns, centaurs, and giants— really live and breathe. Given this extra portion of life, perhaps readers are not surprised to learn that in Narnia the planets are not just celestial bodies that cross the sky each night but are, in some unspecified sense, great lords and ladies with distinct personalities associated with them. In *The Voyage of the Dawn Treader*, Lewis will introduce Coriakin and Ramandu, characters who were previously stars shining in the sky. There Eustace will state, "In our world a star is a huge ball of flaming gas," to which Ramandu will reply, "Even in your world, my son, that is not what a star is but only what it is made of" (209).

Here in chapter four, Caspian sees the planet Tarva, the Lord of Victory, as he passes near to Alambil, the Lady of Peace, in what Cornelius foresees as a "fortunate" meeting, one that means "some great good for the sad realm of Narnia" (50). In chapter six, Glen- storm the Centaur will interpret this same conjunction to mean "the time is ripe" for the Old Narnians to rise up in battle (78).

If we make the distinction between *astrology* (the study of the supposed influence the stars and planets have on human—or, in this case, Narnian—affairs) and *astronomy* (the study of the stars and planets as physical objects), then what, if anything, should we make of Lewis's brief inclusion of astrology here in *Prince Caspian?* Several observations are worth making.

First, Lewis's animation of the planets and stars can be seen as another manifestation of the way Narnia overflows with vitality. An even more vivid animation of the planets is at the heart of Lewis's space trilogy, which also shows a cosmos that is the opposite of empty and barren.

Second, as Paul Ford has argued, "In the Chronicles, Lewis recov- ers a medieval worldview" (104). The swords, shields, and armor used in Narnia are clearly medieval, as is the royal court with its kings, queens, and nobles. Another part of this medieval view, as Lewis explains in *The Discarded Image*, involves the belief that each planet "is a conscious and intellectual being" (115), and that these celestial bodies "affect terrestrial bodies, including those of men" (103). Lewis is drawing on what he refers to in *English Literature in the Sixteenth Century* as "the older conception" of nature (4), a worldview that sees the universe not as something largely empty and void but rather "tingling with anthropomorphic life." This medieval world will insert itself again at the start of chapter five in the archaic subjects Caspian must study, a list that will include rhetoric, heraldry, versification, and alchemy, as well as lessons on the recorder and a lutelike instrument called a theorbo.

Third, Lewis uses this astrological element to further characterize Doctor Cornelius in his role as a magus, a studier of the stars in the tradition of the magi of the New Testament. When the wise men arrive at the court of King Herod, looking for the one who has been born king of the Jews, they explain, "We saw his star in the east and have come to worship him" (Matt. 2:2).

Fourth, in Doctor Cornelius's study of the night sky, we can find an echo of a rather unknown interest from Lewis's personal life. In his section on autobiographical allusions, Paul Ford quotes from a letter written by one of the girls who stayed at the Kilns, Lewis's home, during the war. In this passage from Ford's book, Margaret Leyland, now much older, recounts, "Lewis himself was a keen astronomer and had a telescope on the balcony of his bedroom. I was privileged to be shown many of the wonders of the universe" (107). Readers may wonder if there were nights when Lewis woke up his young houseguests to show them a similar rare conjunction of the planets visible from the balcony of his house outside Oxford.

Finally, it should be pointed out that the means and ends connected with Cornelius's and Glenstorm's proper studies of the heavens in *Prince Caspian*—studies that may have the appearance of magic to some readers—are diametrically opposed to both the means and the ends that will be associated with Nikabrik, who wants to use magic in chapter twelve to call on the White Witch to serve his own wicked purposes. Doctor Cornelius and Glenstorm, rather than trying to manipulate anything, seek to understand the movements of the heavens and to align their purposes with those revealed there.

The People Who Lived in Streams and Trees

Cornelius has told Caspian that he has been brought to the rooftop in the middle of the night for an astronomy lesson. However, prompted by the prince's earlier questions about Caspian the First, the Doctor's real purpose for the late-night session is to give Caspian a lesson on Narnia's unspoken past. In a very private tutorial, Doctor Cornelius reveals to his pupil, "All you have heard about Old Narnia is true" (51). To his astonishment and delight, Caspian learns that his longing for the talking animals, dwarfs, and dryads from his nurse's tales is more than just longing. He learns that his uncle's world is not all there is.

Earlier in the chapter, the young prince told his uncle about the "nice people" who lived in streams and trees. Lewis will call these creatures by a number of different names. Here on the roof, Cornelius refers to Narnia as the country of "the Waking Trees and Visible Naiads" (51). In chapter nine, Lucy will refer to the spirits of the trees as "Dryads and Hamadryads" (118).

Readers were first introduced to naiads and dryads in *The Lion, the Witch and the Wardrobe*, where they played a smaller role. During Lucy's tea with Mr. Tumnus, he told tales of "how the Nymphs who lived in the wells and the Dryads who lived in the trees came out to dance with the Fauns" (15). As he prepared to escort Lucy back to the lamp-post, Mr. Tumnus warned her that the wood was full of the Witch's spies, noting that even some of the trees were on her side. When Peter, Susan, and Lucy first met Aslan, he was surrounded by a large group of creatures: "There were Tree-Women and Well-Women (Dryads and Naiads as they used to be called in our world) who had stringed instruments" (126). In Pauline Baynes's illustration of this scene in *The Lion, the Witch and the Wardrobe*, these dryads and naiads were depicted as indistinguishable from each other. In the film, the spirit of a cherry tree, made up of blossom petals, waves to Lucy as the children enter Aslan's camp. In a later scene, this same naiad delivers the news of Aslan's death to Peter and Edmund.

Paradoxically, in his portrait of Miraz's Narnia, Lewis is able to evoke two opposing sentiments. On one hand, Miraz's Narnia is a land once filled with spirit that has now been lost. In a poem titled "Victory," from his long poetic work *Spirits in Bondage*, Lewis laments this loss of spirit, writing, "The faerie people from our woods are gone, / No Dryads have I found in all our trees" (7). On the other hand, the spirits who lived in the streams and the trees of Narnia are not completely gone but are merely silenced or put to sleep. We are given indications that perhaps they are still present, waiting to be awakened, and this gives the land the feeling that there may be something more beneath the surface, something just beyond the reach of our senses.

In "Song," another poem from *Spirits in Bondage*, Lewis proposed the idea that the mysterious beauty we encounter in the natural world must have its source in something more than material, that this beauty must be due to some spark of spirit that lives deep down in the physical things we see:

> Atoms dead could never thus
> Stir the human heart of us
> Unless the beauty that we see
> The veil of endless beauty be,
> Filled full of spirits that have trod
> Far hence along the heavenly sod. (50)

Doctor Cornelius tells Caspian, "It is you Telmarines who silenced the beasts and the trees and the fountains" (51). He urges the prince that if he wants to help, he should "gather learned magicians and try to find a way of awaking the trees once more" (53). Here Lewis sets up the rousing of the woods Lucy will witness in chapter eleven.

Why Do You Say My Race?

There are several areas of controversy associated with the Chronicles. One of these controversies involves the assertion that the Narnia stories are racist, a claim drawn from the fact that the Calormenes, the enemies of Narnia in later books, have dark skin. Anyone wanting to make a convincing argument that the stories display racism would need to address four elements.

First, while it is true that many of the Calormenes who appear in the Chronicles are portrayed negatively, an equally substantial list could be made of negative characters who are light-skinned or, to be more exact, are never specified as being dark-skinned. This roster would include the White Witch, the early Edmund, Caspian the Conqueror, King Miraz, the lords Glozelle and Sopespian and most of their Telmarine countrymen, the early Eustace, the bullies and many of the staff at Experiment House, Governor Gumpas, Lord Bar, Uncle Andrew, and the later Susan.

Second, the Calormene characters we get to know best, Aravis from *The Horse and His Boy* and Emeth from *The Last Battle*, are very positive characters and are portrayed no less sympathetically than their fair-skinned counterparts.

Third, and perhaps most significantly, Lewis's characters—human, animal, dwarf, plant, or otherwise—are never portrayed negatively or positively *simply because of their race*. Thus we find both good and bad dwarfs, good and bad trees, good and bad Calormenes, good and bad wolves, good and bad humans from England, and so on. It is consistent with Lewis's nonracist stance that when Lucy looks off into the distance at the end of *The Last Battle*, she sees that Tashbaan too has a place in eternity.

Finally, anyone attempting to label the Chronicles as racist would need to address the strong and unmistakable antiracist attitudes that run through the entire series. One of the most essential aspects of Narnia, which the children discover immediately after entering through the wardrobe, is that it is profoundly multiracial, composed of a diversity of creatures hard to match anywhere—beavers and fauns, giants and mice, dwarfs and dogs. Narnia would not be Narnia if it were inhabited only by badgers.

Here in *Prince Caspian*, Lewis introduces another antiracist element: the mixed-race Cornelius. Doctor Cornelius is aware of the prejudice many dwarfs would have against him and tells his pupil,

"If any of my kindred, the true Dwarfs, are still alive anywhere in the world, doubtless they would despise me and call me a traitor" (52–53). Nevertheless Caspian's tutor urges him, if he should ever become king, to "be kind to the poor remnants of the Dwarf people" (53). The racial prejudice Doctor Cornelius encounters is clearly cast in a negative light, while the acceptance shown him is portrayed favorably. In chapter seven when Nikabrik will attempt to convince the others that Cornelius should be killed because of his mixed-race ancestry, Caspian will immediately declare, "This is my greatest friend and the savior of my life. And anyone who doesn't like his company may leave my army: at once" (88). In addition, the acceptance Cornelius extends to those who differ from him—whether human, dwarf, or mouse—is portrayed positively.

Caspian's lesson ends in a "deep silence" that extends for minutes as the young prince contemplates the implications of what he has learned on the rooftop. In response to his pupil's wish to go on talking, Cornelius warns, "Someone might come looking for us" (55), a stark reminder of what Miraz does to anyone who dares to think differently than he does.

Discussion Questions

The proverb "When the pupil is ready, the master will appear" was cited in this chapter to describe the providential way Doctor Cornelius seems to arrive at just the right moment in Caspian's development. The adage might be said to be equally appropriate in depicting the way many readers discover C. S. Lewis, seemingly by accident, at a point in their lives when they are ready for a certain kind of answer, support, or guidance.

1. What kind of answers, support, or guidance does Lewis give readers—young and old—through the Chronicles? What has Lewis given to you through these stories?
2. Who are some of the "masters" that have appeared in your life just when you were "ready" for them—perhaps in the

flesh, perhaps through their writings—and provided not only instruction but also encouragement, inspiration, and even correction?

In *Prince Caspian*, the four children are older and more mature than they were in *The Lion, the Witch and the Wardrobe*, and accordingly the Narnia they return to is initially less like the fairy-tale world they had first encountered and more like the real world. In his portrait of Miraz's Narnia, Lewis embodies two essential qualities from his own world: a sense of spirit that at one time had been infused into all of creation but was now lost; and a spark of the divine, for eyes that could see it.

3. To what extent does the modern world resemble the silenced, disenchanted, and spiritless Narnia that Miraz rules and the children first encounter on the island?
4. The poet Gerard Manley Hopkins wrote, "The world is charged with the grandeur of God." Can we claim that the real world still retains a spark of the divine? If so, where do we see it?

5

Caspian's Adventure in the Mountains

Thinking, Dreaming, and Longing

Chapter five opens with the news that Caspian and his tutor have had "many more secret conversations on the top of the Great Tower" (56). The more Caspian learns about the old days, the more he dreams of them and longs for their return. In his recent work *Into the Region of Awe: Mysticism in C. S. Lewis*, David Downing claims, "The mystical elements in *Prince Caspian* do not emerge until more than halfway through the story," starting with Lucy's visions (134). However, Downing also observes that one of the defining traits of the mystical is "a habitual sense of yearning, a deep longing for something inaccessible or unknown" (34). It could be argued that here in chapter five, we have a brief window into one mystical element, Caspian's insatiable yearning that fills "nearly all his spare hours," a craving that mirrors the desire felt by Lewis himself when he was young.

In the opening chapter of his autobiography, *Surprised by Joy*, Lewis describes this powerful longing he experienced as a young person and cautions that anyone who has no interest in this kind of episode need read no further, for, as Lewis asserts, "the central story of my life is about nothing else" (17). Lewis found this yearning hard to put into words and hard to categorize. He finally gave this sensation the title of *joy*, defining it in a special way that distinguished it from mere happiness or pleasure, and made it the focus in the story of his early life.

Paul Ford has observed that longing is "one of the most important themes in Lewis's life and thought" and the term Lewis uses "to express the sort of experience within life that opens us up beyond appearances to the transcendent" (291). In the longing to return to Narnia that the four Pevensie children have, Lewis evokes a similar longing on the part of readers, the feeling that "this world is not my home." Lewis reflects on this yearning in *Mere Christianity*, where he argues, "If I find in myself a desire which no experience in this world can satisfy, the most probable explanation is that I was made for another world" (136–37).

Of course, Caspian is not the first character in this story to experience this deep longing. In the previous chapter, Doctor Cornelius told the prince, "My old heart has carried these secret memories so long that it aches with them and would burst if I did not whisper them to you" (53). When asked if any of the Old Narnians might still be left, the Doctor sighs deeply and gives the following account of his yearning: "I have been looking for traces of them all my life. Sometimes I have thought I heard a Dwarf-drum in the mountains. Sometimes at night, in the woods, I thought I had caught a glimpse of Fauns and Satyrs dancing a long way off; but when I came to the place, there was never anything there. I have often despaired; but something always happens to start me hoping again" (53–54).

Peter experienced a similar yearning in *The Lion, the Witch and the Wardrobe*. After Mr. Beaver revealed that Aslan "isn't safe" but "he's good," Peter replied, "I'm longing to see him, even if I do feel frightened when it comes to the point" (80).

Frightened and Small

Earlier it was suggested that beginning with this second Narnia story, Lewis's protagonists will be somewhat more realistic. If in later chapters Caspian will be able to lead an army of Old Narnians into battle, it will be because here in chapter five, the prince learns "sword-fighting and riding" and "how to shoot with the bow" (56), in addition to other skills. Even with this training and practice, Caspian will be no match for Miraz, and it will be the older and more experienced Peter who will be chosen for the single combat.

As part of his informal education, the prince continues to learn the important lesson that things are not always as they appear. He comes to see that his aunt dislikes him and that Narnia is "an unhappy country" with high taxes and stern laws (57). In Caspian's final tutorial up on the Great Tower, he finds out that his Uncle Miraz is not merely a cruel man but a ruthless villain, a usurper who killed his own brother—Caspian's father—and then underhandedly did away with all the great lords who had supported the former king. In *The Lion, the Witch and the Wardrobe*, Aslan promised Mr. Beaver, "All names will soon be restored to their proper owners" (140). This promise will be kept at the end of *Prince Caspian* as well. In the story's final chapter, Aslan will tell the young prince, "Under us and under the High King, you shall be King of Narnia, Lord of Cair Paravel, and Emperor of the Lone Islands" (206).

Here Doctor Cornelius concludes his revelations about Miraz: "And finally he persuaded the seven noble lords, who alone among all the Telmarines did not fear the sea, to sail away and look for new lands beyond the Eastern Ocean, and, as he intended, they never came back" (59–60). Here Lewis sets up the basis for the next Narnia story, *The Voyage of the* Dawn Treader. There Caspian will explain, "When I was a child my usurping uncle Miraz got rid of seven friends of my father's (who might have taken my part) by sending them off to explore the unknown Eastern Seas beyond the Lone Islands" (20). If it is Caspian's duty to right the wrongs his uncle has committed, then since this task is not fully completed at the end of *Prince Caspian*, it must be undertaken later.

Next Caspian learns that he himself is positioned to be the next victim of Miraz's morals of expediency. As Cornelius says, "Now that he has a son of his own he will want his own son to be the next King. You are in the way. He'll clear you out of the way" (60).

With the news of the birth of the new baby, adult readers might wonder how the queen could have been pregnant for months without Caspian knowing it. However, when Caspian later flees from the castle, his absence will not be noticed for several days, and then only because his horse Destrier reappears in the castle stable without him. From this we might conclude that Caspian no longer sees the king on a regular basis, as he did earlier, and that he sees the queen even less frequently, which would explain why he would not have noticed the change in her condition. In addition, as we later find out, Miraz's court is filled with intrigue and backbiting. Perhaps the king and queen have concealed the pregnancy from everyone until the baby was born, out of concern that a rival for power might have tried to preempt Miraz from establishing his dynasty.

Caspian's circumstances share numerous parallels with Edmund's situation in *The Lion, the Witch and the Wardrobe*. Both young boys are promised they will succeed a monarch who first appears to them under the guise of kindness and concern. Both Edmund and Caspian quickly progress from naïveté to awareness as they find themselves fleeing for their lives from their supposed benefactors. In *The Magician's Nephew*, Lewis will have young Digory Kirke follow a similar path. When Digory first meets the White Witch, then known as Jadis, he believes her to be beautiful, brave, and strong. Later, like Edmund and Caspian, he comes to see through the false appearances. In presenting not one but three young characters whose education takes these same steps, Lewis suggests that this progression from unawareness to knowledge is a universal aspect of maturation. Lewis also interjects the insight that evil appears rarely as evil but typically under some other guise. Readers may recall the line from

The Lion, the Witch and the Wardrobe where the narrator explains that it was part of the Witch's evil magic to "make things look like what they aren't" (138).

If a number of protagonists come to learn the lesson that evil rarely appears as evil, we could also argue that a number of them must also learn that good characters are not always what they seem either. Caspian finds that his new tutor is far more than he first appears to be. Trumpkin will learn this same lesson about the four children. Tolkien embraces this same truth: not only does Aragorn turn out to be far more than he first seems to the hobbits, there is also a great deal more to the hobbits themselves than meets the eye.

The skill of discernment is a part of growing up, and from the beginning it is an important issue for Lewis's protagonists. Moments after their first arrival in Narnia, the Pevensies had to decide whether to follow a seemingly innocent robin and then whether to trust a secretive beaver. In *The Silver Chair*, Lewis will have the Green Witch appear as a beautiful woman. In *The Last Battle*, Shift will trick many Narnian creatures into believing that Puzzle is really Aslan.

After equipping his young pupil with what he can, Cornelius sends Caspian beyond the reach of Miraz and out into the wide world. Readers are told that for a short time Caspian feels "brave and, in a way, happy, to think that he was King Caspian riding to seek adventures" (63). If Lewis had stopped with this sentence, *Prince Caspian* would have been a very different book—less realistic and more escapist. But Lewis goes on to add this moving postscript: "But when day came, with a sprinkle of rain, and he looked about him and saw on every side unknown woods, wild heaths, and blue mountains, he thought how large and strange the world was and felt frightened and small."

Lewis will inject a similar realistic note at the start of chapter nine. There after the children and Trumpkin have been traveling all day in the rowboat, the narrator will state, "As they all grew more tired, their spirits fell. Up till now the children had only been thinking of how to get to Caspian. Now they wondered what they would do when they found him, and how a handful of Dwarfs and woodland creatures could defeat an army of grown-up Humans" (114).

Strange Help

Before Caspian's departure, Doctor Cornelius gives him "the magic horn of Queen Susan herself" (62). When Father Christmas originally presented Peter, Susan, and Lucy with their gifts in *The Lion, the Witch and the Wardrobe*, there was no indication that one present was more valuable than another. In the Doctor's claim that Susan's horn is "the greatest and most sacred treasure of Narnia" (61), readers must assume Cornelius is unaware that the other gifts have also survived and are in the treasure chamber at Cair Paravel.

The Doctor presents the horn to Caspian with the declaration, "It is said that whoever blows it shall have strange help—no one can say how strange" (62). The words "it is said" seem to refer to lore passed down through the centuries rather than to Father Christmas's original promise to Susan in *The Lion, the Witch and the Wardrobe*: "When you put this horn to your lips and blow it, then, wherever you are, I think help of some kind will come to you" (108). The existence of this lore suggests that the horn may have been used during the span of years separating the first two books.

Lewis reports only two uses of Susan's horn in the Chronicles. Both times it may be said to have brought this type of strange help—assistance that does not look like what was expected or hoped for but that turns out to be exactly what was needed. When Maugrim, the White Witch's wolf, attacked Susan in *The Lion, the Witch and the Wardrobe*, the horn call brought Peter, someone who has never used a sword before. However, with Peter's coming, not only was Susan saved, but the new high king had his first exposure to battle—experience he would need the next day in his encounter with the forces of the Witch. The only other recorded use of the horn will occur in chapter eight of *Prince Caspian*. When the prince blows the magic horn, his call for help will be answered not by the great warriors that he and his army are hoping for, but by the four children—strange help indeed.

It could be argued that a great deal of the aid in *Prince Caspian*, especially when viewed in retrospect, is this same kind of strange assistance. The exile of Caspian's nurse, though it appears unfortunate to Caspian, could be said to be strange help because it leads to the arrival of Doctor Cornelius. The violent thunderstorm that arrives during Caspian's flight from the castle will not seem much like assistance, nor will his subsequent riding accident, but without these events he would never have been rescued by Trumpkin and Trufflehunter. In chapter ten, the children and Trumpkin will travel to Aslan's How by rowing up Glasswater Creek. While at one point this route appears to have been a mistake—after they narrowly avoid being killed by Miraz's sentries at the Bridge of Beruna—Susan will conclude it was "a blessing in disguise" (135), another way of describing this strange type of help.

Strange help appears not only in *Prince Caspian* but throughout the Narnia stories. Perhaps the best illustration of this unconventional kind of blessing in disguise will be Eustace's transformation into a dragon in *The Voyage of the* Dawn Treader, a painful ordeal but the only way he will be able to achieve his much-needed character transformation.

In literature a theme may be defined as a generalization about life that is stated or implied by a story. In the Narnia stories, we can find a number of themes, or truths about life, Lewis sought to convey. At first glance, it might seem odd to claim that Lewis hoped to present truths about life in the real world through the events and characters of an imaginary land. But in fact, Lewis's insights about life are powerful and deeply moving *because of*, not *despite*, the fact they occur in the make-believe world of Narnia. We are able to see the truth of Lewis's statements about the human condition with greater clarity and poignancy because they are conveyed in a fairy-tale realm.

One of the themes, or generalizations about life, from *Prince Caspian* has already been mentioned: *evil appears rarely as evil but typically under some other guise*. A second theme introduced here could be the following: *help often comes in an unanticipated form, in a manner that is so unexpected and strange that it may be recognized as help only in looking back on it.*

Lewis had much to say about this kind of help in his other writings. In *Letters to Malcolm*, he writes, "It seems to me that we often, almost sulkily, reject the good that God offers us because, at that moment, we expected some other good" (26). This same lesson about accepting the good that is sent to us—however strange or unexpected it may be—plays a central role in *Perelandra*, the second volume of Lewis's space trilogy. In the unfallen world of Perelandra, the native name for Venus, the queen of that world explains the concept to Ransom:

> "One goes in the forest to pick food and already the thought of one fruit rather than another has grown up in one's mind. Then, it may be, one finds a different fruit and not the fruit one thought of. One joy was expected and another is given. . . . If you wished . . . you could send your soul after the good you had expected, instead of turning it to the good you had got. You could refuse the real good; you could make the real fruit taste insipid by thinking of the other." (59)

In chapter eight, Trumpkin will be guilty of initially rejecting the help that was sent because the Old Narnians had been anticipating a very different kind of assistance. He will tell the children, "The King and Trufflehunter and Doctor Cornelius were expecting—well, if you see what I mean, help. To put it another way, I think they'd been imagining you as great warriors. As it is—we're awfully fond of children and all that, but just at the moment, in the middle of a war—but I'm sure you understand" (103).

Lucy too will fall prey to limiting help to the kind she has been expecting, instead of being open to the help sent. As she will complain to Aslan, "I thought you'd come roaring in and frighten all the enemies away—like last time" (143).

The Old Narnians at Last

As Caspian gets farther from Miraz's castle, he enters "a dark and seemingly endless pine forest" and in fear remembers that he is a Telmarine, "one of the race who cut down trees wherever they could and were at war with all wild things" (64). In his portrait of Caspian's wicked ancestors and of Miraz in particular, Lewis will parallel many of the aspects found in Tolkien's villain Saruman. In *The Two Towers*, Treebeard describes Saruman in terms that could easily apply to Miraz, saying, "He is plotting to become a Power. He has a mind of metal and wheels; and he does not care for growing things, except as far as they serve him for the moment. And now it is clear that he is a black traitor. . . . Down on the borders they are felling trees—good trees" (462).

The parallels between the two evil figures continue. Readers learn that in their wanton destruction of the trees, both Miraz and Saruman have silenced the forests. Treebeard tells Merry and Pippin, "Many of those trees were my friends, creatures I had known from nut and acorn; many had voices of their own that are lost for ever" (462–63). Similarly Doctor Cornelius has told Caspian that it was the Telmarines who "silenced the beasts and the trees and the fountains" (51). Lewis and Tolkien suggest that tyrants like Saruman and Miraz will never be satisfied in their desire to dominate. The two oppressors seek to tame even the wild countryside, to subdue it and dominate it. With fitting justice, in both stories it will be the trees, after they have been wakened and roused, that will serve as the main vehicle in the overthrow of the evil regimes that have been abusing them.

When Caspian finally comes to after his riding accident, he finds himself lying on a bed of heather in a fire-lit cave. Lewis has intentionally kept the lighting low so that the prince will only gradually come to realize that he has found the Old Narnians. Like the Pevensies in the first book, Caspian has never seen a talking animal, so readers share his moment of astonishment and delight, similar to the moment when Lucy met Mr. Tumnus and later when the four children encountered Mr. Beaver.

First Caspian hears low voices speaking close at hand. Next he notices that one of the speakers has a "curiously husky, earthy voice" (65). As this person approaches the bed with a warm drink, the shape of his arm and his face seem "wrong." Caspian wonders if he is looking at a mask or if his perceptions are the product of a fevered imagination. Suddenly someone stirs the coals, causing a momentary blaze, and in this moment that combines shock, awe, and delight, Caspian recognizes that he is looking into the face of a badger not a human. By the fire he sees two "real Dwarfs, ancient Dwarfs" (67). Just before passing out, Caspian knows he has found the Old Narnians at last, the very creatures he has been looking for all his life.

Over the next few days as Caspian gradually recovers, Truffle-hunter, Nikabrik, and Trumpkin—the badger and the two dwarfs who have rescued the prince—continue the debate of what to do with him. Nikabrik, a "sour Black Dwarf" (67), continues to insist they kill Caspian, because, according to Nikabrik, Caspian is sure "to go back to its own kind and betray us all." Here Nikabrik, a thoroughgoing racist, is arguing from his own set of values. His words tell readers all there is to know about him. Going back to his own kind and then betraying those who are different is exactly what Nikabrik himself would do. In fact, Caspian wants just the opposite. He wants nothing to do with his "own kind," as he tells the Old Narnians: "I want to stay with you—if you'll let me" (68).

As Caspian recounts his story, Nikabrik learns of the role Doctor Cornelius has played. In a further manifestation of his deep-seated racism, and despite the fact that the details make it clear the Doctor is completely loyal to Old Narnia, Nikabrik replies, "It's all mixed up with that Tutor: a renegade Dwarf. I hate 'em. I hate 'em worse than the Humans" (69). Lewis, a keen observer of human vice, knew that the one thing a racist hates even more than someone of a race different from his or her own is someone who comes from a mixed-race background, whose very being suggests coexistence and harmony. Like racists everywhere, Nikabrik will refer to those who are different from him by using racial epithets. In addition to the term *renegade*, Nikabrik will later call Doctor Cornelius "a half-and-halfer" (88).

In his book *Companion to Narnia*, which I believe is the single best commentary on the seven-volume series, Paul Ford devotes nearly six pages to the issue of sexism in the Chronicles and rightly concludes that Lewis's fiction reveals "a basic sympathy for the equality of women" (388). In his entry titled *racism*, however, Ford offers only a single, four-sentence paragraph that argues Lewis was "a man of his time and socioeconomic class," and had he lived today, he surely would have reconsidered the racial "insensitivity" displayed in the Chronicles (363). David Colbert goes even further, claiming that Lewis's writing is "spiced with bigotry that is anything but unconscious" (166).

However, it could be argued that Lewis's fiction reveals sympathy for the equality not just of women but of all races, a sympathy that goes well beyond that of his time and class. Any discussion of racism in the Narnia stories that fails to point out Lewis's scathing indictment of Nikabrik's vile ethnocentrism here misses the author's position on this topic and the great emphasis he puts on acceptance of diversity.

Who Believes in Aslan Nowadays?

In the chapter on *Prince Caspian* in *The Way into Narnia*, Peter Schakel describes what he sees as the central focus of the novel: "*Prince Caspian*, with its beginning in the ruins of an ancient castle and its pervasive sense of antiquity, of the past, of the old days, of old stories, raises the question of believability: How can we believe in what we cannot see?" (50). Here at the end of chapter five, in what comes as a surprise, readers learn that two of the three Old Narnians Caspian has met do not believe in Aslan. And by defying our expectations here and resisting a simplistic predictability, Lewis adds seriousness and depth to the novel.

It is important to note that it is the virtuous Trumpkin and not his vile counterpart, Nikabrik, who interjects the element of serious doubt into the conversation. When the ever-faithful Trufflehunter asserts that he believes in "High Peter and the rest" as firmly as he believes in Aslan, Trumpkin's reply is, "But who believes in Aslan nowadays?" (70). Throughout *Prince Caspian*, Lewis will present the relationship between belief, reason, and action in its full complexity.

Paradoxically Miraz believes in Aslan, which is why he silences any mention of the great lion and has intentionally built up a buffer of dense woods along the sea, but his belief does not make him moral. Readers may be reminded of the observation from James 2:19 that even the demons believe in God.

Trumpkin, on the other hand, does not believe the stories of Aslan—not here in chapter five when Caspian first meets him, not during the strategy sessions at the Stone Table, and not even after he meets the four children, who appear as living proof that the old tales are true. Nevertheless there is no suggestion anywhere that Trumpkin's disbelief is morally wrong. It would be more accurate to say he is depicted as being on a faith journey, and at each point on this journey readers accept him for where he is. As Jonathan Rogers has noted, "Trumpkin is an honest dwarf, and his doubts are honest doubts" (33). It is significant that in chapter eleven when Trumpkin finally meets Aslan, the lion has no condemnation for the dwarf. Aslan will pretend to be angry, loudly stating, "And now, where is this little Dwarf, this famous swordsman and archer, who doesn't believe in lions?" (154). But the children, and readers also, can tell "he liked the Dwarf very much."

In *Mere Christianity*, Lewis responds to the notion that one could or should believe despite his reason, stating, "A sane man accepts or rejects any statement, not because he wants to or does not want to, but because the evidence seems to him good or bad" (138). He further elaborates, "I am not asking anyone to accept Christianity if his best reasoning tells him that the weight of the evidence is against it" (140). Evan Gibson argues that Lewis's depiction of Trumpkin's skepticism "suggests that Lewis did not believe that honest doubt about spiritual matters is a very serious problem" (161). As Gibson rightly concludes, Lewis's point is that "one who determines to do right will eventually be led right."

Caspian replies to Trumpkin's question of who believes in Aslan with the simple declaration "I do" (70), and he notes that the Old Narnians themselves are evidence that the ancient stories are true.

Trufflehunter affirms his loyalty to Caspian with the qualifica-tion, "As long as you will be true to Old Narnia you shall be *my*

King." Nikabrik's response is to raise the objection that Caspian has "*hunted* beasts for sport" (71), an objection he knows to be misconstrued. When Caspian admits to having hunted non-talking beasts, Nikabrik claims, "It's all the same thing." Trufflehunter vehemently counters Nikabrik's deceit, stating, "No, no, no, you know it isn't." As Jonathan Rogers has pointed out, "One of the hallmarks of Nikabrik's mind is intellectual dishonesty. He trots out specious arguments in support of his prejudices and hatreds, but he won't be convinced by sound reasoning" (33). Rogers argues that this pattern of deceit is characteristic of Nikabrik and observes, "You get the impression that this isn't the first time Trufflehunter has had to say, 'No, Nikabrik, you know that's not true.'"

Lewis ends chapter five with the statement: "There was a great deal more talk, but it all ended with the agreement that Caspian should stay" (71). Nikabrik's opposition to Caspian is overcome for now but will return with even greater stridency later.

Discussion Questions

As noted earlier, in his essay "On Three Ways of Writing for Children," Lewis claimed that fairy tales arouse a longing in the reader "for he knows not what" (38). Deep longing is an important element throughout *Prince Caspian*. In chapter four, the very young Caspian first states, "I wish—I wish—I wish I could have lived in the Old Days" (42). His repetition here could be interpreted as hesitation to say something that will anger his uncle, but it also could be read as a little boy's unyielding desire for something beyond the world he lives in.

In *The Lion, the Witch and the Wardrobe*, after Mr. Beaver tells the children "Aslan is on the move" (67), the narrator breaks in to tell us, "Now a very curious thing happened." Then he describes a feeling that Peter, Susan, and Lucy have of a dream "so beautiful that you remember it all your life and are always wishing you could get into that dream again" (68).

1. How do the Narnia stories evoke a longing when you read them?
2. To what extent can you identify something specific they make you long for, and to what extent do they cause a vague longing for "[you] know not what"?
3. In what ways might the longing evoked by the Chronicles of Narnia be different for younger readers? In what ways might all readers, young and old, experience the same yearnings?

In this chapter, some of the parallels between Caspian and Edmund were noted. Both young characters mistake bad for good and only later realize their error. Lewis, by choosing to go down this same path twice, may be suggesting that this is a common path for all young people.

4. How are Edmund and Caspian initially taken in by the White Witch and Miraz? Why are they unable to see what readers, young and old, quickly realize—that these two are evil and should not be believed?
5. Is this theme—that evil often masquerades as good—something that all young people must learn at some point on their journey?

6

The People That Lived in Hiding

All Sorts of People with Queer Names

In chapter six we find the fulfillment of Caspian's promise that as soon as he was well enough, he should be taken to see what Trumpkin calls "the Others" (71). The subsequent accounts of Caspian's series of meetings—with the Bulgy Bears, Pattertwig the squirrel, the Seven Brothers of Shuddering Wood, the five Black Dwarfs, Glenstorm the centaur, Reepicheep the mouse, Clodsley Shovel the mole, the Hardbiter badgers, Camillo the hare, and Hogglestock the hedgehog—may appear as merely a string of delightful encounters intended for the enjoyment of younger readers, but Lewis uses these incidents to make a highly relevant point. With each new type of character introduced, Lewis advances one of his most important themes: *real community is made up of different types of individuals with different gifts and different abilities.*

With so many new characters to introduce, Lewis makes the most of each detail. As with Trufflehunter earlier, each character is given a name suggestive of his nature. Readers discover that the Bulgy Bears are quite bulgy, that Pattertwig keeps up a running patter as he bounces from branch to branch, and that the Seven Brothers make the Shuddering Wood shudder with their powerful hammering. Glenstorm the centaur is described as living in "a great glen or wooded gorge" (77). Paul Ford further proposes that his name "suggests that he is a force to reckon with, whose sheer weight makes his presence felt on the pastures" (227). The Hardbiters are badgers whose name hints that they, like Trufflehunter, possess a stubborn resolve.

The name of Clodsley Shovel, a mole who spends his time digging through clods of dirt, has a second chuckle for readers who know of Sir Cloudsley Shovel (1650–1707), the famous British admiral who, ignoring repeated warnings that his entire fleet was off course, blindly steered them onto rocks near Sicily. Readers who recognize this historical reference may call to mind the expression "blind as a mole."

As seen earlier with the name Prunaprismia and here again with Clodsley Shovel, Lewis does not limit himself to allusions with which all his readers would be familiar. In fact, his links with literature, history, or old languages are sometimes so obscure that they seem made for the amusement of the Inklings, his erudite writing group. Another example of this practice occurs with the name of Caspian's horse, Destrier, which is an ancient term for a war horse. Paul Ford suggests that Lewis's use of the name Destrier helps to create a medieval atmosphere in the Chronicles (165), a claim that is true only if the reader knows that this word has origins in Old French.

In *The Horse and His Boy*, Lewis will have Shasta explain that in times of war, "Everyone must do what he can do best" (209). The Old Narnians are not quite at war yet, but here in chapter six of *Prince Caspian*, they each give something from their own unique resources. From the bears Caspian receives honey; from Pattertwig he receives a nut. The Seven Brothers of the Shuddering Wood donate mail shirts, helmets, and swords. Glenstorm offers wise advice, and Reepicheep pledges his service as well as that of his band of fellow mice. It is significant that while most of the Old Narnians live in fertile, green surroundings, the five Black Dwarfs are described as living in "a dry, rocky ravine" (76), and they do not give Caspian anything, except for a suspicious and sullen reception.

If He Is Against Miraz

Continuing his portrait of dwarfs as highly capable creatures, Lewis gives readers a brief but dignified portrait of the Seven Brothers of Shuddering Wood, a family of Red Dwarfs whose labor at their smithy makes the ground tremble and results in workmanship "far finer than any Caspian had ever seen" (76). On January 5, 1939, a decade before writing *Prince Caspian*, Lewis and his brother Warnie had gone to see Walt Disney's film *Snow White and the Seven Dwarfs*. In *Surprised by Joy*, Lewis describes how as a boy he had fallen deeply under the spell of Dwarfs but notes that this was "before Arthur Rackham sublimed, or Walt Disney vulgarized, the earthmen" (54). At this point in *Prince Caspian*, Lewis takes the opportunity to present his own seven dwarfs as creatures more capable and consequential than their cartoon counterparts.

The narrator points out that it takes "some time" to convince the Seven Brothers that Caspian is a friend to the Old Narnians and not an enemy like the rest of the Telmarines (76). As Paul Ford has noted, Narnian dwarfs are prone to "hypersuspicion" (185), and even Trumpkin will exhibit this deep tendency of his race. Once convinced, however, the seven Red Dwarfs give the young monarch their unqualified support, crying together, "Long live the King" (76).

Caspian has a very different reception from the Black Dwarfs. We learn that they look suspiciously at the prince and never offer a similar expression of commitment. The eldest merely states, "If he is against Miraz, we'll have him for King" (76), a comment that contains the implied warning that the Black Dwarfs will follow

Caspian only as long as he is advancing their goals. This lack of allegiance by the dwarfs will appear again not only in *Prince Caspian* but also in *The Last Battle*. There a group of renegade dwarfs will tell King Tirian, "No more Aslan, no more Kings, no more silly stories about other worlds" (83). They will then conclude with a statement that fully summarizes the dwarfish predisposition: "The Dwarfs are for the Dwarfs."

Perhaps the most telling comment in the exchange with the five Black Dwarfs comes after one of them suggests that Caspian should be introduced to an ogre and a hag, evil characters who live nearby. When Caspian, Trufflehunter, and Trumpkin reject this idea, Nikabrik disagrees with them and must be "overruled" (77), much as he was back in chapter five when he wanted to kill Caspian. In what is part warning, part threat, Nikabrik boldly declares, "I'll believe in anyone or anything that'll batter these cursed Telmarine barbarians to pieces or drive them out of Narnia. Anyone or anything, Aslan *or* the White Witch, do you understand?" Nikabrik's statement here helps prepare readers for his treachery at Aslan's How in chapter twelve.

In literary works, authors often make use of what is called a foil character. As briefly mentioned earlier in the discussion of chapter four, this is someone who, through comparison, highlights the features of another character. When the comparison is between a main character and a minor character, the minor character is seen as a foil for the first. When the two characters are relatively equal in importance, they can be referred to as foils for each other. In *The Lord of the Rings*, Gandalf and Saruman—two wizards who take differing positions regarding the Ring and the use of power—stand as opposing foils. Tolkien also sets up another pair of foils in Théoden and Denethor. Both aging rulers are faced with overwhelming odds, but while Théoden overcomes his despair and remains resolute, Denethor gives in to hopelessness. To further highlight their contrast, Tolkien places their deaths in adjacent chapters. Théoden dies with honor on the battlefield, while Denethor commits suicide.

Lewis likewise employs a number of foils in *Prince Caspian*. Two of the clearest are Nikabrik and Trumpkin. Although both dwarfs begin as unbelievers, Nikabrik's contempt, negativity, and ethics of expediency are in sharp contrast with Trumpkin's humility, optimism, and morality. In the next chapter, Trumpkin's loyalty and submission serve to further underscore Nikabrik's faithless and self-serving attitude. Trumpkin will tell Caspian, "You are my King. I know the difference between giving advice and taking orders. You've had my advice, and now it's the time for orders" (98). In addition, in chapter eight after Trumpkin is shown his error in underestimating the four children, he both confesses his mistake and expresses his gratitude in a way Nikabrik never would, stating, "Well, I've made as big a fool of myself as ever a Dwarf did. No offense, I hope? My humble duty to your Majesties all—humble duty. And thanks for my life, my cure, my breakfast—and my lesson" (109–10).

What happens to the two dwarfs can be seen as a natural consequence of their contrasting natures. In the encounter inside Aslan's How, Nikabrik is killed as a direct result of his treason, whereas in *The Voyage of the* Dawn Treader, the faithful Trumpkin will be named as regent over all of Narnia while Caspian is away searching for the lords exiled by Miraz.

Though Nikabrik's ethics differ completely from Trumpkin's, ironically they bear a strong resemblance to those of Miraz, Nikabrik's hated enemy. Both are willing to use any means available to advance their ends, including betrayal, treachery, and murder. Because they have their own self-interest as their only guiding principle, both are very willing to use a coup to overthrow the legitimate authority and put themselves in a position of power. Here in chapter six, Trufflehunter points out that the White Witch was a worse enemy than Miraz. Nikabrik's response—"Not to Dwarfs, she wasn't" (77)—perfectly expresses his overriding self-centeredness.

The conflict between the opposing values of the Black Dwarfs and the rest of the Old Narnians in *Prince Caspian* is left unresolved until chapter twelve, when it culminates in a battle to the death between Nikabrik and Trufflehunter, who may be seen as the most differing representatives of the opposing sides. There Trufflehunter will have to remind Nikabrik, "His Majesty is the King to whom you have sworn allegiance" (165). Nikabrik's vow of fealty, like any promise he makes, is good only so long as it profits him. This fact is made clear in his response. He will shrug off Trufflehunter's admonition and claim that his sworn allegiance was merely "court manners."

After Nikabrik's death, Caspian will express regret and note the possibility for Nikabrik's redemption, stating, "He might have become a good Dwarf in the days of peace" (173). Lewis's evil characters are typically not simply evil but, like people who commit evil in the real world, will have some reason for their actions. According to Caspian, Nikabrik went "sour inside" because of his "long suffering and hating," a description that could also explain the attitudes of the five Black Dwarfs Caspian meets here in chapter six.

When Is the Battle to Be Joined?

The narrator points out that the next visit with Glenstorm is "a pleasanter one" than Caspian's encounter with the Black Dwarfs (77). The company hikes from the dry, rocky ravine of the Black Dwarfs into a lush valley, or glen, filled with blooming roses, masses of foxgloves, and the buzzing of bees. In the same gradual fashion that Trufflehunter was introduced earlier after Caspian's accident, here again Lewis gives us a sound that precedes its source. Readers are told that the echo of galloping hooves "grew louder till the valley trembled and at last, breaking and trampling the thickets, there came in sight the noblest creatures that Caspian had yet seen, the great Centaur Glenstorm and his three sons" (78).

Perhaps to preserve their special dramatic impact, Lewis uses centaurs only rarely in the Chronicles, preferring to cast more humble, ordinary creatures—children, beavers, badgers, mice, horses, and Marsh-wiggles—in the major roles. Centaurs, while present, are not given specific names or speaking parts in Lewis's version of *The Lion, the Witch and the Wardrobe*, as they are in the movie. In his use of more common, less majestic creatures as his heroes, Lewis was taking a tack similar to Tolkien who, while including elves and wizards in *The Lord of the Rings*, chose hobbits as his prime focus. As Tolkien himself noted about his own writing, "There are of course certain things and themes that move me specially. The inter-relations between the 'noble' and the 'simple' (or common, vulgar) for instance. The ennoblement of the ignoble I find specially moving" (*Letters* 220).

Perhaps in keeping with his similar strategy of making less majestic creatures his main protagonists, Lewis will have Glenstorm appear only once more in *Prince Caspian*, as part of the embassy to Miraz. There, as Trufflehunter notes, he is chosen because "no one ever laughed at a Centaur" (178). In contrast to the dwarfs, both red and black, who needed to be convinced of Caspian's title, Glenstorm, described here as "a prophet and a star-gazer" (78), already knows who Caspian is and why he has come. Accordingly his first words are "Long live the King."

Caspian, and perhaps readers as well, are somewhat surprised by Glenstorm's very next statement as he tells the company, "I and my sons are ready for war. When is the battle to be joined?" (78). Like Peter before him, Caspian must gradually grow into his title, a fact that adds realism to his character. While Aslan served as Peter's advisor in *The Lion, the Witch and the Wardrobe*, Caspian will be given guidance by a number of counselors. Doctor Cornelius will continue to offer his learned advice. Here Glenstorm's words prod the young ruler to look beyond "an occasional raid" on the unlawful government and to become "more serious." In chapter thirteen, King Peter himself will step in to mentor his young counterpart. Unlike *The Lion, the Witch and the Wardrobe*, which included the coronation of the four Pevensies, *Prince Caspian* will end without a crowning, and in this decision and in the book's title, Lewis implies that, despite Glenstorm's greeting, Caspian still has more growing to undergo before fully assuming his position as king.

Peter Schakel has noted this extended period of maturation for the young prince and sees it as part of Lewis's overall plan for the sequence of three Narnia stories that feature Caspian. Schakel observes:

> The ending, while unifying the plot and themes of the book, does not complete the story of the title character's growth. *Prince Caspian* describes Caspian's initiation and the first steps toward his maturity. . . .

Lewis subordinates his title character in the second half of the book in order to allow his continued growth—in maturity, knowledge of Aslan, and trust in Aslan—to occur in *The Voyage of the "Dawn Treader*," the second book of the "Caspian trilogy." (*Way* 59)

Lewis will choose to have many of his protagonists—not just Caspian but also Peter, Edmund, Lucy, Eustace, and Jill—grow and mature over the course of several books. In doing so, Lewis not only makes their development more detailed and more realistic but also gives readers the chance to get to know them in a deeper way and to identify with them as well.

In answer to Trufflehunter's question of whether it is possible for the Old Narnians to drive Miraz out of Narnia, Glenstorm gives no guarantee but states only that "the time is ripe" (78). As with the prophecies found previously in *The Lion, the Witch and the Wardrobe*, Lewis offers hope—but never complete assurance—that the efforts of the protagonists will be successful, and in doing so, he intertwines destiny and free will. In this same mixture of prophecy and choice, Glenstorm declares somewhat vaguely, "The hour has struck" (79). The narrator concludes the scene with this same blend of hope and ambiguity by noting, "It now seemed to them quite possible that they might win a war."

A Talking Mouse

Lest readers forget the peril that still surrounds the Old Narnians, on the way to the next encounter, the narrator briefly steps in with a reminder of the weak position Caspian's forces are in. We are told, "The next place they were to visit was quite near at hand, but they had to go a long way round in order to avoid a region in which Men lived" (79). Finally, in an area of level fields bordered by hedgerows, Caspian is introduced to the last thing he or readers expect—a large talking mouse.

In *The Lion, the Witch and the Wardrobe*, mice appeared briefly for three pages in chapter fifteen to gnaw away the ropes that bound Aslan. Where they came from and where they went afterward was never explained. They were non-talking mice, presumably non-rational, and how or why they happened to show up was left a mystery. At this point in *Prince Caspian*, Lewis introduces a talking mouse described as "well over a foot high when he stood on his hind legs" (79). It turns out that there is a connection between the non-talking mice from the first book and the mice that appear in *Prince Caspian*, but Lewis will wait until the book's final chapter to reveal it.

In writing the sequel to *The Lion, the Witch and the Wardrobe*, rather than creating everything from scratch, Lewis often took small elements from the first book and allowed them to branch and grow into new elements. In doing so, he lessened the burden of creative innovation and at the same time provided important links between the stories that would establish continuity and pique readers' interest. This is a technique also used by Tolkien in writing the sequel to *The Hobbit*. In *The Lord of the Rings*, for example, the story behind Bilbo's Ring is a somewhat minor aspect in the first narrative, but it develops into one of the key elements that pushes the second story forward. In *Prince Caspian*, readers have already seen how Lewis brought back Susan's bow, an element he had introduced earlier but never put to use. Here in chapter six, Lewis turns once again to the topic of mice in Narnia.

Evan Gibson has called Reepicheep "one of Lewis's most successful creations" (161), an evaluation shared by most readers. Gibson goes on to point out that "although there is a comic element about the High Mouse, he is taken seriously"—by Lewis, by readers, and ultimately by his fellow Narnians, if not always initially. Here in chapter six, Reepicheep has but a single spoken line, but in it Lewis establishes the traits the mouse will be known for—courtesy, sacrifice, courage, and gallantry. Reepicheep bows low and tells Caspian, "There are twelve of us, Sire, and I place all the resources of my people unreservedly at your Majesty's disposal" (80).

Doris Myers has observed that Reepicheep is Lewis's best example of "aristocratic, ethical behavior," and the fact that this grand soul is located in a mouse's body can be seen as Lewis's "touch of Anglican self-mockery" (quoted in Ford 480). Myers goes on to note that through Reepicheep, Lewis introduces into the story "the Renaissance model of a gentleman," one who defends his honor, maintains "a courteous demeanor," and "demonstrates his courage at every opportunity."

In the next Narnia book, Lewis will give Reepicheep not only a larger role but perhaps a few more inches in stature as well. Here in *Prince Caspian*, readers are told the valiant mouse stands well over a foot high. In *The Voyage of the* Dawn Treader, Reepicheep will be described as "about two feet high" (15).

Artistic Unity and the Well-Crafted Novel

After all the meetings have taken place and after everyone has had supper, Trufflehunter wishes, "If only we could wake the spirits of these trees" (80). This is the second time someone has bemoaned the fact that the trees have been put to sleep by the Telmarines' persecution. As was noted, back in chapter four Doctor Cornelius had hoped Caspian might "find a way of awaking the trees once more" (53). A well-crafted novel will display artistic unity, which means everything the author has included has been needed, and everything needed has been included. If the spirits of the trees are to awake later and become not just one factor but the key factor in winning the final battle in *Prince Caspian*, then Lewis must establish the possibility for this in advance in order to make what happens seem both natural and believable. In fact, Lewis will revisit the issue of waking the trees twice more before the final battle.

The vital importance of artistic unity can be seen best when it is lacking—when an author fails to set up an element that occurs later. When that element appears, it seems more like an improbable coincidence than a natural product of what has come before. Greek drama was sometimes particularly guilty of lacking artistic unity. When the protagonists would end up in an impossible situation and need rescuing, the easy solution was to send one of the Greek gods down in a mechanized apparatus to save the day and set everything right. The literary term for this type of resolution is *deus ex machina*, meaning "god from a machine." Some readers may feel that Lewis at least partially resorted to this method when Aslan used "Deeper

Magic" in *The Lion, the Witch and the Wardrobe* with no earlier hints of its existence, a move uncharacteristic of his writing.

Another way to express the idea of artistic unity is the saying, "If you are going to shoot a cannon in Act V, you must put it on the wall in Act I, and if you put a cannon on the wall in Act I, you must shoot it in Act V." Similarly, it could be said that Caspian's later attempt to abdicate his throne near the end of *The Voyage of the* Dawn Treader is in a small way set up by his unsure answer to Miraz's question in chapter four of whether he wanted to become king.

Fauns!

Yet another example of artistic unity can be seen in the dance in the moonlight that Lewis uses to conclude chapter six. Readers may remember the tales Mr. Tumnus had told Lucy near the start of *The Lion, the Witch and the Wardrobe*: "He told about the midnight dances and how the Nymphs who lived in the wells and the Dryads who lived in the trees came out to dance with the Fauns. . . . And then about summer when the woods were green and old Silenus on his fat donkey would come to visit them, and sometimes Bacchus himself" (15–16). Besides setting up the midnight dance here, which everyone but Nikabrik participates in, Mr. Tumnus's stories also help prepare readers for the arrival of Silenus and Bacchus later in chapter eleven.

In a letter Lewis wrote in 1957 to an aspiring author, he offered several tips, among them the advice that to be memorable, names of characters "ought to be beautiful and suggestive" and "not merely odd" (*Letters of C. S. Lewis* 469). Lewis obeyed this guideline with nearly all of his characters, and thus we have unforgettable names like Mr. Tumnus, Caspian, Reepicheep, and Trufflehunter. The exception is found in the Roman-sounding faun names that appear here. Although Pattertwig was sent to invite "all sorts of people with queer names" to the council on Dancing Lawn, the fauns' names—Mentius, Obentinus, Dumnus, Voluns, Voltinus, Girbius, Nimienus, Nausus, and Oscuns—may be *too* "queer." These names are not only immediately forgotten, but this list of them becomes one of the rare descriptive passages in the Chronicles that readers may be tempted to simply skip over.

As Paul Ford has pointed out, "Dances and dancing are the chief means of celebration in Narnia" (153). Besides the celestial dance performed by the planets Tarva and Alambil, which Doctor Cornelius described earlier, there are four additional dances that occur over the course of *Prince Caspian*, and all of these take place here at Dancing Lawn. Here in the final paragraphs of chapter six, Lewis advances yet another key theme: *celebration, joy, and merriment are central to life, not elements reserved only for holidays or vacations.* What may be most noteworthy here is that this festive dance to the music of reedy pipes takes place during a time of oppression, just days before the outbreak of a full-scale war.

Lewis expands on the topic of festivity and safety in *The Problem of Pain*, where he observes, "The settled happiness and security which we all desire, God withholds from us by the very nature of the world: but joy, pleasure and merriment He has scattered broadcast. We are never safe, but we have plenty of fun, and some ecstasy. It is not hard to see why. The security we crave would teach us to rest our hearts in this world" (103). Here in *Prince Caspian*, the dancers are far from safe or secure, but this does not hamper or lessen their celebration.

This merriment contrasts sharply with the somber and repressive tone seen earlier at Miraz's castle. In the preface to *The Screwtape Letters*, Lewis describes the "ruthless, sleepless, unsmiling concentration upon self which is the mark of Hell" (ix). There is no smiling or laughter—at least not the happy kind—depicted at Miraz's castle or among his courtiers, nor are we told about any dancing by moonlight, or by any light. Readers may wonder how festive the fireworks marking the birth of the new prince really were. Although Miraz has tried to snuff out all feelings of joy or freedom, these emotions live on in dances like this one, which presumably have been taking place in secret all along.

The moonlight dance with the fauns is significant for another reason. Like most authors, Lewis put some of himself into a number of his characters. We can find aspects of Lewis in Professor Kirke's occupation and bachelorhood, in the transformations Edmund and Eustace undergo, and even to some extent in Susan's fearfulness. However, if we take Alan Jacobs's proposal about which feature of Lewis's personality was most central, then it could be argued that of all his characters, Lewis was most like Caspian. Jacobs argues that Lewis was above all characterized by "a willingness to be enchanted" and that this aspect "held together the various strands of his life" (xxi). In Lewis and in Caspian, we discover what Jacobs refers to as "an openness to delight, to the sense that there's more to the world than meets the jaundiced eye."

As evidenced by Caspian's declaration to Miraz in chapter four, "All the same, I *do* wish" (42); his first words in Trufflehunter's den, "I want to stay with you—if you'll let me" (68); and "Fauns!" (82), his shout of gladness here at the end of chapter six, Caspian has opened himself to the enchantment and mystery of Narnia that his uncle has tried to destroy. While one kind of enchantment came to Lewis through nature, the prime vehicle for Lewis was story. Jacobs argues that Lewis's unswerving willingness "to submit to the charms of a wonderful story" was fundamental to who he was (xxi). Accordingly one of the first things we were told about the young Caspian was that he liked best "the last hour of the day when the toys had all been put back in their cupboards and Nurse would tell him stories" (41).

Chapter six concludes with Pauline Baynes's illustration of the fauns' dance, clearly showing Caspian joining in with delight. The illustration also shows Nikabrik sitting off to the side with a scowl on his face—a foreshadowing of things to come.

Discussion Questions

In chapter six, Lewis advances one of his most important themes: real community is made up of different types of individuals with different gifts and different abilities.

1. Discuss how diversity in Narnia does not mean simply different colors and sizes but also a diversity of temperaments, personalities, abilities, and opinions.

2. What lessons about diversity in our world might Lewis be trying to teach through his story set in Narnia?

We also get a brief glimpse at another one of Lewis's most important themes: celebration, joy, and merriment are central to life, not elements reserved only for holidays or vacations. When the Witch tempted Edmund with Turkish Delight in *The Lion, the Witch and the Wardrobe*, Lewis was not implying that enjoying sweets is wrong. In fact, his position is just the opposite. Enjoyment of life's pleasures is an essential quality of proper Narnian life, as can be seen in the tea that Mr. Tumnus provided for Lucy, which included "a nice brown egg, lightly boiled, for each of them, and then sardines on toast, and then buttered toast, and then toast with honey, and then a sugar-topped cake" (15).

Throughout the Chronicles and his other works, Lewis suggests over and over that right living involves a certain stance or attitude toward the things of creation, one of great enjoyment but not slavish adoration. One of Narnia's defining characteristics is its merriment and festivity.

3. As you look at the fauns' dance here in chapter six, as well as other times of celebration and enjoyment, what message do you think Lewis may be sending to his readers?

Most critics, even those who do not agree with Lewis's overall themes or insights, agree that Lewis was a master storyteller and a master craftsman whose books for young readers can be pointed to as standards of excellence.

4. Besides artistic unity, which was mentioned in this chapter, what other elements in the Chronicles mark them as being particularly well written?
5. Are there any elements that stand out as being weaker than others? Is this a question younger readers might answer differently than older readers?

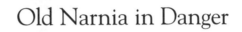

7

Old Narnia in Danger

Various Strange Subjects

Chapter seven opens with a brief description of Caspian's living outdoors at Dancing Lawn, awaiting the council meeting called for midnight three days later. Lewis's narrator describes the prince's experience this way: "To sleep under the stars, to drink nothing but well water and to live chiefly on nuts and wild fruit, was a strange experience for Caspian after his bed with silken sheets in a tapestried chamber at the castle, with meals laid out on gold and silver dishes in the anteroom, and attendants ready at his call" (84). Here we see the beginnings of the second stage of a three-step process common to many hero tales. As Colin Manlove has pointed out, Caspian follows "the pastoral movement of a departure from the court or city to the wildness of nature and then back again with new and redeeming power" (143–44).

In this story of a ruler who finds a pasture preferable to a palace, Lewis may have had in the back of his mind the story of King Fergus, the Irish king who forsook his kingdom to live a simpler life in the wild. Lewis, who as a young man was strongly influenced by the Irish poet William Butler Yeats, certainly knew Yeats's poem "Who Goes with Fergus?" which asks its readers who will go with Fergus to "pierce the deep wood's woven shade" and to "dance upon the level shore," much as Caspian does here.

In addition to Caspian's ambivalent statements about assuming the kingship and his attempt to abdicate in *The Voyage of the Dawn Treader*, one further element that contributes to the perception of Caspian as a somewhat reluctant ruler, much as Fergus was, is the fact that Lewis never depicts him on his throne. Despite appearing as a main character in two Narnia stories and as a lesser figure in a third, Caspian is never shown as a king holding court from his throne in his castle.

Soon the night of the council meeting arrives, and readers are told that gradually by the light of the moon "various strange subjects came stealing into the lawn" (84). Caspian's war council will have a number of elements in common with the Council of Elrond in *The Lord of the Rings*. Both meetings take place about one-third of the way into the story, following hazardous journeys made by young, inexperienced protagonists largely on their own. At both councils, decisions are made that will affect the story's final outcome. Most significantly, both gatherings are heavily multiracial, involving characters with widely conflicting opinions about what course of action is best.

In a manner consistent with their unique traits, the bears, mice, squirrels, moles, and fauns all have differing proposals for what should take place first. Here as Caspian begins to assume leadership, he gets practice trying to govern not the homogenous kingdom of Telmarines his uncle rules over but a Narnia composed of mice and giants, dwarfs and centaurs—a diversity captured well here in Pauline Baynes's illustration of the young prince addressing his circle of various strange subjects.

In his earlier novel *Out of the Silent Planet*, Lewis takes Ransom, his protagonist, to the planet of Malacandra, where three races live in harmony with each other as well as with a fourth nonphysical race called eldil. At one point, a group of sorns, the race of intellectuals, questions Ransom about human life on Earth. One of the key elements they learn from him is that on Earth there is only one kind of rational species, a factor they conclude "must have far-reaching effects in the narrowing of sympathies and even of thought" (102). In *Prince Caspian*, Lewis shows that this narrowing of sympathies due to limited exposure to other races is not limited to the Telmarines. In chapter five when Caspian awoke in Trufflehunter's den, the Old Narnians referred to him as "it" (65). In a choice between a homogenous society—whether all humans or all Old Narnians—or one rich with diversity, Lewis again asserts that real community is made up of different kinds of individuals.

Caspian barely begins to speak when he is interrupted by the announcement that something smelling "like Man and yet not quite like Man" is somewhere near (86). In his first act of command, the prince orders two badgers and three dwarfs to capture the intruder. Indicative of the Black Dwarfs' failure to recognize Caspian's authority, one of them questions the prince's instructions not to shoot and must be commanded by Glenstorm, "Do as you're told." The intruder turns out to be none other than Doctor Cornelius, himself now on the run from Miraz. He brings important news that they all must flee for safety because, as he tells them, "Miraz is on the move. Before midday tomorrow you will be surrounded" (88). His first statement will have a special resonance for readers of *The Lion, the Witch and the Wardrobe*. In a dramatic moment during the first encounter the four children have with Mr. Beaver, he announced, "They say Aslan is on the move" (67). Here Doctor Cornelius's use of the identical phrase highlights the precarious state of the Old Narnians, who find themselves outnumbered, unprepared, and, as far as they know, without help. With Miraz rather than Aslan on the move, the need for Susan's horn to bring assistance becomes even more desperate.

Shakespeare in Narnia?

Imagine a story where an evil traitor kills his brother and steals his crown. After assuming the throne, the usurper pretends to show affection for his late brother's son but in reality seeks to do away with him as well. The nephew soon discovers his uncle's intentions and escapes. In the end, justice is achieved in an unexpected manner. This is the story of *Prince Caspian*. It is also the story of *Hamlet, Prince of Denmark*.

Although technically not his literary specialty, Lewis knew well the plays of William Shakespeare. In fact, in October 1938 he gave a lecture titled "Hamlet: The Prince or the Poem?" which would later be published in a number of collections, including the prestigious Norton Critical Edition of the play. So what can we say about the plot similarities between *Prince Caspian* and *Hamlet*? Are they intended as allusions? First we must ask if any resemblances we find are significant enough for us to claim there is some kind of a connection. Then we must determine if a particular similarity was simply a case of Lewis borrowing and adapting some element he liked from Shakespeare—an aspect of the plot or a turn of a phrase—or whether the association is supposed to add to our reading, to evoke additional thoughts or feelings because of its source.

Marvin Hinten claims that the idea for Miraz to murder his brother and steal his throne is a "plot feature" Lewis "derived" from *Hamlet* (26), a claim that has merit but is difficult to prove. It is hard to say for sure if Lewis intends for us to hear an echo of *Hamlet* in the story of Prince Caspian, as earlier he seemed to echo *Little Dorrit* with the name for Queen Prunaprismia. Perhaps the similarities between these two works will evoke memories in some readers of how a young and inexperienced prince of Denmark learned that appearance and reality are not always the same, a lesson the young Prince Caspian comes to learn also.

Connections between Shakespeare and Narnia might not warrant as much discussion if it were not for the fact that there are several other instances in the Chronicles where there seem to be possible links. In act three of *A Midsummer Night's Dream*, the character Bottom makes a journey into the forest, where he meets Titania's fairies. As he is introduced, Bottom replies, "I shall desire you of more acquaintance, good Master Cobweb. . . . Master Peaseblossom, I shall desire you of more acquaintance too. . . . I desire your

more acquaintance, good Master Mustardseed" (3.1.160–73). Here
in chapter seven of *Prince Caspian*, Doctor Cornelius too makes a
journey into the forest and is introduced to a giant talking mouse, a
character as fantastical as Shakespeare's airy spirits. In words closely
reminiscent of those used by Bottom, Doctor Cornelius says to Reepicheep, "Signior Mouse, I desire your better acquaintance" (89).

In chapter eight of *Prince Caspian*, after Edmund persists in referring to Trumpkin as Our Dear Little Friend, Lewis will have
the dwarf tell him, "No more of that, your Majesty, if you love
me" (111). This closely parallels Falstaff's reply to Prince Hal in
Henry IV, Part I, where Falstaff says, "Ah, no more of that, Hal, an
thou lovest me!" (2.4.283).

In chapter eleven of *The Voyage of the* Dawn Treader, Coriakin will
tell Lucy, "I am a little impatient, waiting for the day when they can
be governed by wisdom instead of this rough magic" (161). The final
two words used here are identical to those Prospero says in act five of
The Tempest: "But this rough magic I here abjure" (5.1.50–51).

Perhaps readers will hear echoes of Shakespeare in these lines,
and in the first example they will find in the Old Narnians the same
dreamlike quality as seen in Shakespeare's woodland sprites. Perhaps they will, in Trumpkin and Edmund's friendship, be reminded
of the affection between Falstaff and Hal. Possibly in Coriakin's
words they will be reminded of Prospero's same desire to go beyond
governing by force.

However, another possible way to treat these somewhat minor
similarities is to see them as merely affectionate borrowings, reflections of previous material that are not intended to change the way
we react to a passage. This is the response taken by Paul Ford in
regard to the term Lewis will use to refer to Reepicheep in chapter
fourteen. Ford argues:

> In *Prince Caspian*, Lewis calls Reepicheep "the Master Mouse," a
> term suitable enough to Reepicheep's station in life but actually
> drawn from Henryson's version of Aesop's lion-and-mouse story in
> the *Morall Fabillis*. No doubt Lewis was tickled by the expression
> and amused by the new currency he was giving it. He may even

have looked ahead with pleasure to the possibility that a few of his child readers, going on to study literature, would meet Henryson's original Master Mouse. (288)

So perhaps we can simply claim that these similarities are not allusions intended to impact our reading, but rather, as Ford proposes, that Lewis was "tickled" by these elements of Shakespeare he echoes, was "amused by the new currency" he was able to give them, and "looked ahead with pleasure" to the chance that some readers would find them someday—in this case in *Hamlet, A Midsummer Night's Dream, Henry IV*, and *The Tempest*.

It is better to miss the literary allusions than to be distracted from the story by chasing down nonexistent ones. In his book *Reading with the Heart*, Peter Schakel rightly claims, "Lewis created in his stories 'secondary worlds' which he expected readers to enter imaginatively and to respond to, initially, with their hearts rather than with their heads" (xii). The key word here is *initially*. On one hand, readers should not be so caught up with tracking down echoes of Shakespeare or any other source that they miss the story. On the other hand, with further readings of the Narnia stories, readers will be well rewarded by using their heads to think about what additional meanings Lewis might have intended.

In *The Way into Narnia*, Schakel goes on to identify numerous parallels to other works but adds this qualification: "I have noted some allusions, ones that are functional and in some way enrich the work. I have not tried to point out every passing verbal echoing of the Bible and other works, ones that may or may not be actual allusions" (121). In this way, Schakel distinguishes between those allusions that affect our reading and those he labels as "merely interesting curiosities."

Aslan's How

Nikabrik rudely interrupts the exchange between Doctor Cornelius and Reepicheep, exclaiming, "Is there time for this foolery?

What are our plans? Battle or flight?" (90). Caspian then gets advice from Trumpkin, the Bulgy Bears, and Glenstorm, before Doctor Cornelius suggests they should quickly travel to Aslan's How, where they can be sheltered if need be. The narrator relates that "all approved of Cornelius's proposal" (91) and in this statement indirectly raises the question of what would have happened had they not all approved of this decision. Although Caspian is frequently referred to as "your Majesty" in this chapter, it is clear his authority is far from firmly established among the Old Narnians.

Doctor Cornelius describes Aslan's How as "a huge mound which Narnians raised in very ancient times over a very magical place, where there stood—and perhaps still stands—a very magical Stone" (91). With the phrase "in very ancient times," Lewis reminds readers once again of the vast scope of time that has passed since the events of *The Lion, the Witch and the Wardrobe*.

As Colin Duriez has observed, Lewis uses Aslan's How as one indicator of "the sweep of Narnia's history" (170). Even in his choice of the term to describe the hill that has been built over the Stone Table, Lewis evokes feelings of a distant past. The word *how*, as Paul Ford notes, comes from "the Old Norse and Old Teutonic name for mound or cairn" (96). Ford goes on to point out that with its "mazelike tunnels, galleries, and caves, all lined and roofed with smooth stones, and carved with ancient writing, snaking patterns, and—everywhere—stone reliefs of Aslan," the suggestion of "similar Celtic shrines and burial places is inescapable" (96). When Peter and Edmund finally enter the mound in chapter twelve, Edmund will whisper, "Look at those carvings on the walls. Don't they look old? And yet we're older than that. When we were last here, they hadn't been made" (162).

Both Tolkien and Lewis deliberately chose to set their stories against a vast backdrop of earlier times. Names of people and places, as well as objects from these distant times, evoke what Tolkien once described as "a past that itself had depth and reached backward into a dark antiquity" (*"Beowulf"* 27). As Tom Shippey explains, Tolkien felt no need to bring all the names that his narrator or other characters mention into the story because "they do their work by suggesting that there is a world outside the story, that the story is only a selection" (68). The evocative details of Aslan's How work in the same way here, and Lewis puts other indications of the past throughout the Narnia stories.

Prince Caspian is set thirteen hundred years after the previous Narnia story, a time Doctor Cornelius now refers to as "the Golden Age" (62). *The Lion, the Witch and the Wardrobe* itself occurred a thousand years after Narnia's creation and a hundred years into the reign of the White Witch. The prophecies and "old rhymes" Mr. Beaver recited in the first tale served as markers there of Narnian history's great sweep (80). In *The Silver Chair*, Eustace and Jill must journey with Puddleglum to "the ruined city of the ancient giants" (25). Even *The Magician's Nephew*, the story of the first events at Narnia's birth, contains Digory and Polly's journey to the ancient land of Charn. There, as Polly exclaims, everything is "all in ruins" (46), and even the sun is dying.

Another illustration of this technique of setting a story against a backdrop of earlier times can be found in *The Fellowship of the Ring*. There Tolkien has Tom Bombadil give the hobbits long knives he has taken from the barrow they were captive in and makes a vague reference to the Men of Westernesse who forged the ancient blades. "Few now remember them," Tom says, "yet some go wandering, sons of forgotten kings" (142). At this point Tolkien's narrator observes, "The hobbits did not understand his words, but as he spoke they had a vision as it were of a great expanse of years behind them."

These half-glimpsed vistas into the distant past, whether of Narnia or Middle-earth, provide, in Tolkien's words, "the impression of depth" (*"Beowulf"* 27). Readers encountered this same "impression of depth" earlier in *The Lion, the Witch and the Wardrobe* when the children first arrived at the Stone Table and the narrator offered this portrait: "It was a great grim slab of gray stone supported on four upright stones. It looked very old; and it was cut all over with strange lines and figures that might be the letters of an unknown language. They gave you a curious feeling when you looked at them" (125). Here in *Prince Caspian*, the strangeness and the unknown

associated with Aslan's How are intended to evoke this same curious feeling in readers as well.

While both authors share this technique, Tolkien more frequently
not only gives the impression of depth but also provides actual depth.
For example, if Tolkien had placed a Stone Table with letters in
Middle-earth, he might very well have included a rendition of the
letters themselves, a history of the language they were written in,
and not only the names of the people who had originally carved
them but also the names of their parents and grandparents. When
we come to a door on the backdrop of Tolkien's stage, he will often
open it for us. In contrast, as Doris Myers rightly asserts, the doors in
Narnia typically "do not open unless the story requires that someone
go through them" (136).

This observation about Lewis's technique of suggesting more
than is stated and not answering every question extends beyond
historical details. Thus, as Myers points out, with Lewis there is
no use in asking questions like, "Since there were no other humans, who ruled Narnia after the Pevensies returned to our world?"
or "Since Caspian the First gained Narnia through conquest and
unjustly destroyed Nature, under what law is Prince Caspian the
rightful king?" (136). Myers's answer to closed doors like these is
that Lewis's stories are "sufficiently powerful" so that we do not
question or perhaps even notice any lack of more adequate explanations (135).

Fortune Began to Turn against Them

In their widely read textbook *Literature: Structure, Sound, and
Sense*, Laurence Perrine and Thomas Arp describe several aspects
by which we can distinguish excellent fiction. They argue that
while enjoyment is the first aim and justification of reading fiction, "unless fiction gives something more than pleasure, it hardly
justifies as a subject of serious study." To have a compelling claim
on our attention, a work must yield "not only enjoyment but also
understanding" (3).

Perrine and Arp then go on to describe two different types of literature. The first type, *escape literature*, is written "purely for entertainment, to help us pass the time agreeably." The second type, *interpretive literature*, is written "to broaden and deepen and sharpen our awareness of life." Escape literature, the authors state, "takes us away from the real world," temporarily allowing us to forget our troubles. Interpretive literature takes us, via the imagination, "deeper into the real world" and assists us in understanding our troubles (3–4).

Having established this distinction, Perrine and Arp emphasize that we must not exaggerate it or oversimplify it. The authors claim that escape and interpretation are not "great bins" into which we can toss any given story (4). Rather, they see them as opposite ends of a continuum. A story becomes interpretive "as it illuminates some aspect of human life or behavior." An interpretive story is one that presents the reader "with an insight—large or small—into the nature and conditions of our existence." It "gives us a keener awareness of what it is to be a human being" and "helps us to understand our world, our neighbors, and ourselves." If we accept Perrine and Arp's distinction, it can be argued that the Narnia stories in general, and *Prince Caspian* in particular, are more than mere escape literature; they possess many of the qualities of interpretive literature.

Before returning to exploring *Prince Caspian*, it would be helpful to note one further distinction Perrine and Arp make. The authors point out that readers of escape literature want the stories they read to be "mainly pleasant" (3). Evil, danger, and misery may appear in escape literature but not in "a way that they need really be taken seriously" (4). One of Lewis's most significant themes and one he develops in each of the Chronicles of Narnia involves hardship and can be stated this way: *the virtuous life is an adventure, one with hardship that must be taken seriously, but one not to be missed because it is the only path that leads to genuine happiness, real fulfillment, and true community.*

As before in *The Lion, the Witch and the Wardrobe*, here in chapter seven of *Prince Caspian*, readers find hardship that must be taken seriously. The narrator reports that shortly after Caspian's force arrives at Aslan's How, "fortune began to turn against them" (92). The narrator tells us that there is fighting "on most days and sometimes by night" and that Caspian's troops on the whole have "the worst of it."

After Peter, Susan, Edmund, and Lucy returned through the wardrobe at the end of the first story, everyone in Narnia may have lived happily for a while but not "ever after." Similarly the happy time of Caspian's life depicted at the start of the chapter, a period in which "he had never enjoyed himself more" (84), soon gives way to a time of difficulty and suffering—and not noble, majestic suffering, but the everyday, unglorious kind. Readers are told, "At last there came a night when everything had gone as badly as possible, and the rain which had been falling heavily all day had ceased at nightfall only to give place to raw cold. . . . The best of the Bears had been hurt, a Centaur terribly wounded, and there were few in Caspian's party who had not lost blood. It was a gloomy company that huddled under the dripping trees to eat their scanty supper" (92, 93–94).

One of Lewis's many strengths is his ability to capture the mundane irritability that springs from this unexciting suffering. Giant Wimbleweather, who is described as "the gloomiest of all" (94), begins to cry over his blunder on the battlefield. His tears soak the sleeping mice and wake them, and their shrill complaints wake the others, bringing about even more complaining. As Wimbleweather attempts to move farther off, he steps on a fox's tail, and the fox bites him. What we find here is not heroic suffering but suffering nonetheless. As the narrator concludes, "Everyone was out of temper."

Lewis explored this same topic earlier in *The Screwtape Letters*. In Letter 30, Screwtape tells his young apprentice that he can "expect good results" from fatigue, but "the paradoxical thing is that moderate fatigue is better soil for peevishness than absolute exhaustion" (166).

Later as the children journey with Trumpkin, Lewis will again accurately portray the bickering and ill tempers that unspectacular discomfort brings. There as well as here, his truthful depiction of the way things actually work in circumstances like these adds a realism to the story and serves to remind readers that everyday distress and the petty squabbling it causes are simply a part of life—even the life of a hero.

One final point about this scene is worth looking at. Throughout the Chronicles, and particularly in *Prince Caspian* as we have seen, Lewis focuses on the process of character development. Lewis's point is that transformation, if it happens at all, happens over time, not overnight, and in the Chronicles it may take place over the course of more than one book. It may be assumed that Reepicheep was among the mice here who responded to being drenched by Wimbleweather's tears with "shrill but forcible voices" (94), causing the giant to tiptoe away to find some place "where he could be miserable in peace."

The reaction of the mice, while understandable, shows nothing of the graciousness and generosity that will typify Reepicheep in the next Narnia story, *The Voyage of the* Dawn Treader. There, in a very similar scene, Reepicheep will reach out to comfort Eustace, his former tormenter. At that point Eustace has been turned into a dragon and, like Wimbleweather, is ashamed to be with the rest of the group. Readers will be told, "He would slink away from the camp and lie curled up like a snake between the wood and the water. On such occasions, greatly to his surprise, Reepicheep was his most constant comforter. The noble Mouse would creep away from the merry circle at the camp fire and sit down by the dragon's head" (102).

Like the other major characters in Narnia, Lewis will have Reepicheep grow and develop over time. While always ready for daring action in *Prince Caspian*, Reepicheep's empathy was presumably something acquired gradually—as it often is in the real world. Here in chapter seven, Lewis ends the scene with Wimbleweather slinking away without a friend to offer a word of comfort.

When Shall I Blow the Horn?

Lewis opens *A Preface to Paradise Lost* with the declaration, "The first qualification for judging any piece of workmanship from

a corkscrew to a cathedral is to know *what* it is—what it was intended
to do and how it is meant to be used. . . . The first thing the reader
needs to know about *Paradise Lost* is what Milton meant it to be"
(1). A similar statement could be made about the Chronicles of
Narnia. As fairy tales, they are intended to have a dual nature. As
Peter Schakel has observed, "the Chronicles will be characterized
by strangeness and wonder" and yet at the same time "must be
believable and have internal consistency" (*Reading* 2).

In his essay "On Stories," Lewis claims that the logic found in a
fairy tale is "as strict as that of a realistic novel, though different"
(13). Although Lewis goes on to offer an illustration of the type of
logic found in one of his favorite fairy tales, Kenneth Grahame's *A
Wind in the Willows*, he never fully explains what he means by the
word *different*. Earlier in chapter five, Doctor Cornelius's last words
to Caspian concerning Susan's magic horn were, "Do not use it except at your greatest need" (62). Now at the end of chapter seven,
a debate takes places about whether or not this time has come.
Caspian states, "We are certainly in great need. But it is hard to be
sure we are at our greatest. Supposing there came an even worse
need and we had already used it?" (96). Readers are never told why
this difference between great and greatest need is so crucial. Perhaps
there is fairy-tale logic here, and readers simply assume that this
stipulation is part of the horn's magic.

Once Doctor Cornelius declares that the horn is to be used only
at a time of greatest need, we may join Caspian in accepting his tutor's directive without question. If so, we are following Doris Myers's
approach mentioned earlier, acknowledging that Lewis's stories are
"sufficiently powerful" to preclude the necessity for more complete
explanations (135).

However, some readers may feel a need to go looking for more
internal consistency and may ask *why* the horn is to be used only
in greatest need. In *The Lion, the Witch and the Wardrobe*, this
restriction was never made in connection with Susan's horn, but
interestingly it was a condition made for her other gift. There
Father Christmas told Susan, "You must use the bow only in
great need" (108). Perhaps in attributing the "only in great need"

aspect to the horn, Lewis was incorrectly remembering this passage from the first book. As Green and Hooper point out, Lewis became aware of a number of inconsistencies he had created in the Chronicles and just a few days before his death met with the editor of the Puffin Books edition of the Chronicles, promising to "connect the things that didn't tie up" (432), a task he was unable to complete.

Should Cornelius's instructions about using the horn only in greatest need be seen as an inconsistency between *Prince Caspian* and *The Lion, the Witch and the Wardrobe*? Perhaps, but an alternate and more satisfying approach is to see it as an expansion or an outgrowth from the first book. In "Foreword to the Second Edition" of *The Lord of the Rings*, Tolkien claimed that his story was a tale that "grew in the telling" (xiii). Lewis employed this same organic process for the Narnia stories. Just as *The Lord of the Rings* expands and, in doing so, somewhat alters the account of Bilbo's Ring in *The Hobbit*, it could be argued that *Prince Caspian* expands on and sometimes alters the elements associated with Susan's horn in *The Lion, the Witch and the Wardrobe*. Not only is the element of greatest need added in the second book, but so is the concept of sunrise as the best time to use the horn.

As mentioned earlier, most readers will simply accept the conditions surrounding Susan's magic horn as being part of Lewis's fairy tale. Here near the end of chapter seven, they may do the same with Doctor Cornelius's mention of "White Magic" (98). Other than its intended contrast with the black sorcery Nikabrik enlists in chapter twelve, this is a term readers simply accept without further direct explanation from Lewis.

Leland Ryken and Marjorie Lamp Mead have rightly pointed out that unlike the magic in the Harry Potter stories, which comes about as the result of "human spell casting, divination, and occult practices," the magical events in Narnia "primarily happen by the power of supernatural agents, preserving a sense that they are manifestations of the power of supernatural beings" (89). Thus Ryken and Mead propose that the good magic that occurs in Narnia, including the help sent in response to the horn, can be seen as "the equivalent of divine interventions or the miraculous in our own world" and as such is "an affirmation of the Christian worldview." At the start of *The Silver Chair*, when Eustace invites Jill to join him in calling on Aslan to take them to Narnia, he will take pains to point out that she should not think they can make Aslan do things. As he explains, "Really, we can only ask him" (9).

In *The Lion, the Witch and the Wardrobe*, Father Christmas explicitly tells Susan, "When you put this horn to your lips and blow it, then, *wherever you are*, I think help of some kind *will come to you*" (168, emphasis added). Yet another new element added to the lore of Susan's horn in *Prince Caspian* is that the help might not necessarily come directly to the horn blower. Chapter seven ends with expressions of loyalty from Pattertwig, who agrees to journey to Lantern Waste, and from Trumpkin, who, despite referring to the use of the horn as "all this foolery" (97), volunteers to make the journey to Cair Paravel and wait there for whatever help may or may not come.

Discussion Questions

In Narnia and in his space trilogy, Lewis intentionally designs communities made up of many different kinds of members. The point was made in this chapter that Lewis implies that exposure to only one kind of rational species can have "far-reaching effects in the narrowing of sympathies and even of thought."

1. Can you think of ways this claim is true in our world?
2. Lewis suggests that modern man's belief that he is the only intelligent species on Earth has not been good for him. Do you agree?
3. How might reading in general, and reading the Chronicles of Narnia in particular, be seen as an antidote for this type of narrowing?

As stated, one of Lewis's most important themes is that the virtuous life is an adventure, one with hardship that must be taken seriously, but one not to be missed because it is the only path that leads to genuine happiness, real fulfillment, and true community.

4. How would you respond to this claim? How does this apply to your own life, which on the surface may seem less adventurous than Caspian's?
5. Why does Lewis feel it is important for us to be reminded of this theme? Has the virtuous life lost some of the esteem it once had?

In *Prince Caspian*, Lewis gives us an insightful portrait of unglorious suffering—cold but not hypothermia, fatigue but not exhaustion, and wetness but not drowning. Peter, Susan, Edmund, and Lucy must endure not starvation but boredom in eating apples several meals in a row. Their main antagonist for several chapters is nothing more monstrous than prickly woods.

6. Could it be argued that in some ways the small, everyday suffering is harder to bear than the greater, more majestic kind?
7. Does Lewis, by allowing his protagonists to give way to petty irritability, make them less inspiring or more?

8

How They Left the Island

More New Elements

As chapter eight begins, readers are reminded that it has been Trumpkin who has been telling the story for the previous four chapters, and that all of Caspian's experiences have actually been an extended flashback. Trumpkin has nearly finished bringing the children up to the present. All that remains to recount is the final blowing of the horn and the story of how Trumpkin was captured.

When the horn was used by Susan in *The Lion, the Witch and the Wardrobe*, readers were told, "At that moment a strange noise woke the silence suddenly. It was like a bugle, but richer" (130). Here in *Prince Caspian*, Lewis expands on this sound, as he has previously with other aspects connected with the horn. Unable to capture the mysterious nature of the sound with ordinary language, Trumpkin must resort to using similes as he tells the children, "I'd been plugging away for many hours when there came a sound that I'd never heard the like of in my born days. Eh, I won't forget that. The whole air was full of it, loud as thunder but far longer, cool and sweet as music over water, but strong enough to shake the woods" (100).

At the start of *The Two Towers*, Tolkien includes a similar call for help. Under attack and badly outnumbered, Boromir sounds his great horn, summoning Aragorn, Middle-earth's high king, to rush in with assistance. Tolkien writes, "Then suddenly with a deep-throated call a great horn blew, and the blasts of it smote the hills and echoed in the hollows, rising in a mighty shout above the roaring of the falls" (403). Like Susan's horn, the horn Boromir blows also brings strange help, assistance that comes in a different form than was expected. Boromir had hoped for aid in defeating the orcs and defending the hobbits. Instead Aragorn arrives after the battle is over. The hobbits have been captured and Boromir has been mortally wounded, but Aragorn is just in time to accept Boromir's confession of wrongdoing, allowing the man of Gondor to die in peace.

As noted earlier, it will be Lewis's intention in *Prince Caspian* to depict more mature protagonists, and one part of this maturity in this second story is that the four children will *help* more and *be helped* less. Because of this, Lewis makes a clear connection between Caspian's use of the horn and the children's disappearance from the train platform: they are like the genie who gets summoned to be of assistance, not the summoner. Lewis has Edmund interrupt Trumpkin's story to ask at what time he heard the horn's mysterious sound. When the dwarf answers between nine and ten, the children respond, "Just when we were at the railway station!" (100).

In the previous trips made to Narnia in *The Lion, the Witch and the Wardrobe*, there was no relationship between the time in Narnia and the time in England. Lucy's first trip was made shortly after breakfast at the Professor's, but as she emerged from the wardrobe, it was nighttime in Narnia. On the second trip, Lucy and Edmund entered the wardrobe on a rainy English afternoon several days later, but in Narnia the sun was just rising.

Now in *Prince Caspian* as Lewis's tale grows in the telling, more organic than rigidly consistent, he uses the similar times in England and Narnia to link the summons for help and the children's disappearance. If Lewis had wanted to be more consistent with the first book, he could have had Edmund say, "Just when we arrived in Narnia," but the need for a dramatic connection here is more satisfying than strict consistency.

Providence and the Effect Intentions Have on Outcomes

Back in the discussion of chapter three, it was noted that Lewis has providence appear in *Prince Caspian* in the guise of coincidence or strange chance, such as when the children arrive just in time to save Trumpkin. Here in chapter eight, providence can be seen in a different form, this time in the effect intentions have on outcomes. Good intentions will be rewarded and evil intentions thwarted in ways that suggest the presence of an outside agency at work.

In his hurry to get to Cair Paravel, Trumpkin makes a mistake by risking "a short cut across open country to cut off a big loop of the river," and he gets caught by the forces stationed at Miraz's last stronghold before the coast (101). In fact, the final outcome of his capture turns out even better than he had planned, as Trumpkin ends up in a boat that Peter and Susan easily recover. Without the soldiers' boat, how would Trumpkin have crossed the channel? Without this boat, how would the children have gotten off the island? It could be argued that because Trumpkin's mistake was well intentioned, the results are even better than if he had not been captured. And in this effect intentions seem to have on outcomes, readers can see either the unrealistic, overly optimistic hand of coincidence or the benevolent hand of providence.

Tolkien introduced providence into *The Lord of the Rings* in a similar way, and the key role providence has in both Middle-earth and Narnia warrants an in-depth look.

In *The Two Towers*, Gandalf sets out to round up Théoden's scattered forces at Helm's Deep. But what actually happens—the arrival of the treelike huorns who change certain defeat into victory—turns out to be even better than he had planned. Gandalf describes the outcome as "better than my design, and better even than my hope" (530). He does not mention the role providence has played, but his words hint at it, as he tells Théoden, "The trees? Nay, I see the wood as plainly as you do. But that is no deed of mine." In the expressions "no deed of mine" and "better than my design," readers can hear the implication that someone or something else was behind what happened.

Earlier in *The Two Towers*, Gandalf had explained to Aragorn about the importance of having right intentions, no matter if, in the end, events do not play out exactly according to the original design. Gandalf commented on Aragorn's choice to devote time to Boromir's funeral and on the decision to pursue the orcs who took Merry and Pippin. Gandalf told Aragorn, "Do not regret your choice in the valley of the Emyn Muil, nor call it a vain pursuit. You chose amid doubts *the path that seemed right: the choice was just, and it has been rewarded*" (489, emphasis added).

Gandalf's point here is that intentions have significance in Middle-earth: if someone sets out to do the right thing, that aim will be honored. Somehow, in a way that is never explained, providence will reward proper intentions. As David Mills describes it, events "work out for the good because the heroes do the right thing," and in this, "some supervening power is clearly at work" (23).

Gandalf's point about the hand of providence honoring intentions in Middle-earth is also Lewis's point in Narnia. Trumpkin also took the path that seemed right, and what happened ended up being better than he had planned. Later in the novel, Peter, much like Aragorn, will have to guide his small band and will make well-intentioned decisions that do not turn out as he had hoped. When he finally encounters Aslan, Peter will express his regrets, saying, "I'm so sorry. I've been leading them wrong ever since we started and especially yesterday morning" (153).

Aslan could have answered Peter using words similar to Gandalf's, such as, "Do not regret your choice to go down the river gorge instead of up, nor call it a vain pursuit. Because of the delay, Nikabrik has finally been forced to play the evil hand he has been concealing, and you are just in time to rid Caspian of this enemy in disguise." Aslan's actual response to Peter after hearing his regrets may hold this implication, but he simply will say, "My dear son" (153).

If providence can be seen in the effect intentions have on out-comes, and if this means that good intentions will sometimes seem to be rewarded in Narnia, what about evil intentions? In the discussion of Miraz's decision to send away Caspian's nurse in chapter four, it was noted how Miraz's evil intentions resulted not in ending Caspian's education about Old Narnia but in furthering it. Gandalf's words mentioned in that discussion—"A traitor may betray himself and do good that he does not intend"—hold the suggestion that the hand of providence can also be seen in the way evil intentions will sometimes seem to be thwarted, both in Middle-earth and here in Narnia.

In *The Two Towers*, Gandalf explains how Sauron's and Saruman's evil designs end up backfiring, stating, "So between them our enemies have contrived only to bring Merry and Pippin with marvelous speed, and in the nick of time, to Fangorn, where otherwise they would never have come at all!" (486). The two hobbits rouse the Ents of Fangorn who, at the last moment, turn the tide in the battle.

Here in the story of his capture, Trumpkin tells the children, "Anyone else would have run me through then and there" (101). But Miraz's seneschal sought to add to the falsehood that the woods are haunted by decreeing that the dwarf receive "a grand execution" and be sent down "to the ghosts." Instead of doing away with him, the "pompous fool" ends up doing good that he did not intend by delivering Trumpkin to the very spot he needed to be at the very time he needed to be there. And, as mentioned earlier, he even provides the boat necessary for Trumpkin to cross the channel and bring the children back to the Stone Table.

If Aslan Wants Us Here

Trumpkin finishes the last bit of his tale, stating, "And then this young lady does her bit of archery—and it was pretty shooting, let me tell you—and here we are" (101). Peter, the first to respond, is astounded by the fact that it was the horn that dragged them from the train platform twenty-four hours earlier. In words full of implication, Peter declares, "I can hardly believe it." Lucy tells Peter, "I don't know why you shouldn't believe it, if you believe in magic at all." It is not that Peter doubts the power of Susan's horn. Peter's problem in believing is due to the fact that *what happened did not take the form he expected.* Peter was expecting that they would be the ones to use the horn to summon help, not the other way around, as he explains, "In the stories it's always someone in our world who does the calling" (102).

The limiting nature of Peter's expectations created a similar problem of disbelief in *The Lion, the Witch and the Wardrobe.* After Lucy and Edmund offered conflicting accounts about Narnia's existence, Peter questioned his younger sister's story and, along with Susan, took the problem to the Professor. It was not that Peter doubted Lucy's general truthfulness. His problem again was due to the fact that what happened did not take the form he expected. The issue was Lucy's claim of a magic country that could be entered through the wardrobe. If such a country existed, Peter expected to be able to travel there at any time. As he told the Professor, "If it was real why doesn't everyone find this country every time they go to the wardrobe? I mean, there was nothing there when we looked; even Lucy didn't pretend there was" (49).

Then Peter went on to assert, "If things are real, they're there all the time" (49). The Professor's only response was to ask, "Are they?" The implication is clear: there will be things that are real, things that are true, that go beyond Peter's expectations. But this will be a lesson it will take Peter several more occasions to learn.

In the next chapter of *Prince Caspian,* Peter's pattern of disbelief will come up again. Lucy will claim to see Aslan indicating that the troupe is supposed to go up the gorge. Peter again will find it hard to believe her because what has happened does not match his expectations, and he will object, "Why should Aslan be invisible to us? He never used to be" (148). Peter's statement sounds very similar to his previous "if things are real, they're there all the time" argument.

Despite the fact that Edmund reminds his older brother of their earlier error, pointing out that when Lucy first discovered Narnia, "none of us would believe her" (128), Peter will persist in doubting that Aslan might behave in ways different from those they have known, and he will then proceed to lead the group down the gorge.

Edmund responds to the knowledge that they have been summoned by the horn with "a chuckle" and adds the mild complaint, "It's a bit uncomfortable to know that *we* can be whistled for like that" (102). His comment sets up Lucy's statement: "But we want to be here, don't we, if Aslan wants us?"

Why does Lucy see Aslan's involvement in bringing the children to Narnia when clearly it was the horn that summoned them? One answer is that perhaps Lucy sees Aslan "at the back of all the stories" in Narnia, as Shasta suggests in *The Horse and His Boy* (208). From this perspective, Aslan governs over all the events that take place in Narnia, particularly those having a supernatural or providential aura about them.

Additionally, Lucy may see Aslan as the source of Father Christmas's gifts. Aslan was clearly aware of them in *The Lion, the Witch and the Wardrobe*—he identified the sound of Susan's horn for Peter, urged Peter to respond to Susan's call and therefore use his new sword, and urged Lucy to use her healing cordial to help Edmund—so perhaps Lucy sees Aslan's intention and his power in the gifts. The children's summons in *Prince Caspian* can be viewed as Aslan calling them through the agency of the horn as earlier he did through the agency of the wardrobe.

Finally, with Lucy's statement, "But we want to be here, don't we, if Aslan wants us?" (102), and the unspoken agreement of the other siblings, a vital link is made between the children and Trumpkin. From this point on, the five are united, not in a submission to Aslan—for Trumpkin does not yet believe in Aslan—but in a shared submission and a shared attitude for proper authority. Regardless of whether they find it pleasant, regardless of their personal preferences, Trumpkin and the children share an allegiance to a cause that goes beyond their own personal interests. This marks them as allies. This also marks them as opponents to figures like Miraz and

Nikabrik, who have no cause other than self. It is revealing that later in the chapter when the children bring Trumpkin down into the treasure chamber, his first words will be, "It would never do to let Nikabrik see this" (104), presumably because of the Black Dwarf's selfish streak.

In the previous chapter, Trumpkin's last words to Caspian were, "I know the difference between giving advice and taking orders" (98). Or to paraphrase Lucy, Trumpkin wants to be at Cair Paravel if Caspian wants him to.

No Help Has Come?

The help Susan's horn has called is the strange kind of help already discussed—assistance that at first does not seem much like help. Trumpkin explains, "The King and Trufflehunter and Doctor Cornelius were expecting—well, if you see what I mean, help. To put it another way, I think they'd been imagining you as great warriors" (103).

If we look back to chapter seven, it is clear that Doctor Cornelius spoke truer than intended when he stated, "We do not know what form the help will take" (96). His best guess was that the horn would call "Peter the High King and his mighty consorts down from the high past." The Old Narnians can certainly be excused for expecting four mighty adults. The last time the Pevensies were seen in Narnia, they had been ruling for years and—without any further direct help from Aslan—had ridded the kingdom of all remnants of the White Witch's army. They had grown into men and women, and under them Narnia had enjoyed a long period of peace and prosperity. In the last account of the four in *The Lion, the Witch and the Wardrobe*, Peter was described as "a tall and deep-chested man and a great warrior," Susan as "a tall and gracious woman," Edmund as "great in council and judgment," and Lucy as "valiant" (183–84)—quite different figures from the four children now sitting on the grass in the ruined hall of Cair Paravel, who are just a year older than when they entered Narnia the first time.

Trumpkin may be somewhat excused for thinking that no help has come, at least from his perspective. Ever since his rescue, it has been he who has been taking care of the Pevensies, rather than the other way around. He was the one who thought to hide the boat, not Peter, and then he provided the children with breakfast, not only catching the fish but cleaning and cooking them as well.

The children are quite irritated at Trumpkin's underestimation of them, so much so that Peter has to step in to calm things down. Susan, the horn's original owner, emphatically points out to Trumpkin, "But it *has* worked" (102). With a bluntness uncharacteristic of her, Lucy tells the dwarf, "You *are* stupid." The only other time she will use language this severe will be in chapter nine after Trumpkin suggests that Lucy has seen an ordinary lion and not Aslan.

Edmund is so angry that he jumps to his feet, declaring, "I suppose you don't believe we won the Battle of Beruna?" (103). Edmund may perhaps be excused for oversimplifying the situation a bit here as he recalls how he battled his way through three ogres and smashed the wand of the White Witch, therefore destroying the enemy's greatest weapon. In fact, he and Peter actually appeared to be *losing* the Battle of Beruna before Aslan arrived and killed the Witch. Nevertheless Edmund's underlying point is valid—he and his siblings are far more than the mere children they appear to be. Regardless of whether they themselves actually won the Battle of Beruna, they would make a valuable contribution to any army.

Before being cut off by his brother, Edmund suggests that his earlier conspiracy with the White Witch might be behind Trumpkin's doubts, stating, "Well, you can say what you like about me because I know—" (103).

In *The Lion, the Witch and the Wardrobe*, after his talk with Edmund, Aslan instructed Peter, Susan, and Lucy, "Here is your brother, and—there is no need to talk to him about what is past" (139). Lewis's use of the dash here adds a pause for emphasis, as though Aslan knew the other three children would be tempted to bring up Edmund's mistake, if not immediately then at some point in time. Readers were told that "no one ever heard" what Aslan said to Edmund in their private conversation, so whether Edmund too was given instructions about talking about his betrayal can only be guessed. Clearly Edmund is about to bring up his past here, and he will bring it up again in *The Voyage of the* Dawn Treader to assure Eustace no mistake is beyond remedy. There Edmund will tell his cousin, "You haven't been as bad as I was on my first trip to Narnia. You were only an ass, but I was a traitor" (110).

Peter stops the argument with Trumpkin from escalating, stating, "There's no good losing our tempers" (103). Readers might recall that on the first trip to Narnia, Peter let his anger make an already bad situation with Edmund become worse. In *The Lion, the Witch and the Wardrobe* when Aslan learned that Edmund had betrayed them to the White Witch, Peter suggested, "That was partly my fault, Aslan. I was angry with him and I think that helped him to go wrong" (128). Here in *Prince Caspian*, Peter has learned the importance of keeping his anger, and the anger of those he leads, under control.

Peter sets up competitions with Trumpkin to demonstrate Edmund's swordsmanship and Susan's skill with the bow, and then afterward Trumpkin recognizes the power of Lucy's healing cordial. But it is not these abilities that are used to help Caspian; they merely establish the fact that Trumpkin has underestimated the children's abilities. After the fencing contest with Trumpkin, Edmund ends up doing relatively little fighting, none of it critical, and Susan will not shoot her bow again. Lucy's cordial will not be used again until the final chapter when the battle has already been won. So exactly how do the four children "help" Caspian? Certainly not in the conventional sense Trumpkin and the other Narnians are expecting. As readers will later see, the four children provide unconventional help that will look more like encouragement than military power. Readers may be reminded of the phrase "not by might nor by power" from Zechariah 4:6, and here Lewis has yet another parallel with Tolkien.

In *The Fellowship of the Ring*, Elrond tells the council that "neither strength nor wisdom" will be the major factor in the war against Sauron and that the quest may be attempted by "the weak with as much hope as the strong" (262). For the most part, Tolkien has the forces of good use unconventional means in the battle for Middle-earth. In one particularly telling example, it is Éowyn, a young woman, and Merry, a small hobbit, who defeat the great Lord of the Nazgûl, the most powerful tool of the enemy.

Before moving on, it is worth noting Lucy's response to her older brother's proposal that they abandon the argument with Trumpkin and instead arm themselves from the treasure chamber. As Edmund begins to object, Lucy whispers to him, "Hadn't we better do what Peter says? He is the High King, you know" (103).

In *Prince Caspian* and the next two books, Trumpkin's actions will be based on simple obedience. But despite Lucy's statement about doing what Peter says, obedience will not be quite this simple for her, Susan, and Edmund. In chapter eleven, Lucy will wake everyone with the news that Aslan has arrived and wants them to follow him. As they debate what to do, Trumpkin will state, "If you all go, of course, I'll go with you; and if your party splits up, I'll go with the High King. That's my duty to him and King Caspian" (148). At that point in the story, Lucy will find the issues of duty and obedience more complicated and will tell her siblings, "I do hope that you will all come with me. Because—because I'll have to go with him whether anyone else does or not" (147). Here in her words to Edmund, Lucy hints there is something more to duty than blind obedience—that capability is also a factor. She concludes her comments about obeying Peter by adding, "And I think he has an idea" (103), an addition that suggests obedience to a leader is partially based on a leader's ability to come up with a good proposal.

The Clop-Clop of Water and the Splash of Oars

In the pages that follow, Lewis reminds readers yet again that the air of Narnia is causing the children to regain their former abilities, which are not some inexplicable gift but were developed during the years of their reign as kings and queens. As they come up the stairs of the treasure chamber, we are told that they look and feel "more like Narnians and less like schoolchildren" (104). As

Edmund prepares for his match with Trumpkin, the narrator points out, "The air of Narnia had been working upon him ever since they arrived on the island, . . . and his arms and fingers remembered their old skill" (105).

After Trumpkin is shown his mistake and sees that there is more to the Pevensie children than meets the eye, the dwarf responds good-naturedly with "a great laugh" and confesses, "Well, I've made as big a fool of myself as ever a Dwarf did. No offense, I hope?" (109). If Trumpkin is to be punished for his offense, particularly for referring to the four children earlier as *little*, his only sentence will be a nickname, or at least nick-initials. When the dwarf objects to being called "Our Dear Little Friend," Edmund suggests calling him the "D.L.F." (111).

Douglas Gresham points out that one facet of the Inklings' personalities was that they "often bestowed nicknames on their friends" (108). Tolkien was called Tollers. To his friends, Lewis was known as Jack, his self-given nickname. The Lewis brothers referred to their tutor William Kirkpatrick as Kirk or The Great Knock. The Eagle and Child, where the Inklings met, was the Bird and Baby. Robert Havard—doctor to both Lewis and Tolkien and, as noted earlier, an Inkling member and the father of Mary Clare Havard—was known by his nickname, Humphrey, and also as the "U.Q.," or "Useless Quack." Lewis and his brother, Warnie, had private nicknames for each other, a practice that began during childhood and stemmed from a warning received from their nurse, Lizzie Endicott. After she threatened to smack their "piggiebottoms," the boys decided that Warnie should henceforth be the Archpiggiebotham and Jack the Smallpiggiebotham, names that were then, like Trumpkin's, shortened to initials: the APB and the SPB. Lewis's work on his volume of Oxford's History of English Literature was a labor of love as well as something he loved to hate, a project he came to refer to by the nickname OHEL.

So when Trumpkin is given his nickname here by Edmund and when it is used later in the novel, readers should see this as a sign of affection. Certainly Trumpkin does. When Susan the Gentle chides Edmund for teasing, the dwarf sees his private name as the sign of friendship it is. He tells Susan that he knows it is only "a jibe" and that a jibe "won't raise a blister" (111).

Now that the Pevensies have proved they are not mere children, the time has come for them to leave the island and join Caspian. Instead of retracing the path Trumpkin took—going north from Cair Paravel and following the Great River to Aslan's How—Edmund suggests, "Why shouldn't we row a little south till we come to Glasswater Creek and row up it?" (111). As he did in the first Narnia book, Lewis will have the middle portion of *Prince Caspian* taken up by a long journey the children must take to the Stone Table.

In structuring the book in four parts—an introduction, followed by a long journey on foot, then action at the destination, and finally a return home again—Lewis was mirroring not only *The Lion, the Witch and the Wardrobe* but also the pattern found in both *The Hobbit* and *The Lord of the Rings*. To help readers in picturing the various routes taken by Lewis's characters, Paul Ford has added a Narnian atlas, created by Stephen Yandell, to the latest edition of *Companion to Narnia*. One of the diagrams, "Narnia's Eastern Peninsula," was specifically made for *Prince Caspian* and shows Cair Paravel now cut off from the mainland by a channel (507). Also included on this map are the northern route taken by the Telmarine soldiers in the boat and the southern course taken by Trumpkin and the four children as they leave the ruins of the former castle.

One confusing geographical element in the journey to Aslan's How is caused by two different meanings for the word *creek*. When Edmund suggests traveling up Glasswater Creek, American readers will picture the children rowing along the coast until they come to a flowing tributary larger than a stream but smaller than a river. British readers will understand Lewis's intention and will see Glasswater Creek as a narrow bay on the ocean, an inlet that extends farther inland than a cove.

Lewis ends chapter eight with the departure from Cair Paravel. Like Caspian in his earlier flight from Miraz's castle, the children begin with high spirits that gradually give way to more realistic feelings. Initially delightful, the sea journey in the hot sun soon becomes tiresome and tedious, causing Peter to speak "shortly" to

Lucy (113). The vast forest on the shore, rather than being beautiful, now simply serves as a sad reminder of the time "when it was open and breezy and full of merry friends."

Discussion Questions

Here in the discussion of chapter eight, the point was made that providence can again be seen, this time in the effect intentions have on outcomes. Good intentions seem to be rewarded. Characters who try to do the right thing are usually successful, while characters with evil intent are often thwarted—though sometimes in unforeseen ways.

1. Do you think the events that come about in Narnia are too positive to be seen as strictly brought about through natural means? And if so, what does this suggest?
2. What kinds of effects are brought about by the characters' intentions in Narnia? By people's intentions in real life?

As pointed out, in this chapter Lucy first suggests the group should obey Peter because he is the high king, and then she implies that their obedience should be based at least partly on the fact that Peter has an idea. Trumpkin's thoughts about duty and allegiance are much more black-and-white.

3. What is Lucy saying through these contrasting views?
4. How do Lucy's and Trumpkin's positions fit certain kinds of believers or stages of belief in our own world? How do they fit your own beliefs at certain times in your life?

9

What Lucy Saw

Wake, Wake, Wake

Back in chapter five, Caspian originally felt "brave and, in a way, happy" as he fled Miraz's castle riding off to adventure (63). Then the next day, as the realities of his situation set in, everything changed. Readers were told that the world turned large and strange, and Caspian felt frightened and small rather than courageous. Here in chapter nine, the four children experience a similar drop in spirits. As they grow more tired and uncomfortable, their thoughts go beyond thinking merely of how they will get to Caspian and instead to what they will do when they find him. In particular they wonder "how a handful of Dwarfs and woodland creatures" will be able to defeat Miraz's professional forces (114).

As the contest with Trumpkin has demonstrated, Peter, Susan, Edmund, and Lucy have more to offer than meets the eye, but the fact remains that their addition to Caspian's forces will not be enough for a conventional victory over "company after company" of Telmarines (92). Of the four, Lucy appears to be "least gifted in those skills that would seem to be most needed in a campaign" as Jonathan Rogers has observed (40). Yet, as Rogers goes on to note, "Lucy's belief will prove to be the bridge by which the invading Aslan reenters Narnia."

As the company leaves the sea and rows up the narrow Glasswater inlet, the landscape once again takes on the silent, empty feeling it had possessed earlier. The excitement and magic that the treasures from Cair Paravel kindled briefly has faded. The banks of the cove grow closer, and the overhanging branches gradually enfold the little band, much as they did at the novel's start. Readers are once again told it is "very quiet" (115). When the children and Trumpkin finally put ashore, they are too exhausted even to light a fire. After "a little silent munching" in the dark, they huddle together in the dead leaves. Somewhat like the slumbering naiads and dryads, they too are soon buried in sleep.

In *Prince Caspian*, there will be no scene that descends into hopelessness with either the depth or the duration of the Stone Table sequence from *The Lion, the Witch and the Wardrobe*. Lewis will not let Caspian or the four Pevensies sink very low before they are given some form of encouragement. Just as the spark of optimism and faith is about to go out, Lucy, the only one unable to sleep, sees "with a thrill of memory" the bright Narnian stars shining through a gap in the overgrown branches (115). Lucy's thrill of longing here is similar to the yearning described earlier in connection with Caspian and leads her to "an odd night-time dreamish kind of wakefulness" (116). Lucy gradually gets the feeling that "the whole forest was coming awake like herself." For reasons she cannot explain, she feels compelled to get up and walk into the woods.

In the creation of Narnia found in *The Magician's Nephew*, Aslan speaks the trees, streams, and animals into consciousness, calling out, "Narnia, Narnia, Narnia, awake. Love. Think. Speak. Be walking trees. Be talking beasts. Be divine waters" (126). In response, readers are told, "Out of the trees wild people stepped forth, gods and goddesses of the wood" (127). Here in chapter nine, Lucy's words echo Aslan's as she exclaims, "Oh Trees, Trees, Trees. Oh Trees, wake, wake, wake" (117). However, just as Lucy's cordial is not sufficient to heal all wounds, so too her words are not enough to bring the spirits of the trees out of the deep slumber brought on by the Telmarines. The still and silent trees surrounding Lucy may remind readers of the frozen statues in the castle of the White Witch from *The Lion, the Witch and the Wardrobe*. In both cases, only the power of Aslan can undo the spell of silence they are under.

Lucy's "great longing for the old days when the trees could talk" (117), is not only similar to Caspian's experience, it also parallels the feelings of longing Lewis himself experienced, particularly because both sets of feelings are fleeting. Lewis chose to call this particular experience *joy* and describes his transitory encounter with it in *Surprised by Joy*: "It is difficult to find words strong enough for the sensation which came over me. . . . It was a sensation, of course, of desire; but desire for what? . . . Before I knew what I desired, the desire itself was gone, the whole glimpse withdrawn, and the world turned commonplace again" (16).

After a brief stirring and a "rustling noise of the leaves," which is "almost like words" (118), Lucy's moment passes. She suddenly feels sleepy herself, and Lewis ends the scene with her snuggled down between Peter and Susan.

What would Miraz have said about Lucy's nighttime experience, her longing to communicate with the trees and her desire for them to awaken? Surely he would have labeled her feelings as nonsense and would have told her, as he did Caspian earlier, "You're getting too old for that sort of stuff" (42). Lewis, of course, would have said the exact opposite. In "The Weight of Glory" he argues, "Our lifelong nostalgia, our longing to be reunited with something in the universe from which we now feel cut off, to be on the inside of some door which we have always seen from the outside, is no mere neurotic fancy, but the truest index of our real situation" (42).

Where's This Bally Rush?

When Lucy wakes, nothing but the memory remains of her mystical encounter the night before. The day begins "cold and cheerless" with everything "damp and dirty" (118). What is more, the children's confusion about where they are—experienced earlier at Cair Paravel—returns with even greater strength. When Trumpkin asks them if they know the way, Susan declares, "I've never seen these woods in my life before. In fact I thought all along that we ought to have gone by the river" (119). Like Peter, readers may wonder why Susan did not voice her opinion before. They also may wonder that if the troupe had gone by the river, and if this path also proved difficult, whether Susan might have claimed she thought all along they should have gone up Glasswater.

Comfort—or, more accurately, the fear of personal discomfort—is gradually becoming Susan's greatest concern. Because Edmund's comment here is said lightly, readers might miss it. When he tells the others, "Don't take any notice of her. She always is a wet blanket" (119), Edmund is speaking more prophetically than he knows. From this point on, Susan's opinions will need to be weighed with the knowledge that anything she says may be traced more to her fear of discomfort and inconvenience than to a commitment to the truth. Lewis will revisit this same temptation in *The Silver Chair*, where Jill and Eustace will be more interested in "baths and beds and hot drinks" than the quest Aslan has sent them on (102).

We have seen this anxious side of Susan before. In *The Lion, the Witch and the Wardrobe* when the children reached Mr. Tumnus's home and the adventure turned unpleasant, Susan's response was, "I wonder if there's any point in going on. I mean, it doesn't seem particularly safe here and it looks as if it won't be much fun either. And it's getting colder every minute, and we've brought nothing to eat. What about just going home?" (59). To her credit, a few moments later, Susan reversed this suggestion and told Peter, "I don't want to go a step further and I wish we'd never come. But I think we must try to do something for Mr. Whatever-his-name-is—I mean the Faun" (60). In *Prince Caspian*, Susan's reversal from fear of discomfort, such as it is, will not come until a good deal later in the story. From the time the company leaves Glasswater until they finally unite with Aslan near the Stone Table, Susan will contribute little besides negativity.

The group's moment of confusion about where they are and Edmund's solution that follows go by so quickly that Lewis's small lapse here might not be noticed. Edmund says, "You've got that pocket compass of yours, Peter, haven't you? Well, then, we're as right as rain. We've only got to keep on going northwest" (119). The fact that Peter just happens to have matches, a knife, and a compass in his pocket has already been discussed. Here Lewis implies that Narnia, a flat world, also happens to have an earthlike magnetic North Pole, allowing Peter's compass to correctly tell their direction. For some readers, this may seem too much of a coincidence.

Edmund concludes by predicting they will arrive at the Stone Table "by eight or nine o'clock" that same morning, in time for a good breakfast with Caspian (119). Edmund's prediction will turn out to be wildly optimistic. Not only does he underestimate the time it will take to hike through the dense, overgrown woods, he also cannot foresee the bear attack and the time needed to take the meat from the carcass for their meal later. Also, none of the children has imagined that the Rush, a minor tributary during their reign, now flows through a nearly impassable gorge.

Susan replies to Edmund's directions and prediction with, "I hope you're right. I can't remember all that at all" (119), a rather feeble response from someone who by now should be more Queen Susan and less a thirteen-year-old girl. Some readers may see sexism in the follow-up remark Edmund makes to Peter and Trumpkin: "That's the worst of girls. They never carry a map in their heads." If there is sexism here, it could be argued that it is Edmund's sexism rather than Lewis's, and that this is the exact kind of comment Edmund, not a perfect character, might realistically make. If readers want to complain that Edmund's comment is mildly sexist, they must also complain about the implication in Lucy's rejoinder: "That's because our heads have something inside them." Anyone who would point to this exchange as evidence that Lewis is antifemale must also find him to be antimale.

A similar exchange will occur in *The Silver Chair*. When Jill cannot help Eustace determine which way is east, he will say to her, "It's an extraordinary thing about girls that they never know the points of the compass" (10). Jill "indignantly" replies that Eustace does not know where east is himself. Whether readers see gender bashing or just ordinary bickering in these two scenes, Lewis makes it clear that uncharitable comments like these are wrong and should be avoided by everyone. When Jill and Eustace are reunited with Aslan in the final chapter of The Silver Chair, Jill will immediately recall "all the snappings and quarrelings" and will want to apologize (236).

A half hour after leaving the camp beside Glasswater, the march is interrupted by Trumpkin, who whispers, "There's something following us" (120). Susan's fearfulness works to their advantage as she urges Trumpkin to join her in readying an arrow on the string, a fortunate request because Susan the Gentle freezes up, leaving Trumpkin to save Lucy from the attack of the bear that had been tracking them. When Susan explains that her reluctance to shoot was due to her fear that it might have been a talking bear, Trumpkin replies, "That's the trouble of it when most of the beasts have gone enemy and gone dumb" (121). Trumpkin may be suggesting that some of the talking animals have become allies of the Telmarines or that they have gone back to their old marauding behaviors. In either case, they have lost the ability to speak.

In The Magician's Nephew, Aslan warns the talking animals not to return to the ways of the dumb beasts, stating, "For out of them you were taken and into them you can return" (128). The Chronicles relate several instances of talking beasts going dumb. In The Last Battle, Ginger the Cat becomes unable to speak after joining forces with the Calormenes and entering the stable, where he unknowingly confronts Tash. At the end of The Last Battle, the talking animals who look on Aslan's face with hatred rather than love are transformed back into ordinary animals. In The Horse and His Boy, the narrator mentions the tale of the Lapsed Bear of Stormness, a talking bear that has turned to wild bear habits but then reforms after a marathon boxing match with Corin Thunder-Fist.

As the boys and Trumpkin skin the dead bear for its meat, Lucy tells Susan about a "horrible idea" the incident has raised in her head, asking, "Wouldn't it be dreadful if some day in our own world, at home, men started going wild inside, like the animals here, and still looked like men, so that you'd never know which were which?" (122). Lucy's comment here has raised a number of critical responses. Paul Ford argues, "The implication is that this has already happened in our own world, as evidenced by the tendency to reduce the highest aspirations of humanity to material and technological terms" (183). Gilbert Meilaender maintains, "Lucy is speculating about an 'abolition of man.' If, by relinquishing their inheritance, Talking Beasts can become Dumb Beasts without changing their external appearance, it is also possible for a human being to become a 'trousered ape'" (180).

Meilaender's reference to a "trousered ape" comes from Lewis's book *The Abolition of Man* (20). In this philosophical work, Lewis describes two contemporary educators who seek to remove human sentiment and thus to produce "men without chests," who look like men on the outside but lack what Lewis calls "magnanimity" on the inside (34). In *That Hideous Strength*, the third volume of Lewis's space trilogy, the character Frost actually seeks to reduce Mark to this level of non-man through a process Frost labels "objectivity," whereby "all specifically human reactions were killed in a man" (296).

There's Nothing For It but a Vote

After filling their pockets with bear meat wrapped in leaves, the band once again sets off toward Aslan's How. It is closer to midday than to nine in the morning when they finally reach the Rush, only to find not the crossable, marshy tributary that they have been expecting and that its name suggests, but a river at the bottom of a steep gorge with impenetrable cliffs.

As Peter looks at the steep rock face across the ravine, he declares, "It's my fault for coming this way. We're lost" (124). At closer inspection, neither of Peter's two statements is quite true. First, it was Edmund who proposed the Glasswater route in the hope of avoiding Miraz's outposts, and despite Susan's claim she knew "all along" that they would get lost, there was no opposition to Edmund's suggestion. So if there is fault, it must be shared by all. Second, as Trumpkin points out, the high king is not lost, just once again limited by his expectations.

As noted earlier, with Lucy's claim in *The Lion, the Witch and the Wardrobe* of having found a magic land that is sometimes there and sometimes not, Peter began a lesson that will take him two books to fully learn: reality will often defy his own limited notions. Just as Aslan is beyond the control of anyone's wants, wishes, or expectations, the wardrobe also turned out to have a will of its own—at least in a metaphorical sense. Just as Aslan is not a tame lion, we could say the wardrobe was not a tame wardrobe, allowing passage only at times of its own choosing. In the Professor's closing words from the first story, he reminded Peter and his siblings that Narnia's magic would not fit their preconceptions, saying, "Of course you'll get back to Narnia again someday," but "it'll happen when you're not looking for it" (188).

Earlier in *Prince Caspian*, Peter found it hard to believe that Susan's horn had called them because he had always thought they would be the ones doing the calling. Peter was also surprised that the prediction of Lilygloves the mole—"You'll be glad of these fruit trees one day"—was fulfilled in an unforeseen way (21). Here in chapter nine he is given not one but two chances to continue his lesson about preconceptions. Trumpkin points out, "You knew this country hundreds—it may be a thousand—years ago. Mayn't it have changed? A landslide might have pulled off half the side of that hill. . . . Or there might have been an earthquake, or anything" (124–25). The boundaries created by Peter's expectations are still evident as he replies, "I never thought of that" (125).

Trumpkin proposes going downstream to the Fords of Beruna, where they are sure to be able to cross. Suddenly Lucy declares that she has had a momentary vision of Aslan indicating they are to go upstream. In the first book, after Lucy claimed to have traveled through the wardrobe, Peter "went in and rapped his knuckles on it to make sure that it was solid" (25). Here in *Prince Caspian*, Peter again initially gives his younger sister the benefit of the doubt and asks, "Where, Lu?" (125). However, when no one else can see Aslan,

Peter is unwilling to accept Lucy's claim because Aslan is acting in a way he has not before—in a way that, like the appearance of the Rush, defies Peter's expectations.

When they finally meet in chapter eleven, Peter will tell Aslan, "I've been leading them wrong ever since we started and especially yesterday morning" (153). One way to interpret Peter's assertion is to see that from the beginning, his leadership has been bound by thinking only in terms of what has come before.

Lucy's claim about Aslan here contains not one but two new elements that are difficult for the others to accept. First, Aslan is visible only to Lucy, something that was never the case in the first story. Second, Aslan communicates his desire that they go upriver in a mysterious, nonverbal way that even Lucy cannot explain, again something he has never done before. When Edmund asks how Lucy knows this is what Aslan wanted, all she can do is stutter, "He—I—I just know by his face" (126).

The illustration that accompanies this passage adds to Lewis's description. In the picture we see Lucy pointing toward the mountain ashes where she claims to see Aslan. Peter, Susan, and Edmund are gazing in the direction Lucy indicates, but Trumpkin is looking at Lucy, perhaps to determine if she has lost her wits. When readers look to where Lucy is pointing, there is no Aslan; we see only what the four others see and so are able to better share their surprise. The question, Peter points out, is whether Aslan was really there. When Lucy declares, "I know he was" (127), her older brother's response is "Yes, Lu, but we don't."

Earlier at Cair Paravel as Edmund began to object to Peter's suggestion to fit themselves with armor from the treasure chamber, Lucy had whispered to him, "Hadn't we better do what Peter says?" (103). As noted earlier, while this simple formulaic obedience to the high king is good enough for Trumpkin, Lewis makes it clear that for the humans in this story, determining proper action is more complicated. When Edmund jumps in here with the suggestion that they decide which way to go by vote, everyone seems to agree that a democratic decision is more appropriate than simply doing what Peter prefers, particularly since this time, unlike in the earlier scene with Trumpkin at Cair Paravel, he does not seem to know what to do.

As has been mentioned, in *Prince Caspian*, much more so than in the first story, the children are frequently confused about where they are and about what they should do, and this reflects an older, more complex stage in life. In this scene at the gorge, Peter faces a truly difficult decision. On one hand, the experienced Trumpkin assures him, "I do know that if we turn left and follow the gorge up, it might lead us all day before we found a place where we could cross it. Whereas if we turn right and go down, we're bound to reach the Great River in about a couple of hours" (127). On the other hand, Lucy alone has claimed to have briefly seen Aslan and maintains that she somehow knows he wants them to travel up the gorge. Edmund, who is ahead of Peter in learning the lesson about preconceptions, points out that Lucy was proven trustworthy on their previous visit to Narnia when her story defied their notions of what was possible. In the end, Peter chooses what fits with the way things have been before and casts the deciding vote to follow Trumpkin's suggestion.

Paul Ford offers a different analysis of this scene, one based on the fact that Lewis considered democracy only the *second-best* form of government. In an essay titled "Membership," Lewis states, "I do not believe that God created an egalitarian world. . . . I believe that if we had not fallen, . . . patriarchal monarchy would be the sole lawful government" (168). And so Ford proposes that the real mistake Peter makes here is to avoid his responsibility as high king and allow a vote at all. Ford argues, "Peter would like to make peace between Lucy, who has seen Aslan, and the others who doubt her vision, but his solution—a vote—is really more of an abdication of his responsibility to make the decision for them. If he had acted on his instinct, he would have chosen to follow Lucy, but he decides on the more logical path" (330).

It is unclear what evidence we have that Peter's "instinct" here is to accept Lucy's unprecedented claim about seeing Aslan. Thus far in both books, Peter's first instinct has been to base his decisions on what has come before, to restrict what might be possible to what he has already experienced.

In *A Preface to Paradise Lost*, Lewis includes an entire chapter titled "Hierarchy," in which he explains what he calls the hierarchical conception, a thought that is "not peculiar to Milton" but one that "belongs to the ancient orthodox tradition of European ethics from Aristotle to Johnson" (73). Lewis writes that according to this view, "Everything except God has some natural superior; everything except unformed matter has some natural inferior. The goodness, happiness, and dignity of every being consists in obeying its natural superior and ruling its natural inferiors. When it fails in either part of this twofold task we have disease or monstrosity in the scheme of things until the peccant being is either destroyed or corrected" (73–74).

Here in *Prince Caspian*, we see hierarchy in practice in Trumpkin's allegiance first to Caspian, then to Peter, and finally to Aslan. Later Lewis will present Lucy's duty to obey Aslan as correctly overriding her duty to her brother the high king. Similarly in *The Silver Chair*, the parliament of owls will advocate violating Caspian's command that no one may go search for his lost son, because Aslan has given special orders to Jill and Eustace that overrule the king's.

But hierarchy in Narnia sometimes holds complications. First, what if one's "natural superior" does not know what to do? As Lewis suggests here at the gorge, advice and even a vote might be in order. Second, what if one's natural superior is in the wrong? Near the end of *The Voyage of the* Dawn Treader, Reepicheep and Lord Drinian will refuse to allow Caspian to leave the ship and will even threaten to bind him until he comes to his senses. Finally, what if it is unclear who the superior is and who the inferior is? In *The Voyage of the* Dawn Treader, Edmund will question Caspian's authority, saying, "I'm no subject of yours. If anything it's the other way round. I am one of the four ancient sovereigns of Narnia and you are under allegiance to the High King my brother" (128).

So when is it permissible to act against the authority from one's superior? Lewis suggests that in a less-than-perfect society, the notion of hierarchical obedience is not without its problems.

A further issue arises from Ford's assertion that Peter, in choosing to go down the gorge, decides on the "more logical" path.

In the first story, the Professor asked Peter to follow logic, not abandon it, in believing Lucy's story about finding a world in the wardrobe. The Professor's famous words from *The Lion, the Witch and the Wardrobe* fit the situation at the Rush perfectly: "Why don't they teach logic at these schools? There are only three possibilities. Either your sister is telling lies, or she is mad, or she is telling the truth. You know she doesn't tell lies and it is obvious that she is not mad. For the moment then and unless any further evidence turns up, we must assume that she is telling the truth" (48). Peter responded to the Professor by asking, "But do you really mean, sir, that there could be other worlds—all over the place, just round the corner—like that?" (50). Here in *Prince Caspian*, we might phrase Peter's question this way: "But do you really mean that Aslan might not act the same way every time? That he might appear to only one of us rather than to all four? And that he might communicate with one of us in a way that does not involve words?" The Professor's answer from *The Lion, the Witch and the Wardrobe* provides a good answer here as well: "Nothing is more probable" (50). It could be argued that the "more logical" path would be to follow Lucy.

If Peter is guilty of incorrectly assuming Aslan will always act in the same way, he is not alone. Even Lucy, who is closest to Aslan, will to some extent be caught in this same kind of thinking. In the next chapter when she meets Aslan, she will complain, "I thought you'd come roaring in and frighten all the enemies away—like last time" (143). Aslan's reply echoes the Professor's point and serves to drive home the message about not being limited by prior expectations. Aslan tells Lucy, "Things never happen the same way twice," a lesson about the nature of faith that both Peter and Lucy will come to learn before the story's end.

Two lesser aspects of this scene may go unnoticed because the other elements are so dramatic. First, Susan, who later will confess that at some level she knew Lucy was right, attempts to coerce Peter into voting her way here, a further step away from virtue. She says, "And now it's your turn, Peter, and I do hope—" (128). Second, Trumpkin almost has to force Peter to make a decision and cast his vote, yet another sign that Peter is not yet the high king in command.

Chapter nine ends in confusion and anguish. Peter's concluding words are not the words of a leader. Without confidence or even clarity, he tells the rest, "I know Lucy may be right after all, but I can't help it. We must do one or the other" (128). As they set off downstream rather than up, Lucy trails behind with tears reminiscent of those she shed in the first story when her siblings would not believe her astonishing claim.

Discussion Questions

As noted before, Lewis put something of himself in each of the four children. He shared the longing that Lucy feels, as well as many of Susan's fears. As a youth he was as obnoxious as the younger Edmund, and throughout life he fought to overcome his preconceptions, much as Peter does. In this chapter, we see Peter once again doubting something because it does not fit his expectations. He cannot believe Aslan would appear only to Lucy, because he has never done that before.

Near the end of *A Grief Observed*, Lewis records his experience of a mysterious moment that he states can be described only in similes, for "otherwise it won't go into language at all" (81). His experience was like that of a man who thinks he is in a dungeon and suddenly hears a sound that proves he is not in a cellar but free, or like that of a man in the dark who hears the sound of laughter close at hand, indicating there is a friend just beside him.

After making these comparisons, Lewis lists the many obstacles that keep him from fully admitting this experience: "Five senses; an incurably abstract intellect; a haphazardly selective memory; *a set of preconceptions and assumptions so numerous that I can never examine more than a minority of them*" (81–82, emphasis added). Lewis wonders, "How much of total reality can such an apparatus let through?" (82).

In a moving conclusion, Lewis argues, "Images of the Holy easily become holy images—sacrosanct. My idea of God is not a divine idea. It has to be shattered time after time. He shatters it Himself. He is the great Iconoclast. . . . Could we not almost say that this shattering is one of the marks of His presence?" (83).

1. Which of the children's preconceptions and assumptions are shattered by events and characters in Narnia?
2. What might Lewis be saying about our preconceptions? How does life in our world go beyond our expectations?
3. How might our expectations need to be shattered from time to time? In what ways might our encounter with literature—such as the Chronicles of Narnia—serve to shatter our expectations?
4. Finally, how does this topic relate to the humility humans ultimately must have about their own understanding and to the command that we are to walk by faith and not by sight?

10

The Return of the Lion

The Bridge of Beruna

The walk down the gorge quickly becomes a winding, difficult scramble through dense undergrowth and over slippery boulders. As morning turns to afternoon, readers are told, "No one was talking any more about breakfast, or even dinner, with Caspian" (130). Another conflict erupts, again showing a less-than-rigid hierarchy, as Peter, Edmund, and Trumpkin are in favor of stopping to cook the bear meat, while Susan wants only "to get *on* and finish it and get out of these beastly woods" (132).

Although readers are reminded once again that the air of Narnia is making the four Pevensies more like the kings and queens they formerly were—and thus more fit for the strenuous journey—as the hardship increases, Susan's nobility actually seems to decrease. It is significant that the narrator mentions that Lucy is "only one-third of a little girl going to boarding school for the first time, and two-thirds of Queen Lucy of Narnia" but says nothing here about Susan (132).

Earlier in the discussion of Peter's statement from chapter one that they might be "anywhere" (5), it was noted that in *Prince Caspian* Lewis violates his former rule of making Narnia strange but not too strange, familiar but not too familiar. Here in chapter ten, because Miraz has driven the Old Narnians underground or into exile and has silenced the trees and streams, the landscape, while at times beautiful, now holds nothing more than the familiar landscape of England would. The description of the troupe's journey down the gorge could have come straight from a walk in the Lake District. The narrator comments, "For an afternoon's ramble ending in a picnic tea it would have been delightful. It had everything you could want on an occasion of that sort—rumbling waterfalls, silver cascades, deep, amber-colored pools, mossy rocks, and deep moss on the banks in which you could sink over your ankles" (130). It is telling that Peter and Trumpkin are struck not by the sight of a faun carrying parcels or a talking beaver, as in the first book, but by an ordinary eagle. Back in chapter one when they first reached the seashore, Peter had declared, "This is good enough" (6). If Narnia is meant to be more than simply another England—and it is—then this description of the river gorge, while exquisitely pastoral, is not "good enough." And this is why the children have been called: to help return Narnia to its enchanted condition.

Suddenly the gorge gives way to open country as the Rush rounds a bend and joins the Great River. "At last!" Susan declares (132), and in her voice readers can hear exasperation and impatience, emotions that have characterized her ever since she got up that morning. Perhaps to show the contrast in attitudes, two chapters later Lewis will have the badgers standing as sentinels utter the same words when Trumpkin announces he has brought "the High King of Narnia out of the far past" (161). When the badgers declare, "At last. At last," readers will hear not exasperation but the animals' patient yearning through not just the two days since the horn was blown but through years of persecution.

The "broad and shallow" place the children knew on their last visit as the Fords of Beruna is still there but now is spanned by "a long, many-arched" bridge (132). In chapter fourteen, Miraz's forces will retreat here in hopes of crossing to the town of Beruna, where they can defend themselves behind its "ramparts and closed gates" (197). They will be shocked to find that the bridge, which now seems so imposing and so permanent, has completely disappeared.

Peter and Edmund are cheered by the sight of the spot where the Battle of Beruna was won hundreds of years previously on their first visit. The wars and battles from the first two Chronicle stories will not be named at the time they are fought but will be given names elsewhere. The civil war fought in *Prince Caspian* will be referred to as "the great War of Deliverance" in chapter sixteen of *The Last Battle*. The final battle in *Prince Caspian* will be called "the second Battle of Beruna" in chapter one of *The Voyage of the* Dawn Treader. To avoid confusion, the battle fought at the end of *The Lion, the Witch and the Wardrobe*—the one Peter and Edmund recall here as the Battle of Beruna—has been renamed by Narnia scholars as "the first Battle of Beruna."

Bottles and Battledores

As the troupe makes its way toward the bridge, suddenly they find themselves under attack as arrows begin to whiz around them. Here again Lewis uses his familiar technique of providing a sound before a sight. In this case the children hear a noise "rather like the stroke of a woodpecker" before actually seeing the arrows (133). The word *battledore* from Trumpkin's exclamation "Bottles and battledores!" (135) refers to an ancient type of badminton racket, perhaps indicating that the dwarf feels a bit like a shuttlecock being batted back and forth—first being captured on his way to Cair Paravel and now being attacked on his way back to Aslan's How.

As they crawl back uphill through the bracken, only one arrow finds its mark, as the narrator points out: "One struck Susan's helmet with a sharp ping and glanced off" (134). Perhaps Lewis includes this minor detail merely to provide a dramatic element of realism. However, some readers may remember that when Susan shot at the soldier who was about to drown Trumpkin, her arrow also struck on his helmet and bounced off. In *The Horse and His Boy*, Lewis will include a scene in which Aslan attacks Aravis, leaving a row of deep scratches on her back. These wounds match the stripes from the whipping Aravis had caused a household slave to receive, "tear for tear, throb for throb" (201), and this identical injury will be inflicted by Aslan to make Aravis more aware of her wrongdoing.

Lewis is not suggesting here that Susan was wrong for shooting the soldier. It is her increasingly self-centered attitude she needs to become more conscious of. Susan has been snapping at her siblings to get out of the woods and down to this very crossing as fast as they can. In *The Problem of Pain*, Lewis makes his well-known declaration, "God whispers to us in our pleasures, speaks in our conscience, but shouts in our pains; it is His megaphone to rouse a deaf world" (83). While the arrow pinging off Susan's helmet does not inflict much pain, it at least has the potential to get her attention.

Is there enough evidence to suggest that Lewis is making some kind of statement through the fact that Susan is the only one hit in the attack? Probably not, but there are two other elements that may suggest this is more than just a random detail. First, on the very next page, Peter says of his mistake in leading them that way, "I ought to have my head smacked" (135)—the very thing that just happened to Susan. Second, after the arrow attack, Susan's improper attitude immediately takes a turn for the better. She will go so far as to declare that the Glasswater route, the focus of so much of her complaining earlier, is a "blessing in disguise." Whether caused by the arrow or not, this positive shift in Susan will not be lasting. In the very next chapter, her attitude will be worse than ever.

Readers may agree with Peter's suggestion here that he ought to have his head smacked, although a better time for knocking some sense into him would have been earlier in the day when he chose to disregard Lucy's claim to have seen Aslan. In some ways, the unpredictable events that transpire in *Prince Caspian* will come as a smack in the head to Peter and will eventually bring him to a better understanding of the limitations he has been putting on things.

When they are finally out of range of the sentries' arrows and have a moment to catch their breath, Trumpkin points out, "If we'd gone my way, we'd have walked straight into that new outpost, most likely; or at least had just the same trouble avoiding it," and he concludes, "I think this Glasswater route has turned out for the best" (135). Once again, the children have come through a difficult experience that later can be seen as strange help.

Lucy, who is not one to gloat, merely comments, "I suppose we'll have to go right up the gorge again now" (135). Peter then gives voice to what Lucy is too courteous to say herself: "That's the nearest you've got today to saying *I told you so*" (135–36). Peter and the others, while tacitly admitting Lucy was right this time, fail to learn their lesson that events will not always conform to their expectations. In the next chapter, Lucy will again claim to see Aslan, and they will again respond with skepticism.

As the journey continues, the narrator observes, "There is no need to describe how they toiled back up the gorge. It was pretty hard work, but oddly enough everyone felt more cheerful" (136). It does seem odd that even though now they are scrambling up the rocky gorge rather than down and must retrace the very route they just covered, the children and Trumpkin are more upbeat. While the narrator suggests this lift in spirits is due to thoughts of supper and the fact that everyone is getting a second wind, there might be a third factor at play. Perhaps part of the optimism is due to the fact that they are now back on the right track and going in the direction Aslan wants them to.

In *The Silver Chair*, a similar surge in optimism is felt by the typically doleful Puddleglum. Despite the fact they have fallen into a dark cavern and been captured, the Marsh-wiggle comforts Jill, saying, "Now don't you let your spirits down, Pole. There's one thing you've got to remember. We're back on the right lines. We were to go under the Ruined City, and we *are* under it. We're following the instructions again" (148).

Later that night after the troupe is woken for a moonlight march, led by Lucy who is following Aslan, Peter will have another uplift. As they forge ahead, Peter, who at this point still cannot see Aslan, will declare, "I don't feel half so tired now" (151).

Here in chapter ten, the positive feelings continue on through supper and into bedtime. Readers are told, "It was a truly glorious meal. And, of course, no washing up—only lying back and watching the smoke from Trumpkin's pipe and stretching one's tired legs and chatting. Everyone felt quite hopeful now about finding King Caspian tomorrow and defeating Miraz in a few days" (136–37). This scene prefigures the great feast Aslan will provide after the concluding battle in chapter fifteen. There too the fellowship and camaraderie following the meal will be the most enjoyable part, as the narrator will explain: "The best thing of all about this feast was that there was no breaking up or going away, but as the talk grew quieter and slower, one after another would begin to nod and finally drop off to sleep with feet toward the fire and good friends on either side" (213).

Here in chapter ten, even though they are nearly back to where they started earlier that morning, the children and Trumpkin are heading in the right direction and, in fact, are much closer to achieving their goal than they realize. Before the night is over, they will reach Caspian in a manner they never expected.

I Do Believe They're Moving

Lucy is woken up from a deep sleep with the feeling that "the voice she liked best in the world had been calling her name" (137), a voice that first reminds her of her father's voice and then of Peter's. In this scene, readers may find echoes of an Old Testament story found in the third chapter of 1 Samuel. There the young boy Samuel, like Lucy, is woken in the night by a voice calling him. In a way paralleled here in *Prince Caspian*, Samuel twice thinks that it is someone else, in his case his elder guardian and father figure, Eli. In the end, Samuel learns that it is not Eli's voice but the voice of God that has been calling him. A further parallel between the two stories occurs after Samuel hears what God has to say and is reluctant to tell Eli what he has learned. Similarly, Lucy also will be hesitant to tell her siblings about what she is told.

Lucy wakes but does not immediately get up. Instead she is described as "looking straight up at the Narnian moon," which the narrator notes "is larger than ours" (137). What should we make of these two details Lewis inserts? Perhaps here in *Prince Caspian*, the moon is just the moon, and Lucy is simply appreciating its splendor. However, given the scene earlier where Doctor Cornelius pointed out the planets Tarva and Alambil as living beings, readers might wonder if Lucy's interest involves something more than astronomical beauty.

In chapter fifteen after the victory feast, readers will find this detail: "All night Aslan and the Moon gazed upon each other with joyful and unblinking eyes" (213). About this scene Paul Ford has observed, "It is difficult to determine Lewis's intention or the meaning of this beautiful image. If the overall meaning of *Prince Caspian* is the liberation of nature from the fetters of fear and technology, then this image suggests the ultimate reconciliation of the rival principles of creation, symbolized by the Lion or sun or masculinity, and the moon or femininity" (66). Having suggested this possibility, Ford can offer only the somewhat vague conclusion that "some great communion is going on in this scene."

Ford must be vague because Lewis himself is vague about what, if anything, the moon may represent, both in chapter fifteen with Aslan and here in chapter ten with Lucy. If readers look beyond *Prince Caspian* for clues, there may be a further hint that the Narnian moon has some special significance, one that again will be suggestive but difficult to interpret in a specific way. In *The Voyage of the Dawn Treader* when Eustace describes his meeting with Aslan, he will state, "One queer thing was that there was no moon last night, but there was moonlight where the lion was" (106).

Lucy hears her name called again, and this time she sits up, "trembling with excitement but not with fear" (137). Looking over at the nearby stand of trees, she declares, "Why, I do believe they're moving. They're walking about" (138). While everyone else was sleeping the night before, Lucy had been present when the trees almost came alive. Now Lucy, again the only one awake, sees the fulfillment of not only her vision from the previous evening but also of the earlier hopes of Doctor Cornelius and Trufflehunter.

In chapter four, Cornelius had urged Caspian to "gather learned magicians and try to find a way of awaking the trees once more" (53). In chapter six, Trufflehunter had expressed the same hope but implied that this task was beyond the ability of the Old Narnians, maintaining, "We have no power over them" (80). It will take Aslan to wake the trees, and since in *Prince Caspian* he will do none of the fighting, this action becomes the primary form of as-sistance he will provide. Susan's horn has "worked" (102), as Susan insisted to Trumpkin—it called the children. And, as Dr. Cornelius had speculated, it also called "Aslan himself from oversea" (96). However, the actual help that the children and Aslan provide takes somewhat unexpected forms.

The first tree Lucy notices here looks like "a huge man with a shaggy beard and great bushes of hair" (138). Lewis's description bears a close resemblance to Tolkien's Treebeard, the Ent that Merry and Pippin meet in *The Two Towers*. There, in the hobbits' first encounter with Treebeard, he is described as a "large man-like" figure with "a sweeping grey beard, bushy, almost twiggy at the roots" (452). Other similarities with Tolkien's saga will be seen later as Lewis will use the unconventional force of the trees' power as the key element in the climactic battle scene.

One further affinity Lewis and Tolkien share is an intentional vagueness in describing the enchanted trees. In *Prince Caspian* and throughout the Chronicles, it is not clear whether all the trees have spirits in them, nor is it clear whether these are two separate creatures—a tree and a tree spirit—or if Lewis intends them to be one being. Paul Ford points out some of the other confusing aspects about this issue:

> Lewis never makes a clear distinction between Dryads, Hamadryads, and Tree-People. In *The Lion, the Witch and the Wardrobe*, he states

that Tree-Women and Dryads are synonymous, although in later use they seem to be separate entities. In *The Magician's Nephew* some wood-gods become the husbands of the daughters of King Frank and Queen Helen. A case can be made for Tree-Women also being Dryads, as Dryads are nymphs and nymphs are always female; but it is difficult to determine what Tree-Men are. To add to the confusion, *dryad* is from the Latin *drus*, meaning "oak." Throughout the Chronicles, oaks are male. (181)

In the end, Lewis leaves the exact nature of the trees and tree spirits a mystery, as the narrator simply states here in chapter ten that at one moment they seem to assume "friendly, lovely giant and giantess forms" (139), and then the next moment they all look "like trees again."

Aslan, You're Bigger

Lucy pushes past the dancing trees because she wants "to get beyond them to something else" (139), to the "dear voice" that has called her. She steps out from among the "shifting confusion of lovely lights and shadows" into a smooth grassy area, and there, in one of Lewis's most moving expressions of love and delight, Lucy and Aslan are reunited. We are told, "She rushed to him. She felt her heart would burst if she lost a moment. And the next thing she knew was that she was kissing him and putting her arms as far round his neck as she could and burying her face in the beautiful rich silkiness of his mane" (141).

This scene has additional poignancy for readers of *The Lion, the Witch and the Wardrobe* who remember the narrator's description of the journey at night back to the Stone Table: "And so the girls did what they would never have dared to do without his permission, but what they had longed to do ever since they first saw him—buried their cold hands in the beautiful sea of fur and stroked it and, so doing, walked with him" (150).

Here in *Prince Caspian*, Aslan responds to Lucy's caresses by touching her nose with his tongue and then breathing his warm breath "all round her" (141). After his return to life in *The Lion, the Witch and the Wardrobe*, Aslan made a similar gesture of affection to Susan: "Aslan stooped his golden head and licked her forehead. The warmth of his breath and a rich sort of smell that seemed to hang about his hair came all over her" (162). Later in the first story, Aslan also breathed on the Narnians who had been frozen into statues by the Witch and brought them back to life.

Aslan will breathe on people four times in *Prince Caspian*. After Lucy he will breathe on Susan in chapter eleven. Aslan will also breathe on Edmund, although this detail will be mentioned after the fact, as readers will learn in chapter thirteen: "Aslan had breathed on him at their meeting and a kind of greatness hung about him" (179). Aslan will also breathe on the first Telmarine to go through the door back to Earth, and "a new look" will come into the man's eyes (219).

In these scenes where Aslan breathes on someone, giving the person greater strength and courage, some readers may find a parallel with the New Testament story where Jesus breathes on his disciples. In John 20:22, Jesus meets these followers who are gathered behind locked doors, breathes on them, and says, "Receive the Holy Spirit." Paul Ford has suggested that Aslan's breath is "the chief symbol of the Spirit's activity in the Chronicles" (92). In *C. S. Lewis: A Companion and Guide*, Walter Hooper also sees Aslan's breath as suggestive of the Holy Spirit but acknowledges that the association is an indirect one (440).

Lucy's first comment to Aslan here in chapter ten is "You're bigger" (141). Aslan explains that he has not changed since their last meeting, but rather it is Lucy's perception that has expanded. The inference is that even now, Lucy does not perceive him as he truly is. Aslan states, "Every year you grow, you will find me bigger," and the implication is that Lucy's limited awareness will limit how much of him she can see. This statement is in keeping with Lewis's point made throughout *Prince Caspian*: reality—including the reality about Aslan—will always be bigger than our awareness of it. In *The Last Battle*, Reepicheep will issue the invitation "Come further up and further in" (203), and this call can certainly be seen as a summons to grow into a greater consciousness and understanding.

Aslan's statement here holds another important insight. Lewis does not have Aslan say, "Every year, you will find me bigger" but "Every year *you grow*, you will find me bigger" (141, emphasis added). It has been a year since Lucy has seen Aslan, but it is possible for people to be another year older without growing. Aslan's promise is that Lucy's perception of him will continue to grow only as long as she herself continues to develop. Like physical growth, spiritual or psychological growth can reach a stopping point in some people. In Susan's case, it could be argued that this kind of growth has not merely stopped but perhaps has regressed, at least for now.

In *Mere Christianity*, Lewis describes this growth believers are to undergo, writing, "Christ never meant that we were to remain children in *intelligence*: on the contrary. He told us to be not only 'as harmless as doves,' but also 'as wise as serpents.' He wants a child's heart, but a grown-up's head" (77).

So if Lucy is seeing Aslan not as he truly is here but as only a smaller version of him, one bound by her own limitations, does Lewis ever give a hint of an Aslan who is less limited? Do readers ever get a glimpse of what Aslan may really be like? The answers to these two questions are yes and perhaps.

In *The Voyage of the* Dawn Treader, Aslan will appear to Lucy as an albatross and later to Edmund, Lucy, and Eustace as a lamb. He will appear to Shasta as a cat in *The Horse and His Boy*. But except for the fact that they demonstrate Aslan is not restricted to simply his lion appearance, none of these other three forms can necessarily be said to be any "bigger."

However, toward the end of *The Horse and His Boy*, Aslan will first appear to Shasta as a lion surrounded by a golden light. Then just for a moment before he disappears, the lion form changes, as readers will be told: "Then instantly the pale brightness of the mist and the fiery brightness of the Lion rolled themselves together into a swirling glory and gathered themselves up and disappeared" (166). What exactly this "swirling glory" is, Lewis leaves unexplained, which is appropriate since this mysterious form Aslan assumes goes beyond the comprehension of Shasta, who serves as a witness to this event.

As Aslan greets the great procession of characters at the very end of *The Last Battle*, the narrator will note, "As He spoke He no longer looked to them like a lion" (210), but Lewis will reveal no more than this. One further indication that Aslan is more than the lion he appears as here in *Prince Caspian* will come at the end of *The Voyage of the* Dawn Treader. There Aslan will tell Edmund and Lucy that they have made their last trip to Narnia. But before he sends them home, he reveals that they will meet him in England, explaining, "There I have another name" (247). What name Aslan goes by in Edmund and Lucy's world and what form he might take there is left unspoken. No matter how readers choose to interpret Aslan's statement, the point is clear that Aslan is more than Lucy's perception of him here in chapter ten.

Lucy starts to blame her sister and brothers, saying, "They're all so—" but is stopped by Aslan before saying what exactly their flaw was. Readers can complete Lucy's statement for her: they are all so limited by what has come before. And, as has been noted, this causes them to reject anything that does not fit their expectations— including the fact that Aslan might appear to only one person. The lesson, as Aslan has to teach even Lucy here, is "things never happen the same way twice" (143).

You Have Work in Hand

There were very few moments in *The Lion, the Witch and the Wardrobe* when Lucy was alone. Except for the brief time entering and exiting the wardrobe and the walk to Mr. Tumnus's house on her second visit, readers never saw Lucy all by herself. She was accompanied on the journey to meet Aslan, she was with Susan at the Stone Table, she traveled with Aslan and Susan to the Witch's castle to free the statues, and then she returned to the battlefield with the reinforcements. In the final chapter, Lucy hunted for the White Stag with her three siblings.

The Lucy we meet in *Prince Caspian* has grown significantly since the first story. Her new maturity is reflected in the fact that she has twice gone into the woods alone, and now she has a second vision of Aslan, whom she alone can see.

In a similar manner, Caspian needed a time when he too faced life on his own. After learning he must flee the castle immediately, the young prince's first response to Doctor Cornelius was, "You'll come with me?" (61). The answer Caspian's tutor gave him fits Lucy's situation here as well: "You must be very brave. You must go alone and at once."

Lucy's older stage in life is also seen in the fact that her decisions are now more complex than in the first book. Aslan tells her, "We must not lie here for long. You have work in hand, and much time has been lost today" (142). Lucy goes on to protest, "I couldn't have left the others and come up to you alone, how could I?" A look from Aslan forces Lucy to conclude, "Oh well, I suppose I *could*."

What was inconceivable in the first story—that Lucy needed to take action that is not merely independent of her older siblings but also in opposition to them—now becomes an essential component of Lucy's development. In the first story, Lucy was invited by Peter to be the leader on their arrival in Narnia. Now she must take the lead—with or without Peter's invitation or approval.

Like most young people making the journey beyond childhood, Lucy initially resists this increased responsibility and complains that she thought Aslan would simply "come roaring in and frighten all the enemies away" (143), much as he did in the first story. Of course, Lucy would like Aslan to do everything. Everyone would like this. But then those he does things for would not mature as they need to.

While it was appropriate for Aslan to take most of the responsibility in the first book, in *Prince Caspian* he will intentionally do less for the children. In chapter thirteen, Peter will tell Caspian that Aslan wants them to do what they can on their own.

Evan K. Gibson has noted, "If the plot of *The Lion, the Witch and the Wardrobe* is 'Aslan does all,' the plot of *Prince Caspian* could be called 'Aslan does nothing.' Both are exaggerations, but they emphasize the difference between the two stories" (162). In the first book, the prophecy Mr. Beaver recited promised "wrong will be right, when Aslan comes in sight" (79). Here in the second story, Gibson suggests, "Although the great lion appears and does some guiding and awakening, his disciples are left largely to their own swords and wits in dealing with the enemy. . . . The tasks which they are sent to do, they must do on their own." Even in the following scene when he is standing close by, Aslan will send Lucy to wake the others and deliver his message.

In Lucy's wish that Aslan would behave like he did the last time, we may also hear the human desire for predictability, a topic Lewis examined at greater length in *Perelandra*, the second book of his space trilogy. On the planet Perelandra, the King and Queen have been forbidden to permanently live on what is called the Fixed Land and instead must spend each night on the floating islands that ride the seas. When Ransom meets the Queen in the book's final chapter, she explains, "The reason for not yet living on the Fixed Land is now so plain. How could I wish to live there except because it was Fixed? And why should I desire the Fixed except to make sure—to be able on one day to command where I should be the next and what should happen to me? It was to reject the wave . . . to put in our own power what times should roll towards us" (179). Lucy's wish for Aslan to behave the same every time goes against Mr. Beaver's observation at the end of *The Lion, the Witch and the Wardrobe* that Aslan "doesn't like being tied down" (182)—tied down like a tame lion to the wishes and expectations of others.

In the final book he completed, *Letters to Malcolm*, Lewis comments on the human desire to have God act in the same way every time, writing, "We are always harking back to some occasion which seemed to us to reach perfection, setting that up as a norm, and depreciating all other occasions by comparison. . . . It would be rash to say that there is any prayer which God *never* grants. But the strongest candidate is the prayer we might express in the single word *encore*" (26–27). In *Perelandra* Ransom labels this desire as "clinging to the old good" instead of taking the new good that comes in a different manner (71).

Lucy fails to see that by not simply frightening all the enemies away, Aslan has her best interests in mind. What Lucy and her siblings need is for Aslan to stay more on the sidelines this time, allowing them—in some ways forcing them—to do what they can on their own. Yes, it would be easier and more pleasant simply to have Aslan do everything, but then the Pevensie children would never grow up and would never fulfill their potential.

In *The Problem of Pain*, Lewis writes about wishing that God did not have such high plans for us: "It is natural for us to wish that God has designed for us a less glorious and less arduous destiny; but then we are wishing not for more love but less" (38). In our wanting a God who will pamper rather than push, Lewis further suggests, "We want, in fact, not so much a Father in Heaven as a grandfather in heaven" (35).

After some encouraging magic from Aslan's mane, Lucy declares, "I'm sorry, Aslan. I'm ready now" (143). Aslan then tells her, "Now you are a lioness." While Aslan's choice of animal for comparison here may simply be his way of noting Lucy's lion's share of courage to face the task ahead, it may be more. In envisioning a glorious but arduous destiny for Lucy, Aslan is planning for her in some ways to become more like him.

Aslan concludes with the statement, "And now all Narnia will be renewed" (143), a comment that will refer not only to the trees and streams but also to Peter, Susan, Edmund, and Lucy, who are part of Narnia as well.

What Would Have Happened?

Amid the details of Lucy's dramatic meeting with Aslan, in the short span of five lines, Lewis introduces one of his most intriguing topics: the effect of wrong choices and the question of "what if?"

Lucy comes to understand that she made a wrong choice earlier in not leaving the others in order to follow Aslan up the gorge. She asks, "You mean that it would have turned out all right—somehow?

But how?" (142). Aslan responds, "To know what *would* have happened, child? No. Nobody is ever told that."

In this exchange Lucy actually *is* told something about what would have happened: Aslan does mean it would have turned out all right somehow. Lucy is never told exactly *how* it would have turned out all right because this is not the point. The point is that she should have followed Aslan and left what happened next up to him. A similar statement is made in *The Silver Chair* where Puddleglum will have to remind Eustace, "Aslan didn't tell Pole what would happen. He only told her what to do" (167).

In the next Narnia book, Lucy will need to repeat this lesson. In chapter ten of *The Voyage of the* Dawn Treader, she will use magic to spy on a friend named Marjorie, who in a moment of fear and weakness speaks unkind words about Lucy. After Aslan makes it clear Lucy has misjudged her friend, she will worry, "Have I spoiled everything? Do you mean we would have gone on being friends if it hadn't been for this—and been really great friends—all our lives perhaps—and now we never shall" (159). In a reference to this scene from *Prince Caspian*, Aslan will answer Lucy, "Child, did I not explain to you once before that no one is ever told what *would have happened?*" (159–60).

In *The Magician's Nephew*, Lewis will expand on this issue, making the point more clearly that dwelling on what would have happened is a trap, one that must be consciously avoided. In chapter four, Polly and Digory come across a golden bell with a hammer next to it and these words:

> Make your choice, adventurous Stranger;
> Strike the bell and bide the danger,
> Or wonder, till it drives you mad,
> What would have followed if you had. (54)

Digory succumbs to the temptation, declaring, "We can't get out of it now. We shall always be wondering what else would have happened if we had struck the bell. I'm not going home to be driven mad by always thinking of that." Polly refuses to be taken in and tells Digory, "Don't be so silly. As if anyone would! What does it matter what would have happened?" (55).

Lewis adds complexity to this issue when later Aslan will actually seem to reverse his rule about not telling anyone what would have happened. In chapter fourteen of *The Magician's Nephew*, Aslan reveals answers to not one but three "what if?" questions. First, if Digory had eaten one of the silver apples, as the Witch had urged him to, he would have lived forever but in endless misery. Second, if anyone had stolen an apple to protect Narnia instead of being bidden to take it, this would have made Narnia into "another strong and cruel empire like Charn" (191). Finally, Aslan tells Digory that if he had stolen an apple for his mother, "it would have healed her; but not to your joy or hers."

The difference between these incidents—where Lucy is not told what would have happened but Digory is—can be found in the difference of the original actions. In *Prince Caspian* and then again in *The Voyage of the* Dawn Treader, Lucy does something wrong and wants to know what would have happened if she had acted properly. Aslan's response to this situation is to state that her focus should be not on what would have happened if she had done the right thing but on right action in the future. As he tells Lucy here in chapter ten, "Anyone can find out what *will* happen" (142). Telling Lucy what would have happened would have produced only further self-reproach and guilt.

Unlike Lucy, Digory did the right thing—he brought an apple back to Aslan as he was told. To reinforce this proper behavior, Aslan explains how narrowly Digory avoided catastrophe. This knowledge will be a helpful influence should Digory be tempted again later in life.

While Lucy is not told what might have happened, readers may wonder what difference it would have made if she had followed Aslan the first time. Certainly the party would have reached Caspian earlier, perhaps in time to keep Nikabrik from his attempted coup, perhaps ultimately allowing the rebellious Black Dwarf to be healed of the sourness and hatred that characterized him. Caspian himself will speculate, "If we had won quickly he might have become a good

Dwarf in the days of peace" (173). Lewis himself was not averse to sometimes speculating about what might have happened. In *Perelandra* Lewis provides an answer to the question "What would have happened if Eve had not succumbed to temptation?"

Then Why Can't I See Him?

Lucy returns to the camp and tells first Peter and then Susan that Aslan has come and wants them "to follow him at once" (144). After these two take little notice of her, she moves on to Edmund, who wakes up and attempts to see Aslan himself. Unlike earlier when Lucy claimed that Aslan had appeared to her only briefly, now she maintains, "I can see him all the time. He's looking straight at us" (145). Edmund then raises a question readers might also be wondering: "Then why can't I see him?"

When Lucy asked if the others would see Aslan, he responded, "Certainly not at first. Later on, it depends" (143). It depends on what? Why can Lucy see Aslan right away while the others cannot?

Lewis never offers a direct answer. Peter Schakel has proposed, "What a person sees depends on who he or she is and what he or she is looking for. . . . Because Lucy's companions do not believe Aslan is present, they do not see him" (*Way* 56). This claim may be true, but it does not fully explain why Lucy saw Aslan in the first place—she certainly did not believe he was present across the gorge before she saw him.

Jonathan Rogers adds a further distinction to the element of belief, claiming, "Openness to Aslan's plans—whatever they might turn out to be—is a key component of faith. You might say such openness *is* faith. Aslan is not a tame lion, after all, and he can't be expected to stick too closely to anyone's preconceived notions of how he ought to do things" (43). It is this element of receptivity to Aslan's plans and a corresponding lack of rigid adherence to one's own beliefs about what is possible that determines what each character in Narnia can or cannot see.

In *The Voyage of the* Dawn Treader, Edmund will try to tell Eustace about Aslan and will point out, "Lucy sees him most often" (111). Lucy, it can be argued, is the one who is always most open to elements that fall beyond her preconceived notions. When Lucy went through the back of what seemed to be an ordinary wardrobe and discovered a new world, she had no trouble accepting its reality. Likewise, she had no difficulty accepting an invitation for tea from a faun wearing a red woolen muffler and carrying an umbrella and brown-paper parcels.

Lewis will revisit the issue of seeing and believing twice more in the Chronicles. In *The Magician's Nephew*, this becomes an issue of *hearing* and believing as Uncle Andrew will hear "nothing but roaring" in Aslan's song and only "barkings, growlings, bayings, and howlings" in the animals' speech—because this is all he expects to hear. As Rogers observes, Uncle Andrew "lives so fully within his mind's closed system that new and unexpected inputs just don't get through" (149–50). Then in chapter thirteen of *The Last Battle*, appropriately titled "How the Dwarfs Refused to Be Taken In," Lewis will tell how the dwarfs can see only the black darkness of the stable instead of the sky, trees, or flowers apparent to everyone else. Aslan will explain, "Their prison is only in their own minds, yet they are in that prison; and so afraid of being taken in that they cannot be taken out" (169).

Although certainly not to the same extent as Uncle Andrew or the dwarfs in the stable, here at the end of chapter ten, Peter, Susan, and Edmund are locked in the prison of what their minds say is possible. Since Aslan always appeared to them all during their first adventure, they conclude he must appear in this way again.

The limitations Peter, Susan, and Edmund put on Aslan's appearance in the guise of reason actually go beyond what is reasonable. In *The Lion, the Witch and the Wardrobe* when Peter and Susan went to the Professor about Lucy, he pointed out there were only three possibilities: either Lucy was lying, was mad, or was telling the truth. Here Susan proposes that Lucy has been dreaming. Edmund suggests a different explanation to Lucy, stating, "You've got dazzled and muddled with the moonlight. . . . It's only an optical what-do-you-call-it" (145). Susan's and Edmund's assertions are easily disproved by the fact that Lucy claims to continue seeing Aslan. In the next chapter, when it becomes clear that Lucy is not dreaming, Susan will offer an even more illogical explanation: she will claim that Lucy is simply making it all up to be "naughty" (147). Unfortunately, the Professor is not present to insert his good sense about Lucy as he did in the first story.

Thomas Senor has described the children's disbelief this way: "Once again, Lucy has remarkable experiences that she reports to her siblings. And once again they find her story incredible" (34). But as Senor argues, the others should look on Lucy's present claim that she can see Aslan quite differently than they did her earlier claim that there was a world in the back of the wardrobe. As Senor observes:

> They now believe all kinds of wild things they didn't believe before they came to Narnia. They believe, for instance, that animals can speak, that trees can become fully animated, and that at least one lion has been killed and come back to life. Now, given all these current beliefs that previously they would have regarded as absurd, the claim that this powerful, resurrected lion could appear selectively to Lucy seems not only not to contradict any deeply held background beliefs but coheres reasonably well with what they do know. In these circumstances, believing Lucy is a no-brainer. Shame on Peter and Susan!

Readers have no trouble believing Lucy, and so they too are disappointed that Peter and Susan, and to a lesser extent Edmund, cannot see that she is telling the truth.

In *The Voyage of the Dawn Treader* after someone wonders if Eustace, who at this point has gone missing, might have been killed by wild beasts, Rhince will reply, "And a good riddance if he has" (88). To this Reepicheep will respond, "You never spoke a word that became you less." Here Lewis closes the chapter with words from Edmund that merit a similar negative evaluation. Lucy's brother says to her, "Oh, bother it all. I do wish you wouldn't keep on seeing things" (146). Given that Lucy's first report of "seeing things" was her account of Narnia, what Edmund should have said to his younger sister was, "I do wish you would keep on seeing things."

Discussion Questions

In this chapter, Aslan refuses to tell Lucy what would have happened, but he never explains the reasons behind this refusal, leaving readers to wonder a bit about it.

1. What are some ways that dwelling on what would have happened can be detrimental?
2. If dwelling on what could have happened is largely detrimental, why do some people in our world get caught up in it? How might someone stop this pattern of thinking?

In this chapter, it was claimed that a rigid adherence to one's own beliefs about what is possible may determine what each character can see.

3. To what extent is this true in our world?
4. What sort of things can a person "see" only if he or she is open to them?
5. What sort of remedy or remedies might there be for someone who has limited "sight"? What sort of things have helped you to see beyond what you thought was possible?

11

The Lion Roars

On the March, Then

Lucy finally gets everyone up and delivers her message again, this time to the whole group. "And I do hope that you will all come with me," she concludes. "Because— because I'll have to go with him whether anyone else does or not" (147). Once again Lucy's siblings fail her by doubting her story, just as they did after her first vision of Aslan and as they did in the first story. While the reactions of all three of Lucy's siblings are disappointing, as the narrator points out, "Susan was the worst" (149). In fact Susan's reply to her sister, "Don't talk nonsense" (147), has a tone reminiscent of the response Miraz made to Caspian in chapter four: "That's all nonsense, for babies" (42).

Trumpkin's position is similar to Susan's, except it lacks her venom. In one of his few alliterative expletives that seem to have a clear meaning, Trumpkin claims Lucy's talk of a lion that none of the others can see is "all bilge and beanstalks" (148). To his credit, Trumpkin adds the qualifier "as far as I can see." He also makes it clear that if the others choose to follow Lucy's proposal, he will go along willingly, putting what he claims is his "private opinion" aside—a stance that makes his attitude the opposite of Susan's.

Even though he has been given good reason to, it is clear that Trumpkin has not varied his beliefs about Aslan since he commented in chapter six, "Who believes in Aslan nowadays?" (70). In chapter seven, Trumpkin declared the magic horn, King Peter, the Stone Table, and even Aslan himself to be nothing more than "eggs in moonshine" (96)—literally a dish of eggs baked in sweet oil and verjuice—a term used by the Elizabethans to refer to an idea that is mere fantasy. Since making his declaration, Trumpkin has seen half of the items from his list erased. Having witnessed with his own eyes that the horn and King Peter are definitely not eggs in moonshine, Trumpkin should be more open to the possibility that perhaps Aslan will be more than bilge, water that collects in the bottom of a ship, and more than beanstalks, an out-of-place reference perhaps to the fairy tale of Jack and the Beanstalk.

Peter too finds it hard to believe Lucy's story, but for a different reason than Trumpkin. Peter doubts Lucy here not because he disbelieves in Aslan, but because, as he claims, Aslan "never used to be" invisible to them (148). As noted earlier, being locked into things happening the same way every time has been Peter's downfall before. Will Peter ever learn this lesson? One indication that he does learn will come in the book's final chapter, where he will come to the realization, "It's all rather different from what I thought" (221).

Neither King Peter nor King Edmund acts particularly kingly here. Edmund is described as being annoyed at losing his sleep. Peter, despite knowing that Lucy is feeling wretched and that "whatever had happened, it was not her fault," is described as being unable to say something nice to his favorite sister (149). The high king seems to have forgotten that just a few hours before, he declared Lucy "a hero" (135). Edmund sulkily admits that until they do as Lucy wants, "there'll be no peace" (148), and so Peter wearily concludes, "On the march, then."

Supposing *I* Started Behaving Like Lucy

Near the start of chapter five of *The Lion, the Witch and the Wardrobe*, the narrator commented that Edmund "was becoming a nastier person every minute" (45). Here in *Prince Caspian*, this same assessment could be made about Susan. In the first book, Susan had to tell her younger brother, "Do stop grumbling, Ed" (5). Now it is she who has become the group grumbler.

Susan's disrespect becomes so great that Trumpkin has to step in and say, "Obey the High King, your Majesty" (149), although there is nothing majestic about Susan at this point. Two pages later after Lucy and Edmund have scrambled down the gorge, Peter chastises his sister: "Oh, buck up, Susan. Give me your hand. Why, a baby could get down here. And do stop grousing" (151). Readers may remember that earlier when Susan objected to going down into the treasure chamber, Peter had to instruct her, "It's no good behaving like kids now that we are back in Narnia. You're a Queen here" (23).

Queen Susan the Gentle from the first tale has at this point disappeared, and in her place is Susan the Fearful, Susan the Grouch, Susan the Grouser. Susan finally threatens, "Supposing *I* started behaving like Lucy" (149). The irony is that Susan would do well to make her actions more like those of her younger sister.

While Lucy would not say *I told you so* after the trek down the gorge turned out to be a failure, Susan has shown little of her sister's graciousness. In chapter one, Susan suggested they should save the sandwiches. Then later when everyone was hungry, she let the others know it was "a pity" they had eaten the sandwiches so soon (11). In chapter nine, Susan whined to Peter, "I knew all along we'd get lost in these woods" (124). By contrast, as Lucy will lead the troupe on the night march, she will bite her lip and not give voice to "all the things she thought of saying to Susan" (149).

Paul Ford suggests that sibling rivalry may be partly behind Susan's harsh words: "Susan grows increasingly grouchy, going even so far as to consider refusing to cooperate further until she gets the kind of respect Lucy is getting" (417). Another factor seems to be

Susan's tendency to put on what she falsely believes to be a more adultlike posture—we are told that Susan's rebuff to Lucy is made in her "most annoying grownup voice" (145). Like a mother or a governess, she tries to correct Lucy for what she labels as mischief here, and then makes a point of reminding her, "It's four to one and you're the youngest" (148).

In the end, Lewis never makes it entirely clear exactly what has caused the decline in Susan's character since the group's departure from Cair Paravel, what has made her, in Edmund's words, such a "wet blanket" (119). Several pages later, Susan herself will offer a confusing and convoluted explanation that is partly an apology for her conduct and partly an excuse—and, in the end, neither. Susan will tell Lucy:

> "I've been far worse than you know. I really believed it was him—he, I mean—yesterday. When he warned us not to go down to the fir wood. And I really believed it was him tonight, when you woke us up. I mean, deep down inside. Or I could have, if I'd let myself. But I just wanted to get out of the woods, and—and—oh, I don't know." (152–53)

When Susan meets Aslan later in this chapter, he will offer an even vaguer explanation for her wrong turning. All that Aslan will say about what was behind Susan's behavior is, "You have listened to fears, child" (153–54). Exactly what fears, Lewis never says.

Oh, Aslan!

"He's beating his paw on the ground for us to hurry. We must go *now*," Lucy concludes. "At least I must" (148). As has been suggested from the start, *Prince Caspian* involves a later period in the four children's lives, a time when they face more difficult tasks and more complicated decisions. Doris Myers notes that *Prince Caspian* raises "issues of choice and obedience that were glossed over in the first Chronicle" and points out that in this second story, "the choices are not so black and white" (135).

In the name of duty, Trumpkin earlier set aside his own individual viewpoint on what should be done and volunteered to go to Cair Paravel to await the help he was sure would not be coming. Here in this scene, Lucy must do the opposite. She must hold firm to her personal conviction to go immediately—no matter whether Peter allows it or not. To complete the picture, Susan, who seems to believe that Lucy has not seen anything, is told by Trumpkin to disregard her own viewpoint here and obey Peter.

While Susan's attitude is at fault, her assertion "I might threaten to stay here whether the rest of you went on or not" (149) would not be wholly out of line if she truly believed Lucy was mistaken. At the start of The Last Battle, a flock of birds will bring the news to Tirian that "Aslan is here, Aslan has come to Narnia again" (17), and Lewis will make it clear that the last king of Narnia will fall into error because he is too ready to believe this claim without adequate evidence.

What Lewis is suggesting throughout Prince Caspian is that while questions of duty and obedience may sometimes be simple, they may at times be quite complicated, particularly as those facing these questions become older and the choices they face become more complex.

Begrudgingly—more so on Susan's part, less on Edmund's—the troupe takes a first step and follows after Lucy. Aslan, not only invisible but also silent to everyone else, leads the way back along the top of the gorge, finally plunging over the edge, where they discover "a steep and narrow path going slantwise down into the gorge between rocks" (150). Gradually, in the reverse order of their levels of disbelief, the others come to see Aslan—Edmund first, then Peter, and finally Susan and Trumpkin—as they at last reach Aslan's How, the hill "they had been trying to reach ever since they left Glasswater" (152).

In an expression of the good side of Susan's character, immediately after seeing Aslan and realizing she has been wrong, she turns to Lucy and says, "I see him now. I'm sorry" (152). Lucy responds in typical Lucy fashion, not with a reprimand about how Susan should have acted but with the three words, "That's all right." On both adventures Lewis has brought real, not idealized, children to

Narnia, the kind we can identify with, the kind who can and will make mistakes. And when mistakes are made, Lewis makes it clear that the first step toward making them right is a genuine apology with no qualifications.

A corresponding scene occurred in *The Lion, the Witch and the Wardrobe* where Edmund encountered the others after realizing his error. There readers were told, "Edmund shook hands with each of the others and said to each of them in turn, 'I'm sorry,' and everyone said, 'That's all right'" (139). As has been pointed out, this apology was omitted in the first film. It is to be hoped that Susan's important apology to Lucy here will not be passed over in the second movie.

As noted earlier, Lewis set up as a contrast two utterances of "At last," one from Susan and the other from the badgers in chapter twelve. Here we see another time where Lewis uses paired expressions with opposite intonation. In chapter six, when Trufflehunter declared they should not have Aslan as a friend if they brought in the ogre and hag, Trumpkin had responded, "Oh, Aslan!" (77). In the dwarf's words was the implication of Aslan's irrelevance. Here in chapter eleven, Lewis repeats this phrase with a very different meaning as Edmund and Peter each finally see the great lion and exclaim, "Oh, Aslan!" (151, 153).

Next Lewis reprises the scene from the first book where Peter, Susan, and Lucy arrived with the Beavers for their meeting with Aslan. This time, although everyone is both very glad and very afraid—just as they were previously—Peter does not hang back and make excuses about who should go first as he did in the first story. The actions of the others are also significant, as the narrator states, "The boys strode forward: Lucy made way for them: Susan and the Dwarf shrank back" (153).

Lewis has Aslan say strikingly few words to the children in this touching encounter. When Peter confesses to having been leading the company wrong ever since they started, Aslan's response—"My dear son" (153)—seems to suggest that any mistakes Peter may have made were the kind that should and would be overlooked. Edmund, unlike Peter, has no great need to apologize and in fact says nothing in this scene—perhaps allowing his cry of "Oh, Aslan!" two pages earlier to serve as his greeting. Aslan simply tells him, "Well done," words referring to Edmund's earlier support of Lucy.

Neither of the Pevensie brothers has been perfect in attitude, words, or actions up to now, but Lewis makes it clear in this encounter that Aslan does not require or expect perfection. Certainly it could be said that the boys' hearts have been in the right place. Though they have not always succeeded, they have always tried to do what was right. Peter will not return to Narnia in the next book, but Edmund will, and again he will make mistakes from time to time.

Aslan's words to Edmund may remind readers of the parable of the talents from the New Testament. In this story, a master travels from his own country, leaving various servants in charge. Upon his return, the master praises those servants who have been "good and faithful" with the same pronouncement, "Well done" (Matt. 25:21). The master then makes it clear that diligence in carrying out one's duties—particularly when he is away and his representatives must function on their own—is essential for more significant tasks in the future. Both of these points have relevance for Edmund, who has performed well while Aslan has been away and who, with his older brother out of the picture, will be given greater responsibilities in the next book.

In *The Magician's Nephew*, Aslan will also pronounce "well done" to young Digory Kirke after he successfully returns with the apple (180). In Digory's case, like Edmund's, proving faithful in this task will lead to additional duties in other books as a mentor to the younger characters.

After his affirming words with the boys, there is an "awful" pause before Aslan finally says, "Susan" (153). Susan is so distressed she can respond only with her sobs. Aslan tells her she has been listening to fears but does not elaborate further. He simply breathes on her and tells her to forget them. Finally Aslan asks, "Are you brave again?" (154).

Susan's response to Aslan's question, while brief, is revealing. All Susan can say is that she is "a little" braver (154). In all other occurrences of Aslan's breathing on someone in *Prince Caspian*, there is a perceptible and often dramatic change in the individual. In the most recent instance and in stark contrast to Susan, Lucy afterward declared she was ready for the difficult task of confronting the others and was described as a lioness. In *The Last Battle*, Emeth will describe the effect of Aslan's breath on his fears this way: "Then he breathed upon me and took away the trembling from my limbs and caused me to stand upon my feet" (189). The fact that Aslan's breath has only a questionable effect on Susan's fearfulness here does not bode well for her.

Lewis claimed that when he wrote *Prince Caspian*, he did not necessarily have a third book in mind; but since at the end of this book Edmund and Lucy's return to Narnia is mentioned, it is likely that Lewis foresaw *The Voyage of the* Dawn Treader, but nothing beyond that. As a result, it would be hard to argue that when Lewis wrote this scene where Susan seems unable to be helped very much by Aslan's breath, he had already planned she would cease to be a "friend of Narnia" in *The Last Battle* (154). However, this scene and Susan's lapse in attitude during the journey from Glasswater makes it clear that she has definitely undergone a negative change of heart.

Paul Ford maintains that in scenes like this and others, Lewis provides "a faint foreshadowing that all is not right with Susan" (416), a foreshadowing that leaves the door open to the possibility that Susan will not return to Narnia at the end of the series. Ford argues, "Her fall from grace seems sudden and, to the extent that this appears so, shows an uncharacteristic lapse of style on Lewis's part. However, a careful rereading of her story shows that her fall is much better prepared for than some critics think" (414–15).

Aslan's final encounter is with Trumpkin. When the lion calls his name, the dwarf gasps out, "Wraiths and wreckage!" (154), a vague reference to the ghosts that Trumpkin had been told lived in the woods along the sea and to the fact that his old views about Aslan have now been completely shattered. The narrator describes Trumpkin's actions this way: "He did the only sensible thing he could have done; that is, instead of bolting, he tottered toward Aslan" (154).

In this description, we can hear echoes of Lewis's own encounter with God as told in *Surprised by Joy*, where he describes himself as darting his eyes "in every direction for a chance of escape" (229). Lewis refers to himself there as the most "reluctant convert in all England," and here, as Jonathan Rogers notes, Trumpkin could be given a similar title of "Narnia's most reluctant convert" (45).

Trumpkin could also be called a Doubting Thomas, someone who refuses to share the belief all those around him have until he is confronted with physical evidence he cannot ignore. Here Aslan gives the dwarf a good shake and tosses him high in the air before asking, "Son of Earth, shall we be friends?" (155). Lewis will include a similar scene in *The Horse and His Boy* where Aslan will tell a disbelieving Bree, "Draw near. Nearer still, my son. Do not dare not to dare. Touch me. Smell me. Here are my paws, here is my tail, these are my whiskers. I am a true Beast" (201). In a notable difference from the story of Thomas found in the New Testament, Aslan includes teasing and joking in this encounter. He is having fun with Trumpkin, pretending to roar and be angry as he playfully mocks the dwarf's somewhat exaggerated view of his own self-importance as a "famous swordsman and archer" (154).

Trumpkin says exactly one word to Aslan in the entire book. Here he answers the great lion's question of whether they will be friends with "Yes." And from this point on, without any lapses in this story or those that follow, Trumpkin *will* be friends with Aslan.

We Have No Time to Lose

Aslan was present in five of the seventeen chapters of *The Lion, the Witch and the Wardrobe*. Here in *Prince Caspian* he will be on the scene for only three and a half chapters. Even more telling, after their meeting here—an encounter that takes less than three pages from start to finish—Peter and Edmund will not see Aslan again until the final chapter, when the battle will be over. Paul Ford has noted that in *Prince Caspian*, "Aslan demonstrates his dependence on people or beings besides himself" (61). The other side of this claim, as has been noted all along, is that in *Prince Caspian* the children are required to do more on their own than in the first book.

After saying just three words to Peter and two to Edmund, Aslan straightaway sends the boys and Trumpkin on to their next duty with the admonition, "We have no time to lose" (155). In these words, readers may simply hear the statement that a pressing task is awaiting—Peter, Edmund, and Trumpkin will arrive just in time to thwart Nikabrik's takeover attempt. But readers may also hear a gentle chiding in Aslan's words, the reminder that if the group had followed Lucy the first time, they would have arrived much earlier.

Aslan does not offer to go with the boys and Trumpkin. He merely tells them, "Hasten into the Mound and deal with what you will find there" (155). Aslan does not tell what the danger is or even that what they will find is dangerous. He does not tell them how they are to "deal with" what they find. The narrator concludes, "Neither of the boys dared to ask if Aslan would follow them. All three drew their swords and saluted, then turned and jingled away into the dusk."

At a corresponding moment in *The Lion, the Witch and the Wardrobe*, readers were told that Aslan "went on to outline two plans of battle" against the Witch (146), and that "all the time he was advising Peter how to conduct the operations, saying things like, 'You must put your Centaurs in such and such a place' or 'You must post scouts to see that she doesn't do so-and-so.'" Here in *Prince Caspian*, Peter and Edmund must continue to make decisions and overcome obstacles without any advice from Aslan, as they have since their arrival.

This is not to say that in the first story the children never had responsibilities; they merely had fewer. In *The Lion, the Witch and the Wardrobe*, Aslan intentionally had Peter fight the Witch's great wolf alone, telling the others, "Back! Let the Prince win his spurs" (130). In addition, after Peter received Aslan's advice on the upcoming battle, he half-asked, half-hoped, "But you will be there yourself, Aslan" (146). In fact, for most of the first Battle of Beruna, Aslan was not there, just as from this point until the end of *Prince Caspian* he will not be with Peter, Edmund, and Caspian. In this way, as previously noted, he will continue to allow them the opportunity to grow and mature on their own.

In *The Screwtape Letters*, Lewis has Screwtape describe how by gradually doing less for them, God allows his children the opportunity to grow. The senior devil tells Wormwood that in the beginning, "He will set them off with communications of His presence" (40). Screwtape then adds, "But He never allows this state of affairs to last long. Sooner or later He withdraws, if not in fact, at least from their conscious experience. . . . He leaves the creature to stand up on its own legs." What is the purpose of these times of difficulty when the person feels as though he or she is facing hardship alone? Screwtape concludes, "It is during such tough periods, much more than during the peak periods, that it is growing into the sort of creature He wants it to be."

Is It a Romp?

Although they do not have the same pressing time constraints as Peter and Edmund, Aslan and the girls have their own work to do. Aslan turns to the task that has been pointed to through much of the story, and with a great roar that shakes the earth and is heard all over Narnia, he wakes the spirits of the streams and trees from their long sleep. The river nymphs and the river-god himself raise their heads and shoulders above the water. The tree people, who are freer to move about than the spirits of the streams, rush to Aslan, crowding around him in a dance of "bowing and curtsying and waving thin long arms" (157).

Others soon join the throng. The first is a wild boy in a fawn-skin whom Lucy identifies as Bacchus. He has vine leaves wreathed through his curly hair and is accompanied by girls who are described as being "as wild as he" (158). Next, an "old and enormously fat" man appears, riding a donkey. Lucy points out that this second character is Silenus and reminds Susan that Mr. Tumnus had told them about these two figures long ago.

During Lucy's tea with Mr. Tumnus in *The Lion, the Witch and the Wardrobe*, he told her stories of Narnia before the land was shackled with the restrictions of the White Witch. In addition to the midnight dances, which Lewis has already depicted in *Prince Caspian*, Mr. Tumnus described the summertime visits of Silenus and Bacchus, when "the whole forest would give itself up to jollification for weeks on end" (16).

As Paul Ford notes, "As much is done to free Narnia from Telmarine tyranny by the return of dancing and celebration as by the actual combat" (451). Because Bacchus and Silenus are figures from Greek and Roman mythology with numerous and wide-ranging associations, it may be difficult to fully outline all that Lewis intends to evoke by including them here. These two figures are always associated with revelry, and certainly Lewis uses their appearance to make it clear that with Aslan's return, the merriment that was driven underground or limited to furtive displays at midnight has returned in overflowing fullness. In this scene, we have again another expression of a theme seen earlier in *Prince Caspian*: celebration, joy, and merriment are central to life, not elements reserved only for holidays or vacations.

The White Witch, King Miraz, and, in our own world, the sour, unsmiling type of Christian share a common element: the hatred of any expression of authentic gaiety. They are killjoys, unswerving in their dedication to eradicate all "jollification" from their own lives and even more so from the lives of those around them. And this is one of the most distinctive characteristics of their dominance: they seem to have a merriment detector that is set off whenever others are enjoying themselves. Earlier it was noted that there is no smiling or laughter depicted at Miraz's castle or among his courtiers. Aslan's return here and Caspian's subsequent establishment as king must be marked not merely by a different ruler but by a completely different atmosphere.

Why do the White Witch and Miraz abhor the sight of anyone who is simply having an enjoyable time? One reason is that their perverted version of happiness seems to require that they take happiness away from others as a vampire takes life from its victims.

Another reason is that Aslan wants the creatures of Narnia to be happy, to have fun, and to celebrate and enjoy life. Since this is what Aslan wants, his opponents must want the opposite.

Lewis's narrator points out that Bacchus is known by "a great many names" (158). One of the names listed—Bromios—means "he of the loud shout." Readers are told "everybody was laughing: and everybody was shouting out, 'Euan, euan, eu-oi-oi-oi.'" Paul Ford notes that *Euan* is a Greek surname for Bacchus and that *euoi* is "an interjection, a shout of joy" (110). Bacchus's loud shout will be heard again in chapter fourteen, where it will cause the piglike boys at the school to begin "howling with fright and trampling one another down to get out of the door" (202). Here in these loud shouts of joy in chapter eleven, we find a fitting declaration of liberation from the tyranny of the Telmarines, who have sought to silence the streams, the trees, the Old Narnians, and anyone else who dared give voice to forbidden ideas.

In the previous chapter, Aslan had promised, "Now all Narnia will be renewed" (143). Here in chapter twelve, readers see the first fulfillment of this promise. Silenus's call for "Refreshments!" is met with a profusion of climbing vines that produce grapes "overhead and underfoot and all around" (159), symbolic indicators that through Aslan's power, Narnia is being renewed, revived, refreshed, and restored.

A second sign of the renewal Aslan brings can be found in the playfulness that breaks out here. Everyone joins in something like Tig (Tag in American English), Blind Man's Buff, or Hunt the Slipper—games that are played without opposing sides and have no winner or loser. When Aslan himself came back to life in *The Lion, the Witch and the Wardrobe*, he incited a similar romp, challenging Susan and Lucy, "Catch me if you can!" (163).

Lewis will revisit elements of this scene in *The Silver Chair* when the Earthmen are freed from the spell of the Green Lady and their playfulness immediately is restored. Golg's description of their former condition shares much in common with Narnia under the control of Miraz or the White Witch. Golg will tell Rilian and the others, "We couldn't do anything, or think anything, except what she put into our heads. And it was glum and gloomy things she put there all those years. I've nearly forgotten how to make a joke or dance a jig" (201). With the Green Lady's death, her control will suddenly be broken, as Miraz's control is broken in *Prince Caspian*. Golg describes the Earthmen's liberation this way: "Then came a great crash and a bang. As soon as they hear it, everyone says to himself, I haven't had a song or a dance or let off a squib for a long time; why's that? And everyone thinks to himself, Why, I must have been enchanted" (200).

Objections to Bacchus

Throughout his reign, Miraz has sought for ever-tighter control over his subjects, over what they may say and do, and even over what they may think. For the young Caspian, this meant a ban on anything Miraz labeled as nonsense. In his desire for control, Miraz has sought to banish, tame, or destroy anything wild, including unrestrained gaiety, symbolically exiling Bacchus and his unfettered merrymakers from Narnia. Earlier it was suggested that while in the first Narnia story it was always winter but never Christmas, in the second story we find summer but no May Day or Fourth of July. Here in chapter eleven, the holidays finally arrive, and the dramatic appearance of the boy reveler and his entourage functions much as Father Christmas's appearance did in *The Lion, the Witch, and the Wardrobe*—as a first sign of a weakening of the tyrant's hold on the land and as a harbinger of greater good still to come.

Lewis intended that the scenes of celebration in *Prince Caspian* would be enriched by these inclusions from classical mythology. He hoped his readers, young and old, would enjoy the scenes with Bacchus, his girls, and Silenus. However, their appearance may cause some readers to hit a bump in the narrative.

First, some may be uncomfortable with the intoxicated, orgiastic carousing associated with Bacchus and Silenus in Greek and Roman mythology. In answer to this objection, it should be noted that Lewis places their riotous behavior in Narnia clearly under

Aslan's supervision. In *Prince Caspian*, the appearance of Silenus and Bacchus will be associated with wine but not drunkenness. Their presence will provoke wild dancing but not sexual impropriety.

Lewis was fully aware that revelry for its own sake can escalate without limit. He has Edmund make this clear in his observation, "There's a chap who might do anything—absolutely anything" (158). Lewis was also aware that without some authority higher than itself, celebration can take a negative turn toward debauchery. In the exchange between Lucy and Susan that closes the chapter, Lewis points out the need for a governing influence to keep license from degenerating into licentiousness. Susan states, "I wouldn't have felt safe with Bacchus and all his wild girls if we'd met them without Aslan" (160). Lucy, speaking for Lewis as well, firmly answers, "I should think not."

A second objection that other readers, Tolkien chief among them, may have is to the mixture of mythologies we find in the Chronicles, as well as to fictional characters from the real, or primary, world—figures such as Bacchus here or Father Christmas on the first visit—appearing in the fictional, or secondary, world. Tolkien's now-legendary response to Lewis's blend of myths, recounted by Green and Hooper, was "It really won't do, you know!" (307).

A third kind of objection to Lewis's inclusion of Bacchus, Silenus, and the Maenads, as the madcap girls will later be identified, is simply that many modern readers, young and old, will fail to recognize them. Because of this, their arrival here may become a distraction. We get a definite feeling we should know who they are, but unless we can identify them, we may be temporarily pulled away from the story. This objection, to the extent it is valid, raises the question of whether Lewis ever considered inventing his own Narnian versions of these figures.

A fourth and final form of objection comes from readers who view all mythology outside the Judeo-Christian tradition as diabolic, or at least as something young people should not be exposed to or influenced by. These readers have a very different perspective on mythology than Lewis, who, in *The Problem of Pain*, declares that he has "the deepest respect" for pagan myths (63). In *Miracles* Lewis explains that for him myth is not "diabolical illusion" but, at its best, a "real though unfocused gleam of divine truth falling on human imagination" (134).

As the chapter ends, the sun is just rising. Susan and Lucy join the others who are flopped down breathless on the grass, facing Aslan, waiting "to hear what he would say next" (160). Aslan's next words will be "We will make holiday" (197), but readers will have to wait awhile before Lewis will resume this strand of the story. In the next two chapters, Lewis will tell what takes place after Peter, Edmund, and Trumpkin go into the mound.

Discussion Questions

A number of factors seem to have contributed to Susan's downturn in this chapter—among them sibling rivalry, excessive concern with being adultlike, petty frustration at having to climb through tangled woods, and irritability from missing a night's sleep.

1. To what degree is Lewis correct in suggesting that this kind of downward spiral is often brought about by not one but a number of factors, with the small, mundane elements contributing as much or more as the larger ones?
2. How do the mundane aspects of life—concerns about food, sleep, or comfort—often have substantial effects on our behaviors regarding other people?

Prince Caspian is a story of a land that has lost not only its enchantment but also much of its mirth. In both of these losses, Narnia could be said to reflect the modern world.

3. To what level would you say the modern world has lost some of its mirth?
4. Has real mirth been replaced by less genuine forms of merrymaking? If so, what are some of these replacements? How do they differ from the real thing?

Doris Myers has suggested that by linking Aslan with Bacchus and Silenus here, Lewis is making it clear that Aslan "is on the side of freedom, celebration, and plenteousness rather than uncomfortable Sunday clothes, long-faced piety, and self-denial" (139).

5. Are some Christians more sullen and humorless than they should be? If so, what might be some reasons for their attitude? What insights might *Prince Caspian* hold for their situation?

12

Sorcery
and Sudden Vengeance

For Shame, Dwarf

After greeting the two badgers standing lookout at the entrance to the mound, Trumpkin is given a torch and leads Peter and Edmund into the tunnel network, described as a "cold, black, musty place" (161). Despite the fact that the Stone Table is revered as the site of Aslan's resurrection, the location—now called Aslan's How—has all along been more associated with death than life. In *The Lion, the Witch and the Wardrobe* when Peter, Susan, and Lucy first saw the Stone Table, it was described with sinister connotations, as "a great grim slab of gray stone" (125). Before Edmund's dramatic rescue in the first book, the White Witch complained she would have preferred to hold his ritual slaying there because, as she told her dwarf, "that is where it has always been done before" (135). Here as Peter and Edmund follow Trumpkin into the darkness, we are told they encounter "an occasional bat fluttering in the torchlight and plenty of cobwebs" and have the feeling of going "into a trap or a prison" (161–62).

Edmund points out the ancient carvings on the walls and comments, "And yet we're older than that. When we were last here, they hadn't been made" (162). Peter's reply is, "Yes, that makes one think." What might Edmund's observation here be prompting Peter to think about? When they left Narnia the first time, the Professor told the children they would return someday, but Peter never imagined they would return to Narnia "out of the far past" after thirteen centuries had come and gone (161). In *Hamlet* the Danish prince tells his university friend, "There are more things in Heaven and Earth, Horatio, than are dreamt of in your philosophy" (1.5.167–68). Here Peter is provided with further evidence that there are more possibilities than those anticipated by his philosophy, and his response to Edmund suggests he is rethinking some of his former assumptions.

Trumpkin's concern in the previous chapter about the lack of sentries has helped to prepare readers for the fact that the war is not going well for Caspian's troops. Peter, Edmund, and Trumpkin hear an angry discussion as they approach the central chamber and decide to listen outside for a moment before making their presence known. A voice Trumpkin identifies as Caspian's is heard explaining, "You know well enough why the Horn was not blown at sunrise this morning. Have you forgotten that Miraz fell upon us almost before Trumpkin had gone, and we were fighting for our lives for the space of three hours and more? I blew it when first I had a breathing space" (163).

In the heated discussion between Caspian, Cornelius, and Trufflehunter on one side and Nikabrik and his two strange allies on the other, careful readers can find one of the rare typographic errors in the modern edition of the Chronicles. In the passage just quoted, the first edition has Caspian saying "at sunrise *that* morning," rather than "at sunrise *this* morning." Clearly it has been three full days since Trumpkin left and the horn was blown. In chapter eight, Trumpkin left "in the gray of the morning" and plugged away for "many hours" before hearing the sound of the horn between nine and ten in the morning (100). Trumpkin passed the first night hiking, as he noted, "I kept on all night—and then, when it was half light this morning I risked a short cut . . . and was caught" (101). After being rescued, Trumpkin spent his second night away camped near the end of the Glasswater inlet with the four Pevensies.

On the next page, comments by Trufflehunter make the inconsistency caused by the change from *that morning* to *this morning* quite evident. The badger complains that they had all agreed to keep the horn's purpose secret, but "*that* same evening everyone seemed to know" (164, emphasis added).

Nikabrik replies to Caspian by complaining that he is unlikely to forget the desperate battle with Miraz since, as he claims, "My Dwarfs bore the brunt of the attack" (163). Trufflehunter reprimands Nikabrik's readiness to distort the facts and corrects his misrepresentation of what happened, stating, "For shame, Dwarf. We all did as much as the Dwarfs and none more than the King." Nikabrik's intentional perversion of the truth is nothing new. In chapter five, Nikabrik tried to malign Caspian for hunting non-talking beasts by making the absurd claim that there was no difference between them and the talking animals, that "it's all the same thing" (71). There too Trufflehunter had to correct Nikabrik's attempt at deception, emphatically stating, "No, no, no. You know it isn't."

Jonathan Rogers has described Nikabrik's readiness to twist the truth without reservation when doing so will advance his own purposes:

> Nikabrik has left all scruples behind. His logic is characteristically specious, full of false either/or contrasts that always leave out the true option. Either the Ancient Kings and Queens didn't hear the horn, or they can't come, or they are enemies. Or, as Trufflehunter adds, they are on their way. Either Aslan is dead, or he is not on the Old Narnians' side, or he is being held back by some stronger force. Or, Trufflehunter might have suggested, Aslan has sent help already. (45–46)

In response to Trufflehunter's correction, Nikabrik does not offer evidence to support his assertions, because there is none. The Black

Dwarf merely sneers, "Tell that tale your own way for all I care" (163), as though the truth is merely a matter of opinion. A few pages later, Nikabrik will put forward yet more false claims, stating, "Who is sent on all the dangerous raids? The Dwarfs. Who goes short when the rations fail? The Dwarfs" (169). Trufflehunter will counter, "Lies! All lies!"

Powers besides the Ancient Kings and Queens

Nikabrik declares that the appeal for assistance from Aslan has failed, and so they must look to other powers. He now intends to use the hag he has invited to bring back the ghost of the White Witch. Nikabrik claims that Aslan has not acted because Aslan has not worked within the time limits Nikabrik himself has set up. The Black Dwarf is taking a position opposite of that which Peter will assume in the next chapter. In his first statement as the high king in command, Peter will maintain, "We don't know when he will act. In his time, no doubt, not ours" (175).

Nikabrik's plan is flawed in two critical respects. First, Susan's horn has not failed. Trufflehunter is correct in saying that help, in the form of Peter and Edmund, is even now literally "at the door" (164), and Aslan and the girls are nearby. Second, any attempt by Nikabrik to use the spirit of the White Witch against Miraz would have been followed by a rude awakening. "When your sword breaks, you draw your dagger," Nikabrik suggests (167)—as though the great powers of first Aslan and now the Witch are available to him to use as he likes, as his own weapons to further his cause. Despite Nikabrik's claim that the White Witch "got on all right with us Dwarfs" (169), readers of *The Lion, the Witch and the Wardrobe* would find it hard to conclude that the Witch and the dwarfs got on very well at all. In fact, the dwarfs were used by the Witch as slaves and tolerated only as long as they obeyed her every order. Caspian is correct when he declares she would be "a tyrant ten times worse than Miraz" (169).

"We want power," says Nikabrik, telling the others not to take fright at the name of the White Witch "as if you were children"

(168). In *That Hideous Strength*, Lewis tells of a similar plan by the N.I.C.E. to harness the power of higher beings they call "microbes"— creatures who are in reality the dark eldila, or devils, of Earth—to accomplish their goals. Their failed attempt ends with the leaders of the N.I.C.E. becoming subject to the microbes rather than the reverse. Similarly, in *The Magician's Nephew*, Uncle Andrew comes under the command of Jadis within moments after his magic rings allow her to come to London.

Like all deceivers, Nikabrik mixes truth with falsehood. His evaluation of the weakness of their situation is correct, as he tells the others, "This Telmarine boy will be king of nowhere and nobody in a week unless we can help him out of the trap in which he sits" (165). Concerning Aslan's actions following his last visit, he observes, "We hear precious little about anything he did afterward. He just fades out of the story" (168). Here again Nikabrik's account is accurate. As far as readers are told, Aslan has been gone without a trace for thirteen hundred years, and during this time there is little indication he has been present in any form to answer the prayers or ease the suffering of his followers. Although Aslan intervenes here to save Caspian's life, he seems not to have done anything to prevent the murder of Caspian's father or to prevent the extinction of Narnia's beavers. Lewis is telling a fairy tale here and so never explains what, if anything, Aslan did between the two stories.

Readers might find a possible hint of Aslan's ongoing providential activity in Doctor Cornelius's statement in chapter four: "I have often despaired; but *something always happens* to start me hoping again" (54, emphasis added). In chapter fifteen there will be another suggestion of Aslan's watching over Narnia in his statement to Reepicheep: "*I have sometimes wondered*, friend, whether you do not think too much about your honor" (208, emphasis added).

Murder at Council

Nikabrik's accusations continue to escalate until he finally concludes, "And so, if you can't help my people, I'll go to someone who can" (169–70). Nikabrik shares with Tolkien's Saruman a willingness to let the ends justify any means. In *The Fellowship of the Ring*, the corrupted wizard tells Gandalf, "A new Power is rising. Against it the old allies and policies will not avail us at all. . . . There need not be . . . any real changes in our designs, only in our means" (253). Here Nikabrik is willing to resort to necromancy, conjuring up the spirit of the dead Witch, if it will further his cause.

Caspian draws his sword, asking, "Is this open treason, Dwarf?" (170). Caspian is right to prepare for violence, for surely Nikabrik intends to go through with his plans to resort to sorcery, whether the council agrees or not. Nikabrik has invited the hag in order to summon the spirit of the Witch. Since earlier the prince refused the invitation even to meet a hag, presumably Nikabrik has brought the werewolf along in anticipation that the others will attempt to stop him from using any sorcery-related help. Earlier the hag stated she would be willing to use her magic against the enemy only "if it was agreeable to all concerned" (165), but it is obvious Nikabrik is determined to use her, even if it means treason.

Rather than responding to the prince's question about treason, Nikabrik implies that it is Caspian's actions, not his own, that are criminal, charging, "Murder at council, eh? Is that your game?" (170). Nikabrik is known for stating things in the way that best suits him, with little regard for truth. It is doubtful he believes Caspian is bent on murder here. Perhaps Nikabrik makes this charge in order to provoke an attack that will allow him to do away with Caspian and seize control.

Without waiting for an order from the council, the werewolf tells the hag to begin the process of summoning the Witch, saying, "Call her up. We are all ready. Draw the circle. Prepare the blue fire" (170). Violence erupts, and Peter, Edmund, and Trumpkin rush in to help.

If *vengeance* is punishment inflicted in retaliation for an injury or offense, then *sudden vengeance* from the chapter's title is the death of Nikabrik for his treason and attempted rebellion. The hag receives her due from Trumpkin as she is about to choke Doctor Cornelius. To balance Trumpkin's defeat in the fencing match with Edmund and in Aslan's jibe that he was a "famous swordsman" (154), Lewis makes a point of showing the dwarf's fighting prowess in his combat with the hag: "At one slash of Trumpkin's sword her head rolled on the floor" (171).

In *The Magician's Nephew*, Digory will declare that wicked and cruel people of his uncle's sort are always "paid out in the end" (27–28). He concludes by telling his uncle that such punishment would "serve you right" (28). Lewis purposely serves up justice and punishment for wrongdoers in Narnia, a practice he advocates in his essay "On Three Ways of Writing for Children," where he writes, "Let villains be soundly killed at the end of the book" (39–40). Lewis will have Miraz meet his own form of sudden vengeance two chapters later, when he will be stabbed in the back by Glozelle in retribution for an insult.

Your Majesty Is Very Welcome

After order is restored, we witness the meeting between Caspian and Peter. Though it was earlier questioned by Trumpkin, the strange help that Susan's horn has called becomes clear. As the girls and Aslan work elsewhere, the high king is presented here as the answer to Miraz and as his opposite. Miraz as lord protector was supposed to put Caspian onto his throne, not seize it for himself. Here, in contrast, Peter states, "I haven't come to take your place, you know, but to put you into it" (173).

Caspian, Trufflehunter, and Cornelius by themselves would have been outmatched in a fight with Nikabrik, the hag, and the werewolf. But although it is apparent Aslan intended them to arrive earlier than they did, Peter, Edmund, and Trumpkin have arrived in time to change the outcome of this bloody clash. After the group did not follow him the first time, Aslan appeared a second time. Had the group still refused to follow, it could be argued that Aslan would have taken further action to ensure that the help Caspian called for would be on hand when the moment of need arose.

Peter greets Trufflehunter with, "Best of badgers. You never doubted us all through" (173). Trufflehunter claims to deserve no credit for holding on, stating, "I'm a beast and we don't change." But he is being overly humble. All talking beasts have the potential for wrongdoing, as was made clear in Trumpkin's earlier statement that some of them had "gone enemy" (121). Trufflehunter could have doubted, but he chose to believe.

In *Prince Caspian*, as in the first story, readers find the three types of creatures typically found in fairy stories: those such as Aslan, who are by their nature good; those like the hag and werewolf, who are by their nature evil; and those like the humans, dwarfs, and talking beasts, who have the capacity for both good and evil. While Caspian speculates here that Nikabrik might have become good if they had won quickly, there is no suggestion of a similar possibility of redemption for the other two killed.

Back in chapter six, Trumpkin made it clear he would not be part of any project that enlisted evil creatures as allies. There when the Black Dwarfs suggested introducing Caspian to "an Ogre or two and a Hag" (76), Trufflehunter pointed out, "We should not have Aslan for friend if we brought in *that* rabble" (77). Then Trumpkin jumped in to add, "What matters much more is that you wouldn't have me." Here in chapter twelve, the arrangements for the bodies of the hag and the werewolf also reflect their evil status. Peter orders, "Let the vermin be flung into a pit. But the Dwarf we will give to his people to be buried in their own fashion" (174).

This will be the last mention of Nikabrik, the Black Dwarf who went bad, or, as Caspian says, went "sour inside" (173). There is no account of any regret on his part for his wrongdoing or any request for forgiveness. However, in the scene from *The Last Battle* where creatures pass either to Aslan's left and disappear into his shadow or to Aslan's right and enter a new country, Lewis will include two elements that have relevance here.

First, among those who pass on the right will be a character named Poggin, a dwarf who reverses Nikabrik's pattern and leaves the other dwarfs to give his allegiance to the king. His mirror symmetry with Nikabrik will serve to emphasize the importance of free will, personal choice, and individual responsibility—three of Lewis's favorite subjects.

Second, as Eustace watches which creatures pass to Aslan's right, he will notice some "queer specimens" among them (176)—queer because, based on their earlier wicked actions, Eustace would have expected them to pass to Aslan's left side instead. Readers will be told, "Eustace even recognized one of those very Dwarfs who had helped to shoot the Horses. But he had no time to wonder about that sort of thing (and anyway it was no business of his) for a great joy put everything else out of his head." Whether Nikabrik, who has been dominated by hatred for most of his final days, ever makes it to Aslan's country, Lewis never tells.

The only virtue remaining in Nikabrik at the time of his death was a concern—it would be hard to call it a love—for his own kind. Nikabrik allowed this virtue to expand until it became the greatest virtue, erasing all others. In this way he became like another of Lewis's villains: Professor Weston from the space trilogy. Near the end of *Out of the Silent Planet*, the great Oyarsa, or ruler, of Mars has a long conversation with Weston, trying to understand the reasoning behind the scientist's depraved actions. The Oyarsa maintains that there are laws all sentient beings know, "pity and straight dealing and shame and the like" (137). He points out that Weston is willing to break all of these laws except "the love of kindred," which he notes "is not one of the greatest laws." As this law became the only law and moral principle for both Weston and Nikabrik, it became bent and distorted and, in the end, led to evil not good.

The chapter ends with the long-awaited breakfast with Caspian. The boys produce cold, day-old bear meat from their pockets, and from the Old Narnians' stores everyone gets a lump of hard cheese and an onion. Although we are told that Caspian and Cornelius are thinking of venison pasties, and Peter and Edmund of buttered eggs and coffee, there is no complaining. Aslan is finally on the move, and although there is hardship still to come, they are all where they are meant to be.

Discussion Questions

In his book *J. R. R. Tolkien: Author of the Century*, Tom Shippey writes of a belief in Western thought that asserts that evil exists, that it is not merely the absence of good, and furthermore that "it has to be resisted and fought, *not by all means available, but by all means virtuous*" (134, emphasis added). Miraz, of course, has evil means and evil ends. He has used murder, imprisonment, deception, and exile to establish and keep his unlawful hold on power. Nikabrik, although fighting against Miraz, shares his willingness to use any means available—good or evil—that will advance his cause.

1. What is Lewis saying about means and ends here in Narnia?
2. What application might Lewis's message have in the real world? Can you think of examples where people with good ends allow them to justify the means they use to achieve them?
3. Lewis suggests that any cause that uses immoral means is ultimately unstable. Here Nikabrik's attempt at a coup precipitates his death. Later Miraz's rule will crumble from within. What can we say about the ultimate fate of regimes or institutions in the real world whose survival is based on dishonest practices and impure means?

Nikabrik has allowed one virtue—concern for his own kind—to outweigh and therefore effectively erase all others. As he follows his single moral principle, it leads to evil not good.

4. Where do we see people in our own world who mirror Nikabrik's situation, who take one virtue as their only principle and blindly follow it, ignoring all other moral laws?

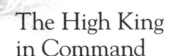

13

The High King in Command

He Would Like Us to Do What We Can on Our Own

Immediately following their meager breakfast, Peter turns to the problem at hand. He delivers the encouraging news that Aslan is nearby with the girls and that he will act—but in his own time, not when they expect. Peter's words indicate that he has learned not to limit Aslan, that where Aslan is concerned, one should be open to the unexpected. In the meantime, Peter concludes, "He would like us to do what we can on our own" (175). Peter is now both ready and able to take action independently, which is exactly what Aslan has been preparing him for all along.

Since Caspian's forces are not strong enough to beat Miraz in a conventional battle, Peter must come up with an alternative method to confront the enemy. As has been mentioned, in *The Lion, the Witch and the Wardrobe*, Lewis presented an earlier time of life and a simpler world. There in the first Battle of Beruna, Peter simply threw his forces against those of the Witch in the best manner he could devise. Here in the second book, this is largely the strategy Caspian has been using, with a notable lack of success. Peter, now a more sophisticated leader, must devise a more sophisticated strategy. He states, "Very well, then, I'll send him a challenge to single combat" (175). As the narrator points out, "No one had thought of this before."

Back in chapter three, readers were told, "The Dwarf at once took charge" (36). Chapter thirteen's title, "The High King in Command," reflects the growth that has taken place in Peter. As Bill Davis has observed, at this point Peter's earlier "lack of resolve and indecisiveness" is "set aside," and from here on he will be more "resolute" (111–12).

In the Chronicles that follow, the forces of good typically will be at a numerical disadvantage, so they must rely on their leaders' cleverness and imagination since sheer physical force is not an option. In *The Voyage of the Dawn Treader* when Edmund, Lucy, Eustace, and Reepicheep are taken captive by a slave trader named Pug, Caspian will ask for advice from the more experienced Lord Bern, who will suggest, "Your majesty must work by a show of more power than you really have, and by the terror of the King's name. It must not come to plain battle" (48). Bern and Caspian then come up with an elaborate scheme to overthrow not only Pug but also Gumpas, the governor of the Lone Islands.

Given the Telmarines' numerical superiority and Miraz's expected unwillingness to meet anyone from Caspian's force as an equal, Peter knows that his challenge is likely to be rejected. However, Peter also knows that even a rejection will take time, giving him the opportunity to inspect Caspian's troops, to strengthen their position, and to come up with another idea—if Aslan has not acted by then.

Have You Pen and Ink?

Peter's written challenge to Miraz contains a number of significant elements. To contrast with Miraz's unlawful usurpation of the crown, Peter establishes his own rightful claim to his four titles. He is high king over Narnia "by gift of Aslan" (176). He is emperor of the Lone Islands "by election" since, as readers will learn in *The Last Battle*, this territory was given to King Gale following a decision by the Lone Islanders themselves after he delivered them from a dragon. Peter is lord of Cair Paravel "by prescription," a common-law title based on possession and use. Finally, he is knight of the Most Noble Order of the Lion "by conquest"—by his victory over the wolf in the first story.

In chapter fifteen, Aslan will tell Caspian that he is to be awarded three of Peter's titles as monarch, stating, "Under us and under the High King, you shall be King of Narnia, Lord of Cair Paravel, and Emperor of the Lone Islands" (206). After Caspian's proven valor in the final battle, Peter himself will bestow Caspian's fourth title—knighthood of the Order of the Lion. Since they are granted by Aslan and Peter as well as by the laws of the Telmarines, all of Caspian's titles will be legitimate, and the rightful order of succession will be reestablished.

Here Peter refers to Miraz as the son of Caspian the Eighth, who was Caspian's grandfather. Presumably Miraz was not the eldest son, since Caspian's father was made the rightful king. Next Miraz is called sometime, or formerly, the lord protector of Narnia, a title describing his limited role while Caspian was a child. This designation, like Miraz's claim to be king, is tainted since it was a title only by self-appointment; readers may remember that earlier Trumpkin told Caspian that Miraz "called himself" lord protector (59). Finally, Peter says Miraz is "now styling himself King of Narnia" (177), a reminder that Miraz is not the true king, but a king only in the sense that he calls himself one.

Next Peter outlines the terms of the combat, or monomachy, as he calls it. Although many readers may encounter the term *monomachy* for the first time here, Lewis borrowed the term and the practice from a long tradition. Marvin Hinten notes, "It would be impossible to determine an individual source for this plot device, since the concept of single combat between on-looking armies occurs in so many cultural traditions" (27). Hinten goes on to cite several famous examples, including Patroclus and Hector from *The Iliad*, and David and Goliath from the Old Testament. A further example of a literary monomachy Lewis would have been familiar with, one from Latin rather than Greek, is the battle between Aeneas and Turnus in *The Aeneid*.

Peter writes to Miraz, "It is our pleasure to adventure our royal person on behalf of our trusty and well-beloved Caspian in clean wager of battle to prove upon your Lordship's body that the said Caspian is lawful King under us in Narnia both by our gift and by the laws of the Telmarines" (177). Back in chapter four, Caspian was urged by Doctor Cornelius to "try to be a King like the High King Peter of old, and not like your uncle" (54). In *The Voyage of the* Dawn Treader, Caspian will follow Peter's lead and, using words similar to Peter's, will suggest that one way he can prove he is truly King Caspian would be through a monomachy. He will tell Lord Bern, "If your Lordship will give me a sword I will prove on any man's body in clean battle that I am Caspian, the son of Caspian, lawful King of Narnia, Lord of Cair Paravel, and Emperor of the Lone Islands" (46). Caspian will emphasize one other facet of monomachy in this scene—that providence will assist the proper victor, and the truth of a dispute can be settled through this means.

Next Peter points out Miraz's double treachery—he killed Caspian's father and then seized the crown. Peter declares that Miraz's murder of his own brother was not only "unnatural" but also "bloody" (177). Readers are not told exactly how the murder took place, but, given Miraz's cowardly ways and the indication that it was bloody, perhaps it was a knife in the back or a hunting "accident." In *Hamlet* Claudius kills his brother by pouring poison in his ear. In the play's final scene, justice is served as Claudius is killed by his own poison. Similarly Miraz will be appropriately served justice in the end with a bloody, underhanded death from the hands of someone close to him.

At this point, Peter makes what may seem an odd request. He tells Doctor Cornelius not to forget to put the letter *h* in the word *abominable*, thus spelling it *abhominable*. During the Renaissance, in an attempt to give evidence of elite status, it became fashionable to

Latinize one's English as much as possible by emphasizing a word's Latin roots or its presumed Latin roots. One way to interpret Peter's spelling request is to see it as a way of using courtly English in the challenge, the dialect "in which he had written such things long ago in Narnia's golden age" (176). Here Peter may simply be making sure that the word is given its prestige spelling.

In Act 5, scene 1 of Shakespeare's *Love's Labors Lost*, Holofernes and Nathaniel discuss Don Armado, with whom Nathaniel has been conversing. They make fun of his pronunciation, which Holofernes labels as "abhominable" (5.1.24). Holofernes then jests that Don Armado would leave out the *h* of this word and would pronounce it "abominable." Whether Lewis is alluding to this passage or not, as Marvin Hinten rightly suggests, "Peter's caution to include the *h* is a warning not to come across as language-flawed bumpkins in writing the challenge" (28).

There is another, somewhat convoluted way to understand the high king's inserted *h*. English took *abominable* from Latin via Old French. The original Latin form was *abominabilis*, meaning "deserving abhorrence." But a folk etymology—a widespread erroneous belief—about its derivation sprang up, incorrectly identifying the Latin root as *ab homine*, which means "away from man." Thus by inserting the *h* here, Peter may be calling attention to the fact that Miraz's action was inhuman, the action of a beast rather than a human. With the modern word *abominable*, we have the less severe meaning of "detestable" or "distasteful."

Peter finishes the challenge to Miraz with the closing, "Given at our lodging in Aslan's How this XII day of the month Greenroof in the first year of Caspian Tenth of Narnia" (178). Greenroof is the only month with a distinctively Narnian name in the Chronicles. The few other times where a month is mentioned, the Narnian calendar mirrors the British one. For example, in *The Voyage of the Dawn Treader*, an old sailor from the Isle of Galma will tell Caspian, "You get some ugly weather rolling up from the east in January and February. And by your leave, Sire, if I was in command of this ship, I'd say to winter here and begin the voyage home in March" (212). In *The Silver Chair*, the narrator will note that Caspian's wife is stung by the great serpent after she and Rilian go out riding in the north parts of Narnia on "a May morning" (57).

Narnia, although a flat world rather than a round world like ours, seems to have the same length of day and the same seasons as Earth. It makes sense that the Narnian months would have English names, for presumably they were given them by King Frank and Queen Helen, the London cabbie and his wife who became Narnia's first rulers. So where does "Greenroof" come from? Perhaps it is the courtlier name for June or July. Perhaps there is an extra month in the Narnian year and thus the need for an extra name. Perhaps Lewis envisioned creating Narnian names for all the months but never got around to it. In any case, the formal tone of Peter's challenge needs a date in the closing to make it official, and Lewis seems to have felt that "this XII day of the month July" did not sound quite right.

Glozelle and Sopespian

After the challenge is written, all that remains is deciding who should deliver it. Edmund is named as the official message bearer. Peter describes him as "sometime King under us in Narnia" (177), a reminder that, despite Miraz's earlier claim that this was impossible, Narnia had two kings and two queens who served concurrently during its Golden Age, showing that power need not be absolute but can be shared. Peter chooses Wimbleweather as one of the heralds who will accompany Edmund, as much to help cheer the giant up after his earlier mistake as for his impressive looks. After briefly considering Reepicheep—someone "who can kill with looks" (178)—Peter selects Glenstorm as the third messenger. As Trufflehunter points out, "No one ever laughed at a Centaur," and the implication is that the Telmarines, who judge only by what they can see, would simply have laughed at the valiant mouse.

An hour later, we are introduced to Glozelle and Sopespian, "two great lords" in Miraz's army (178). We meet the foppish cavaliers as they are "strolling along their lines and picking their teeth after breakfast." After doing away with his brother, Miraz methodically weeded out the virtuous Telmarines who were still loyal to the former king or his proper heir, gathering followers such as Glozelle and Sopespian, who, like him, would gladly put their own advancement ahead of allegiance.

Earlier when Trumpkin learned that the two soldiers commissioned to execute him had escaped, he warned, "That may mean trouble later on. Unless they hold their tongues for their own sake" (36). Since there was no counterattack, it can be assumed the soldiers did not report Trumpkin's escape, putting their personal good ahead of the good of the kingdom. It is no surprise that here in chapter thirteen, Glozelle and Sopespian provide further evidence of the regime's unstable foundation. Since Miraz made an illegal grab for power for his own sake, what moral reservations would stop those around him from following his example?

Glozelle's name suggests someone who "glozes" or "glosses over," someone who creates a deceptive appearance. Glozelle proposes to Sopespian that, under the pretense of concern for Miraz's safety, the two of them might be able to use a form of reverse psychology to trick Miraz into accepting Peter's challenge. Then if Miraz kills Peter, the war is won. If Miraz loses, Glozelle implies that, contrary to the terms of the monomachy, they would continue the battle against the Old Narnians and, in his opinion, "should be as able to win it without the King's grace as with him" (180).

Glozelle makes a weak attempt to justify his betrayal, complaining, "Not forgetting that it was we who first put him on the throne. And in all the years that he has enjoyed it, what fruits have come our way?" (180). The validity of Glozelle's complaints must be weighed in light of who is making them. Despite Doctor Cornelius's earlier statement that Miraz himself killed Caspian's father, here Glozelle suggests that he and Sopespian were responsible for obtaining the crown for Miraz. Certainly Miraz's two courtiers seem more intelligent than their king, as they will easily manipulate him into accepting a challenge he was inclined to ignore. But if they are more intelligent, why put him on the throne in the first place? Perhaps they needed Miraz because of his relationship to the former king.

Since Miraz is the prince's uncle, it may have been easier to first get him appointed as lord protector and then to assume power in gradual steps.

As Edmund and the others approach, the narrator points out that none of Edmund's classmates would have recognized him because "a kind of greatness" hangs about him (179), a result of Aslan breathing on him when they met. Miraz appears to be blind to this greatness, but Glozelle and Sopespian are able to see it. Sopespian notes that Edmund is "a kinglier man than ever Miraz was," a comment that comes as no surprise to readers.

In Council with Miraz

Back in chapter seven, readers were taken inside Caspian's war council, where a wide variety of creatures offered a wide variety of suggestions before a consensus was reached. Here in chapter thirteen, Miraz holds a council that contrasts greatly with his nephew's. Miraz has sent for only two of his courtiers. All three men are Telmarines, so there is none of the diversity seen at Caspian's assembly. Also, Miraz has sent for Glozelle and Sopespian more for confirmation and affirmation than for their suggestions. He has all but decided what policy to follow and, in the end, does exactly the opposite of what he believes his counselors are recommending.

When the two lords arrive at his tent, Miraz exclaims, "See what a pack of nursery tales our jackanapes of a nephew has sent us" (181). Miraz's nursery-tales slur refers to the challenge's claim that it comes from High King Peter and was delivered by King Edmund. Earlier Sopespian saw Edmund as a "fell warrior" (179). Now Glozelle states, "If the young warrior whom we have just seen outside is the King Edmund mentioned in the writing, then I would not call him a nursery tale but a very dangerous knight" (181).

Rather than discussing Edmund's appearance and potential fighting ability in a rational manner and reconsidering his own view in light of this, Miraz simply dismisses Glozelle's point with derision, exclaiming, "King Edmund, pah!" (181).

Critics of Lewis who would like to argue that the Chronicles of Narnia are sexist or racist should note that Lewis's good characters rarely show prejudice, and if they do, it is a mark of their human imperfection and seen only when they are young and still developing. Most significantly, any prejudice in sympathetic characters is never put forth as something to be emulated. Critics should also note that the wicked characters in Narnia are frequently sexist, racist, or both.

The racism of the White Witch was pointed out by Nikabrik in the last chapter, as she "stamped out the Beavers" (169). Miraz's racism has been more widespread. His defining domestic strategy has been a policy of genocide, as he has sought to eliminate the dwarfs, the talking trees, and, in fact, any creature not a Telmarine. Here in his meeting with Glozelle and Sopespian, Miraz's sexism also becomes evident. First, he ridicules Glozelle for believing "old wives' fables" (181). A page later, he will further mock Glozelle for talking "like an old woman" (182). Finally, he will deride both lords for their "womanish" counsels (183). With comments like these and Miraz's overriding drive to dominate all those around him—male or female—it is not hard to imagine what Miraz's relationship with Queen Prunaprismia must have been like.

Earlier Peter, Susan, and, to a lesser degree, Edmund would not believe Lucy's story until they saw Aslan for themselves. Now Miraz refuses to believe what is clearly visible. When Miraz asks Glozelle if he believes the old stories "about Peter and Edmund and the rest" (181), Glozelle claims, "I believe my eyes." Miraz's program of deception has finally become a program only of self-deception. He has spread lies about Narnia's past for so long that when a giant, a centaur, and King Edmund himself actually appear before him, he can only continue to suggest they are nursery tales.

In his chapter on evil in *The Lord of the Rings*, Tom Shippey points out that Tolkien's orcs "have no self-awareness or capacity for self-criticism" (133), an observation that holds true for Sauron and Saruman and Lewis's villains as well. The White Witch from the first story, and now Nikabrik and Miraz in *Prince Caspian*, all illustrate the old saying "no one does evil in his own eyes." Here

Miraz calls his nephew a "jackanapes" (181), an impertinent or saucy child, when it is Miraz whose actions have been out of line. It is only from Miraz's self-serving point of view that Caspian's fight to regain what is rightfully his can be seen as impertinence. Since Miraz has the greater troop strength, Sopespian suggests, "It gives your Majesty excellent grounds for a refusal without any cause for questioning your Majesty's honor or courage" (183). Miraz's concern about his honor and courage shows a double lack of self-perception, for he is wanting in both qualities. His underhanded usurpations of not only his brother's crown but also his young nephew's have shown him to be not just dishonorable but also uncourageous.

In an instance of the pot calling the kettle black, the cowardly Miraz claims it is his two lords who are the cowards and calls them "lily-livered" (183). Readers familiar with *Macbeth* may be reminded of the scene where Macbeth, another unlawful king who gained his crown through a deceitful regicide, calls one of his attendants a "lily-livered boy" (5.3.17). In this scene, Macbeth claims that he himself will not fear "the boy Malcolm" until "Birnam Wood remove to Dunsinane" (5.3.2–3), a reference to the prophecy that Macbeth's downfall will come when the forests of Birnam Wood come alive and move. The prophecy is fulfilled through soldiers who carry branches in front of them. Miraz's own downfall will occur after the newly awakened trees come alive and take up position behind the Old Narnians.

Like Miraz, Glozelle and Sopespian illustrate a notable lack of capacity for self-criticism. After Miraz storms out of the tent, Glozelle declares, "I'll not forget he called me coward. It shall be paid for" (184). The two lords' plan to get rid of Miraz by tricking him into accepting Peter's challenge shows a notable lack of bravery. In addition, Glozelle's choice of payback—a knife in the back after Miraz trips and lies helpless—will be one of the most cowardly acts in all of the Chronicles.

Earlier in the discussion of chapter seven, it was noted that one of Lewis's central messages is that the virtuous life is not boring, as sometimes may be implied, but is a real adventure. Here in Miraz's evil circle, Lewis completes the picture, showing that a life without virtue is not glamorous, fun, or exciting but rather, as Kath Filmer has noted, is "petty, spiteful, dominating, and devouring" (51).

In the preface to the 1961 edition of *The Screwtape Letters*, Lewis invites his readers to picture hell as a state where everyone is consumed with "the deadly serious passions of envy, self-importance, and resentment" (ix), a description brought to life here in the portrait of Miraz and his inner circle. Lewis continues:

> On the surface, manners are normally suave. Rudeness to one's superiors would obviously be suicidal; rudeness to one's equals might put them on their guard before you were ready to spring your mine. For of course "Dog eat dog" is the principle of the whole organization. Everyone wishes everyone else's discrediting, demotion, and ruin; everyone is an expert in the confidential report, the pretended alliance, the stab in the back. (x)

In the end, as Filmer further points out, Lewis shows that evil is "ultimately self-destructive" (51). In Miraz's case, the deceiver will be done in by deceit. The cowardly murderer will himself be murdered in a cowardly manner. The usurper is about to be usurped. Lewis's point is that, had the coup been successful, the cycle would simply continue. At some point, Glozelle would try to do away with Sopespian, and Sopespian would try to remove Glozelle. Miraz spoke correctly when he suggested that in a government like his there could never be "two Kings at the same time" (44). In Miraz's government, everyone wants to be his own king.

Marshals of the List

All that remains is to determine which Old Narnians will serve as marshals of the lists, the roped-off area for the ritual combat. The marshals are a traditional part of the monomachy to ensure that there is no duplicity. The fact that the three Old Narnian marshals will be unable to prevent the treachery planned by Glozelle and Sopespian may be traced to three factors. First, Peter does not have an endless list of great warriors to choose from in Caspian's army.

He chooses a giant, but a rather small and dim-witted one. Second, Peter chooses to honor the old rules, which state that bears have a right to serve as marshals, even though the bear he must choose is a sleepy one who cannot even remember to stop sucking his paws. Finally, the wicked plans the two lords hatch are initially directed against their own king not Peter. So even Glenstorm, the one highly capable marshal, will be completely taken by surprise.

Lewis's main use of this final scene of choosing marshals, a scene that covers much of the same ground as the earlier choice of heralds, is to further develop Reepicheep's character. If later Aslan will tell Reepicheep, "I have sometimes wondered, friend, whether you do not think too much about your honor" (208), then readers need to see some of this excessive concern. In chapter fifteen Reepicheep will declare, "A tail is the honor and glory of a Mouse" (208). Here in chapter thirteen, Reepicheep, who puts himself forward to be selected, is thinking too much about his own honor and glory.

In *The Voyage of the Dawn Treader*, a more seasoned and mature Reepicheep will serve as the moral compass for the expedition. In that story he will be on a quest to reach the utter East in order to fulfill a prophecy that stated, "Where the sky and water meet, . . . doubt not, Reepicheep, to find all you seek" (21). However, here in *Prince Caspian*, Reepicheep declares to Peter, "Sire, my life is ever at your command, but my honor is my own" (186), making it clear that at this point the valiant mouse is seeking something very different.

Discussion Questions

In this chapter we meet Miraz's counselors, Lord Glozelle and Lord Sopespian.

1. How do leaders who use immoral means to achieve their ends ultimately undermine their authority?
2. How does a me-first leader create an unstable foundation for power? How does an others-centered leader create a stable foundation for his or her leadership?

3. Where do we find each type of leader in the Chronicles? In life?

In this portrait of the inner workings of the Telmarine court, Lewis depicts evil not only as dominating and devouring but also as petty and spiteful. Here we see the following theme: *a life without virtue is not glamorous, fun, or exciting but rather is petty, spiteful, dominating, and devouring.*

4. Where do we see other evidence of this theme in the Chronicles? In life?

14

How All Were Very Busy

Before the Battle

Lewis closes chapter thirteen with Edmund and Peter in private conversation. Edmund half-states, half-asks his older brother, "I say, I suppose it *is* all right. I mean, I suppose you can beat him?" (187). In fact, it is not clear who has the advantage in the match-up between Peter and Miraz. Peter acknowledges the uncertainty of the outcome as he answers, "That's what I'm fighting him to find out."

Earlier Edmund was able to best Trumpkin in their fencing match—but Trumpkin and Edmund are much closer in size than Peter and Miraz. The fact that Peter will be facing someone much larger than he is can be seen in Pauline Baynes's illustration of their combat. Why must Peter alone risk his life? As Margarita Carretero-Gonzalez has noted, the higher up in the hierarchy of Narnia one is, the greater his or her "duty toward those who are below" (106). Peter has the highest position and thus the greatest responsibility.

Carretero-Gonzalez has made the following observation about the drawing showing Peter and Miraz and about the two different kinds of communities each monarch represents:

> [This] Baynes illustration offers an interesting contrast between the monolithic worldview imposed by the Telmarines who support King Miraz, and the diversity displayed by the Narnians who stick up for Peter in his fight against the king. All the Telmarines wear the same uniform and have assumed a similar posture, whereas the same variety of forms that gathered in the council around Caspian is perceived in the group supporting Peter. One of them, which appears to be a polecat, even looks at the reader as if asking her to join the group. (108–9)

Besides the contrast of diversity and homogeneity, there is another, even more fundamental difference between the two armies: the stark contrast of underlying philosophies.

In *The Screwtape Letters*, Lewis has Screwtape describe what the senior devil calls "the Enemy's philosophy" (94). "He aims at contradiction," Screwtape writes his nephew. "Things are to be many, yet somehow also one. The good of one self is to be the good of another. This impossibility He calls *love*." This philosophy of love, of course, is the philosophy seen throughout Caspian's camp. Trumpkin serves as a foil to Glozelle and Sopespian. He is not just fiercely loyal to Peter but also quite fond of him. As Peter and Miraz take up their positions, the dwarf tells Trufflehunter, "I wish Aslan had turned up before it came to this" (189). Trumpkin's concern for Peter is further seen as he concludes that the Dryads, Hamadryads, and Silvans will be "very useful" for the rest of the Narnians if the Telmarines resort to treachery, but they "won't help the High King very much if Miraz proves handier with his sword." That Peter returns the dwarf's affection becomes clear during the break in the combat. After asking his brother to give his love to "everyone at home" (192), Peter's last words before resuming will be a request that Edmund "say something specially nice to Trumpkin" (193).

While Caspian expresses regret for allowing Peter to fight on their behalf, exclaiming, "Oh, why did we let it happen at all?" (192), Glozelle and Sopespian have purposely manipulated Miraz into accepting the challenge. The two lords, Miraz, and, by extension, the rest of the Telmarine army exemplify what Screwtape calls the "philosophy of Hell" (94). Screwtape explains that, according to this philosophy, "my good is my good and your good is yours. What one gains another loses. . . . 'To be' *means* 'to be in competition.'"

Beneath their glossed-over exterior, the Telmarines do not manifest even the ethnocentrism seen previously in Nikabrik. If, as we are told in *The Last Battle*, the dwarfs are for the dwarfs, then the Telmarines are *not* for the Telmarines—not ultimately. Miraz is for Miraz, Glozelle is for Glozelle, and Sopespian is for Sopespian.

In response to Trumpkin's wish that Aslan had turned up, it should be noted that Aslan *could* have returned to the camp and stopped this encounter; he could have come roaring in like last time—if this had suited his purpose. Instead Aslan has chosen to let Peter fight on his own. Aslan's contribution has been to bring Peter to Caspian and to wake the "hundreds and thousands" of tree spirits who close ranks behind the Old Narnians (189). Like Peter, the Old Narnians and spirits of the trees will do their own fighting in *Prince Caspian*.

Peter and Miraz in Combat

The combat between Peter and Miraz begins, and the advantage goes back and forth. As Doctor Cornelius points out, "Miraz knows his work" (191). After being ahead for a few initial moments, Peter begins taking "some dreadful knocks." Although Peter draws the first blood "just where the arm-hole of the hauberk let the point through," he soon sprains his wrist and is unable to hold his shield properly. At their first break, Peter explains that the only way he can avoid defeat, and presumably death, is to keep Miraz "on the hop" and so tire him out (192). He frankly confesses to Edmund, "I haven't much chance else."

How realistic should combat be in a fairy tale? In particular, how often should the protagonists get wounded or killed—as they would in a real fight? While Tolkien has Aragorn come through battle after battle without a scratch, Lewis has his protagonists take a share of the knocks. During the fighting in the mound, Caspian was bitten by the werewolf. In the skirmishes before this, Trumpkin received a wound described as "very nasty" and having "a good deal of swelling" (103). In the first story, Edmund was at the brink of death before being brought back by Lucy's healing cordial. Here in *Prince Caspian*, Reepicheep will suffer greatly in the ensuing battle and in the next chapter will be described as "little better than a damp heap of fur; . . . more dead than alive, gashed with innumerable wounds, one paw crushed, and, where his tail had been, a bandaged stump" (206). If the good side never suffered any injuries, Lewis's battle scenes would hold no suspense.

Although Lewis's protagonists do get wounded, it should also be pointed out that their injuries are not usually very long lasting. While Tolkien has Frodo endure real suffering on and off for a year and finally need to journey over the sea to be healed, the Narnian heroes are typically back to full strength the next time we see them. Lucy's cordial brings immediate healing whenever it is used. Peter's sprained wrist and Caspian's bite, once they are bandaged, are never mentioned again.

Lewis's narrative technique here in chapter fourteen is to have the onlookers describe the combat so that we share their suspense and concern. Peter takes a blow on his helmet and goes down. A roar goes up from the Telmarine side, but suddenly Peter is back up, so quickly that Doctor Cornelius must ask what happened. Trumpkin dances with delight as he reports, "Grabbed Miraz's arm as it came down. There's a man for you! Uses his enemy's arm as a ladder" (194). Once again Peter has used his greater wits to compensate for the enemy's greater strength.

In the first book, Peter's climactic battle with the White Witch was also described from an onlooker's point of view. In that scene, readers witnessed the scene through Lucy's vantage point and were told, "Both of them were going at it so hard that Lucy could hardly make out what was happening; she only saw the stone knife and Peter's sword flashing so quickly that it looked like three knives and three swords" (176). Here as Peter regains his feet, we find a similar description: "They were certainly at it hammer and tongs now: such a flurry of blows that it seemed impossible for either not to be killed" (194).

Suddenly it is Miraz who goes down, but as readers quickly learn, the usurper has not been struck down by Peter but has only "tripped on a tussock" (194).

At the end of *Hamlet*, Laertes declares that the usurper Claudius is "justly" served for his treachery (5.2.307). For his triple crime of stealing the former king's life, crown, and queen, Claudius is triply punished—his execution comes by way of a sharpened fencing foil, by Laertes's poison on the foil, and by his own poison in a chalice. Here in *Prince Caspian*, Miraz too is justly served. It is appropriate not only that Miraz meets a treacherous death—he will be stabbed in the back by one of his subordinates—but also that this death is doubly ignoble, coming about as a result of his stumbling on a tuft of grass.

In *The Return of the King*, Tolkien portrays the passing away of Théoden, king of Rohan. In his parting words, Théoden tells Merry, "Farewell, Master Holbytla! My body is broken. I go to my fathers. And even in their mighty company I shall not now be ashamed" (824). In Rohan the citizens sing of the glorious deaths of kings who won great renown. In Narnia there will be no songs memorializing the death of Miraz, who tripped on a tussock and was killed by one of his own advisors.

Treachery and Full Battle

Peter cannot honorably take advantage of Miraz's stumble on the grass tuft. Unlike Miraz and Nikabrik, he will use not all means available but only all means virtuous to triumph. This concern for proper means as well as proper ends is one of the major elements that distinguish the good and evil characters. As Edmund comments, "It is what Aslan would like" (194). By contrast, Glozelle and Sopespian have no scruples about using any means available to accomplish their goal of toppling Miraz. Earlier their plan was only to induce Miraz to accept the challenge and then to allow events to run their course. In the time since leaving the king's tent, they have added a more deliberate layer of treachery to their deceit.

In an Orwellian twist of words, Glozelle and Sopespian cry out, "Treachery! Treachery!" and refer to Peter as "the Narnian traitor" (195). Suddenly Peter finds himself facing "two big men running toward him with drawn swords." According to plan, Glozelle rushes first to his fallen king's side. His vile regicide is portrayed with extra poignancy, as readers are told, "But Glozelle stopped to stab his own King dead where he lay: 'That's for your insult, this morning,' he whispered as the blade went home."

Without waiting for the third Telmarine marshal, Sopespian continues on to attack Peter. This will be a fatal mistake, for Sopespian finds he has underestimated the abilities of the young high king. Their encounter, though brief, is one of the most violent clashes in all the Chronicles. We read, "Peter swung to face Sopespian, slashed his legs from under him and, with the back-cut of the same stroke, walloped off his head" (195).

This is the second beheading in *Prince Caspian*, and some critics have raised concerns about the bloodshed depicted in the Chronicles. Earlier "one slash of Trumpkin's sword" took off the hag's head, and the narrator noted how it "rolled on the floor" (171). In his essay "On Three Ways of Writing for Children," Lewis counters the criticism about the violence in fairy tales, disagreeing with the position that we must try to keep out of the young person's mind the knowledge that he is "born into a world of death, violence, wounds, adventure, heroism and cowardice, good and evil" (39). In fact, since young people are certain to encounter cruel enemies in the real world, Lewis argues "let them at least have heard of brave knights and heroic courage."

G. K. Chesterton explores much the same point in his essay "The Red Angel," where he writes of a letter from a woman who complained that it was cruel to tell fairy tales to children because these stories may frighten them. Chesterton disagreed, claiming that fairy tales

> are not responsible for producing in children fear, or any of the shapes of fear; fairy tales do not give the child the idea of the evil or ugly; that is in the child already, because it is in the world already. Fairy tales do not give the child his first idea of bogey. What fairy tales give the child is his first clear idea of the possible defeat of bogey. The baby has known the dragon intimately ever since he had an imagination. What the fairy tale provides for him is a St. George to kill the dragon. (49)

Chesterton concludes that what a fairy tale does is let the young person know that these enemies of man "have enemies in the knights of God," and that there is something in the universe "stronger than fear."

Edmund is the first to reach Peter. Trumpkin takes a position on Peter's other side. The giant, the centaurs, and the dwarf archers are close behind. Ignoring Peter's order to come back, Reepicheep and his band of mice surge into the battle, "dancing in and out among the feet of both armies, jabbing with their swords" (195). The narrator concludes, "Full battle was joined."

Almost before the Old Narnians are "really warmed to their work" (196), they find the enemy giving way: "Tough-looking warriors turned white, gazed in terror not on the Old Narnians but on something behind them, and then flung down their weapons, shrieking, 'The Wood! The Wood! The end of the world!'" There is an "ocean-like roar" as the awakened trees plunge through Peter's forces, pursuing the fleeing Telmarines. This final battle in *Prince Caspian* lasts for little more than a paragraph.

In the first story, Lewis devoted a mere two paragraphs to describing its final battle and then added a third where Peter, in flashback, praised Edmund's role in the fight. Thus far when a director has adapted Lewis's or Tolkien's works for the big screen, the battle scenes have been given greater prominence than in the authors' originals. Most likely these changes are made on the assumption that a cinema audience wants or needs a higher proportion of action than the literary audience. The Narnia stories and *The Lord of the Rings* are similar to symphonies in that they are composed of fast parts and slow, loud parts and soft. However, the screen versions shift the ratio, making the overall result louder and faster.

It is hard to ignore Lewis's strong environmental message throughout *Prince Caspian*. A long series of Telmarine rulers, culminating with Miraz, has attempted to turn Edenic Narnia into something more useful and more under their control. Following the wanton devastation of the forests by the Telmarines, here in the climactic battle scene nature strikes back and has her revenge.

In her essay "Sons of Adam, Daughters of Eve, and Children of Aslan: An Environmentalist Perspective on *The Chronicles of Narnia*," Margarita Carretero-Gonzalez argues that Lewis was "ahead of his time" in "his respect for the natural environment" (93), and that an "environmentally conscious reader" of *Prince Caspian* "will certainly take pleasure in the way Lewis constructs the relationship between human and nonhuman forms of existence" (94). She concludes that we find the concept of "responsible stewardship of the land of Narnia and its inhabitants" in all the Chronicles, and she argues that this becomes Lewis's main theme in *Prince Caspian* (105). Readers may disagree whether responsible stewardship is Lewis's *main* theme in the novel—and perhaps we do the work a disservice by claiming there is a single main theme—but certainly we can say that proper environmental stewardship is one of Lewis's major concerns both here and elsewhere in the Chronicles.

The Telmarines retreat toward the Great River as fast as they can, planning to cross the bridge and make their defense with the aid of their human technology, behind the ramparts and gates of Beruna. But when they reach the river, they find that the bridge has disappeared. In "utter panic and horror," the Telmarines surrender to Peter's forces (197).

What Had Happened to the Bridge?

"But what had happened to the bridge?" the narrator asks (197).

As Lewis asserts in the chapter's title, "How All Were Very Busy," each of the central characters has had work to undertake. Aslan has not abandoned the boys. He has done more than frolic with Lucy and Susan. His efforts have been threefold: 1) to wake the spirits of the trees, thus providing critical reinforcements for the battle, much as he did in the first story; 2) to remove the Telmarines' means of escape; and 3) to return high spirits and celebration to Narnia, a task just as vital as the other two.

In the story of what happened to the bridge, the narrator tells how Aslan's merry party journeys down to Beruna. It is appropriate that the group dances its way there, for, as Paul Ford observes, the town is "the very picture of the pent-up lifestyle imposed by the Telmarines" (65). Here the river-god entreats Aslan, "Lord, loose my chains" (198). Following Aslan's command, Bacchus and his people cause a profusion of plant growth to pull down the bridge, returning the crossing to being once more the Fords of Beruna. This demolition, coming as it does in such a unique and significant manner, advances an important concept Lewis began in *The Lion, the Witch and the Wardrobe*—that right ruling requires a proper stance toward not just the subjects but also the land being governed.

In *The Voyage of the* Dawn Treader, readers will be told how Eustace—before his transformation—likes "bossing and bullying" (4). And it is this deep-seated desire to always be bossing, bullying, and controlling that most characterizes Lewis's antagonists. Their prime motivation, as with Tolkien's villains, is the all-consuming need "to rule them all." A list of Lewis's evil characters reveals this common thread: the White Witch, Miraz, the bullies at Experiment House, the Green Lady, Rabadash, Uncle Andrew, Shift. All want not merely to lead but to control. Paul Kocher's description of Sauron, Tolkien's evil villain, sheds light on this kind of tyrant who "is an obsessed being, driven by his fever to dominate everything and everybody" (58). As Kocher rightly observes, "He cannot rest. He is always on the offensive, always reaching out to draw all life to himself in order to subdue it." It is significant that one of the topics Doris Myers explores in her discussion of the villains of Narnia is "abolishing the controllers" (126), for having control over everything is what they most desire. In the final chapter of *Prince Caspian*, most of those who were in positions of power under Miraz will accept Aslan's offer and leave Narnia because they have "no wish to live in a country where they could not rule the roost" (214).

What is behind this excessive need for control? According to Lewis, fear and hatred has prompted the Telmarines' behavior, although exactly what has produced this fear and hatred is left unexplained. In the next chapter, the Telmarines will make "a great fuss about wading in the river," and the narrator will explain, "they all hated and feared running water just as much as they hated and feared woods and animals" (210).

In *The Lion, the Witch and the Wardrobe*, as Edmund trudged through the snow drifts and over the fallen tree trunks on his way to betray his siblings to the White Witch, he told himself, "When I'm King of Narnia the first thing I shall do will be to make some decent roads" (91). While Lewis has nothing against roads in themselves, here they represent Edmund's attempt to subdue and control nature. Similarly, in *The Great Divorce* Lewis depicts residents from hell who, after their visit to heaven, want "to dam the river, cut down the trees, kill the animals, build a mountain railway, and smooth out the horrible grass and moss and heather with asphalt" (76).

In *Prince Caspian*, one of the first things we learn about the Telmarines is that they are at war with all "wild things" (64). The Telmarines seek to silence all things beyond their control, exterminate them, put them in chains, or force them to be what they are not. King Miraz does not merely mentor the young Caspian; he seeks to fully dominate him, going so far as to dictate what he may talk and even think about. Doctor Cornelius states that he has never forgotten "the long-lost days of freedom" (53), the days before the Telmarines invaded Narnia. Under the Telmarine rule, dwarfs must completely disappear or, like Cornelius, pretend to be human. The Telmarines' oppression extends to the dumb beasts as well. In chapter fourteen, under Aslan's liberation, chained dogs will break their chains, horses will kick their carts to pieces, and "sad old donkeys who had never known joy" will grow suddenly young again (201).

The Bridge of Beruna can be seen as the Telmarines' version of the White Witch's statues—a physical expression of their inordinate desire to dominate. Just as Aslan freed the frozen statues in the first book, here he liberates the river from its "chains" of captivity. Rather than tearing down the bridge himself, Aslan asks Bacchus to release the Great River, for Bacchus represents the epitome of freedom and thus the antithesis of the Telmarines.

In *The Lion, the Witch and the Wardrobe*, Lewis depicted enslavement to sweets (in Edmund's betrayal to get more Turkish Delight) alongside the proper enjoyment of sweets (in the sugar-topped cake Mr. Tumnus provided for Lucy and the marmalade roll the Beavers served). Lewis's point is that sweets in themselves are not bad. Whether they are good or bad depends on our attitude toward them. The same could be said about bridges and other elements of civilization. As Colin Manlove observes, "The Telmarines have established the rule of man in Narnia" and as a manifestation of their dominance have built "towns, roads, and bridges" (142). In *The Silver Chair*, which will take place fifty-three years later, we find that King Caspian has reestablished a proper stance toward his subjects and the land, and in that book the Bridge of Beruna will be standing again, presumably in accordance with Aslan's will.

Beruna to Beaversdam and Back

After freeing the river, Aslan and his joyful troupe set off on a journey of liberation through the town of Beruna, then up the bank of the Great River to Beaversdam, and finally down the river again, back to where they started. This section accomplishes two purposes: it adds to our understanding of Narnia under Miraz the oppressor, binder, and constrainer; and it further portrays Aslan as Miraz's opposite, as one who unties, loosens, and sets free.

At the end of *The Lion, the Witch and the Wardrobe*, readers were told that during the Pevensies' reign, they "generally stopped busybodies and interferers and encouraged ordinary people who wanted to live and let live" (183). Here in the latter part of chapter fourteen, we learn that Miraz, the great interferer and controller, has established a kingdom-wide network of lesser busybodies who do all they can to disrupt any chance to live and let live. For this section, Lewis switches to a sparser style of narration, one more mythic and more in the tradition of an oral fairy tale, a style that D. L. Ashliman describes as containing "few descriptive passages, very sparse dialogue, and virtually no deliberation or reflection" (44). As Ashliman notes, with this style of storytelling, "the adventure itself is the message."

The first stop is a girls' school where the pupils have "their hair done very tight and ugly tight collars round their necks and thick tickly stockings on their legs" (199). Keeping with Lewis's portrait of evil as unexciting, history lessons in Miraz's realm are boring. Keeping with Miraz's policy of lies and deception, history is also "less true than the most exciting adventure story." One student named Gwendolen joins Aslan's group and is relieved of some of her "unnecessary and uncomfortable clothes" (200)—presumably the confining and controlling collars and stockings—while her teacher and classmates flee in fear.

This pattern of liberation is repeated a number of times with less detail. As Paul Ford has observed, "In every instance Aslan's revelry is itself the sword of division that separates those who will permit themselves to be happy from those who are horrified at the thought" (65). Readers are told, "Wherever they went in the little town of Beruna it was the same" (200). Chained dogs break their chains, horses free themselves from their carts, and all join in, making "a larger and a merrier company."

In one yard, a man is beating a boy with a stick. The stick bursts into a flower, the man's arm becomes a branch, and the rest of him becomes a tree. At the troupe's next stop, piggish schoolboys are turned into pigs. As Aslan grants the gift of speech to mice as a reward for biting away the cords that bound him on the Stone Table, so devolution is used as a fitting punishment here and at other times in the Chronicles. In *The Voyage of the* Dawn Treader, Eustace will become a dragon. In *The Horse and His Boy*, Rabadash will be turned into a donkey. In *The Last Battle*, Ginger the cat keeps his feline form but loses the gift of speech. In these instances of devolution as punishment, Lewis is following in the tradition of Beauty and the Beast, the myth of Narcissus, *Pinocchio*, and *The Odyssey* where Odysseus's men are changed into swine.

In keeping with Aslan's practice of not telling anyone any story but their own, we never learn what becomes of the tree man and the pig boys. However, readers will learn of the beneficial effect Eustace's transformation will have on him. The improved Eustace will be a central character in *The Silver Chair*, where he says to Jill, "Wash out last term if you can. I was a different chap then. I was—gosh! what a little tick I was" (5). When Jill wants to know what it was that brought about the change, he will only say that over the holidays "a lot of queer things happened" (6). Perhaps the transformations seen here in chapter fourteen of *Prince Caspian* will have positive outcomes as well.

On the return loop, the group encounters an elderly woman staying in a cottage with her young niece. Bedridden and near death, the old woman tells Aslan, "I have been waiting for this all my life" and asks if he has come to take her away (203). Aslan answers, "Yes, Dearest, but not the long journey yet." Here for the first time Lewis associates Aslan with the afterlife, an association developed further in succeeding books.

Bacchus helps revive the woman with water that he changes into "the richest wine, red as red-currant jelly, smooth as oil, strong as beef, warming as tea, cool as dew" (204). In his essay "Miracles," Lewis suggests that anyone desiring to see water turn into wine in our world can do so easily. He observes, "God creates the vine and teaches it to draw up water by its roots and, with the aid of the sun, to turn that water into a juice which will ferment and take on certain qualities. Thus every year, from Noah's time till ours, God turns water into wine" (29). In the next book, Caspian will order steaming spiced wine to help revive Lucy and Edmund after they are pulled from the cold ocean waters and taken on board the *Dawn Treader*. In *The Last Battle*, the small animals will bring wine to refresh Tirian.

With the old woman riding on his back and Lucy and Susan now running alongside, Aslan and his followers return to the Fords of

Beruna just in time to witness the surrender of what is left of Miraz's army. In contrast to the dour, stifling, homogenous mood of Miraz's busybodies whom they have just overturned, Aslan's band appears "with leaping and dancing and singing, with music and laughter and roaring and barking and neighing" (204). Lewis ends chapter fourteen with an unexpected reunion and one loose thread tied. The old woman turns out to be none other than Caspian's banished nurse. With the oppressor dead, their embrace here signifies the end of his harsh policies. One of Miraz's wrongs is still left unremedied, however, and Caspian will see to it in the next story, when he goes on a quest to find the seven friends of his father's who were sent to explore the unknown eastern seas.

The plot structure of *Prince Caspian* takes the form of a figure eight, with two sets of double-stranded narratives. In the first set, the story of the four Pevensies' return to Narnia ran alongside the story of Caspian's boyhood and exile with the Old Narnians. These two lines came together at Aslan's How. In the second set of double strands, Peter and Edmund joined Caspian's forces while Susan and Lucy went with Aslan. Here at the end of chapter fourteen, the narrative lines are united again. This use of two double narratives is the same structure Lewis employed in *The Lion, the Witch and the Wardrobe*: Edmund separated from the other three in the first half, then all were briefly reunited, then Lucy and Susan went away with Aslan, and in the end everyone came together again. With this final reunion and the final battle near the end in both books, Lewis gives us a double measure of completeness. All that remains is the establishment of the new order and the children's return home.

Discussion Questions

Two opposing philosophies were discussed in this chapter. The philosophy of love holds that *your good is my good; your ill is my ill*. The philosophy of hell, the philosophy of competition, holds that *your good is my ill; your ill is my good*.

1. Where besides in the events of chapter fourteen do we see the philosophy of love in Narnia? In life?
2. Where else, besides Miraz's camp, do we see the philosophy of competition in Narnia? In life?

In the second part of the chapter, we saw that Miraz's subordinates liked to control others and interfere with their lives as much as he did, rather than to live and let live.

3. Where else in the Narnia stories do we find characters who may be classified as interferers and busybodies?
4. Where do we find the real-life counterparts of these dictators and dominators?

15

Aslan Makes a Door
in the Air

At the Sight of Aslan

It is a distinguishing feature of Aslan that no one can remain indifferent to him. Characters may respond with joy and love or fear and hatred, but it is impossible to be unmoved by his presence. In *The Lion, the Witch and the Wardrobe*, the mere mention by Mr. Beaver that "Aslan is on the move" brought about a powerful response in the four children. As readers were told:

> At the name of Aslan each one of the children felt something jump in its inside. Edmund felt a sensation of mysterious horror. Peter felt suddenly brave and adventurous. Susan felt as if some delicious smell or some delightful strain of music had just floated by her. And Lucy got the feeling you have when you wake up in the morning and realize that it is the beginning of the holidays or the beginning of summer. (68)

In Aslan's festive journey from Beruna to Beaversdam in the previous chapter, all those who met him and his merry band were affected—for better or worse. Here in chapter fifteen, the Telmarine soldiers turn "the color of cold gravy" at the sight of Aslan (205), while the Talking Beasts surge around him "with purrs and grunts and squeaks and whinnies of delight, fawning on him with their tails, rubbing against him, touching him reverently with their noses and going to and fro under his body and between his legs."

The narrator adds, "If you have ever seen a little cat loving a big dog whom it knows and trusts, you will have a pretty good picture of their behavior" (205). In this latter image, Lewis is drawing from personal experience, as he himself owned both dogs and cats throughout his life. In *The Four Loves*, he quotes an anonymous source who states, "Dogs and cats should always be brought up together; it broadens their minds so" (36), and in *Letters to an American Lady*, he describes how one of his household kittens had become friends with a new puppy named Guppy and likewise how Guppy's mother was friends with his tomcat Ginger (72).

Next Peter presents Caspian to Aslan, who welcomes the young prince and asks if he feels sufficient to take up the kingship. When Caspian expresses uncertainty about his readiness, Aslan declares that if anyone thought himself sufficient, it would be proof he was not—a valid point in general, and one that raises further doubts about Miraz's fitness to rule. Aslan seems about to announce when the coronation ceremony will take place. He begins, "And your coronation—" (206), but suddenly is interrupted by the arrival of the band of mice bearing their wounded chief. Caspian's coronation is not mentioned again in the story. In *The Voyage of the* Dawn Treader, a story set three years later, Edmund and Caspian will refer to it only briefly in passing (19–20).

Why, after an entire novel about placing the rightful king on the throne, will the story finish without a crowning? Perhaps Lewis thought that ending the second Narnia adventure with a coronation, as he did the first one, would be too repetitious. Perhaps Caspian is not quite ready to be king. As Peter Schakel has noted, "When Peter arrives, he takes command, and he, not Caspian, fights the decisive, character-testing duel" (*Way* 59). Aslan's directive for Peter in the first book, "Let the Prince win his spurs" (130), holds resonance for Caspian here as well. Although technically Caspian will be crowned king sometime in the three-year interval between the second and third books, it could be argued that he does not fully "win his spurs" and become truly kinglike until near the end of *The Voyage of the* Dawn Treader. An old proverb states it is the sea that makes the sailor, and similarly the sea journey Caspian will undertake will be the making of him. As Schakel concludes, although the young prince-king has learned a good deal in his flight into the wilderness and through his military service with the Old Narnians, at the end of *Prince Caspian* he is left with "a great deal more to learn about himself and the world" (*Way* 63).

What Do You Want with a Tail?

"Now, Lucy," says Aslan (207). As in the first story, Lucy must be prompted to use her healing cordial, although perhaps in this instance she is waiting to allow Aslan the opportunity to help Reepicheep himself. After a drop is applied to each of Reepicheep's many wounds, the gallant mouse springs up from his litter with a bow and a twirl of his whiskers, as good as new but without his tail.

"I am confounded," the appearance-conscious mouse tells Aslan, and he asks the lion's indulgence for appearing before him in such an "unseemly fashion" (208). Aslan responds to the contrary, "It becomes you very well, Small One," and there is the hint in Aslan's words that he views Reepicheep's loss as a possible antidote to his vanity. This idea is reinforced a moment later when Aslan comments, "I have sometimes wondered, friend, whether you do not think too much about your honor." As discussed previously, Reepicheep, like most of Lewis's main characters, shows growth over the course of the series. At this point in the Chronicles, he is not the mouse he will later be. Here in chapter fifteen, he asserts that a mouse's mark of "honor and glory" is his tail. In *The Voyage of the* Dawn Treader, Reepicheep will still have his characteristic gallant and dashing air, but his conception of honor and glory will have nothing to do with his appearance.

In chapter twelve of *The Magician's Nephew*, readers are told that Digory, for just a moment, has the wild idea of telling Aslan, "I'll try to help you if you'll promise to help my Mother" (153), but, as the narrator notes, Digory quickly realizes that "the Lion was not at all the sort of person one could try to make bargains with." Here in *Prince Caspian*, Peepiceek, the second in command, does not seek to bargain with Aslan but merely states that he and the other mice will cut off their tails if Reepicheep must go without his. "Ah!" roars Aslan, undoubtedly with amusement, and appears to change his mind, telling the mice, "You have conquered me" (209).

Aslan seemed inclined to leave the chief of the mice tail-less but now declares, "Not for the sake of your dignity, Reepicheep, but for the love that is between you and your people, and still more for the kindness your people showed me long ago . . . you shall have your tail again" (209). Perhaps Aslan has concluded that, as a result of his superficial loss of dignity, the Master Mouse has learned the intended lesson. When we meet Reepicheep again in *The Voyage of the Dawn Treader*, we will find, as Jonathan Rogers notes, an element of "self-forgetfulness" that defines his character (51), a quality Rogers points out will be in sharp contrast with Eustace's "self-absorption" (52). In *The Lion, the Witch and the Wardrobe*, readers were told that after his meeting with Aslan, Edmund "had got past thinking about himself" (141). The same could be said for Reepicheep.

True freedom, Rogers concludes, is "freedom from the self, freedom to turn one's attention outward, toward the things that give purpose and meaning" (52). Those characters in the Chronicles of Narnia who come to this position of self-forgetfulness discover liberty, real liberty. Those who do not—characters such as Miraz, Nikabrik, Glozelle, and Sopespian—remain "trapped in a prison of their own making" (53). If in the third Chronicle Reepicheep demonstrates a greater freedom from vanity, if he possesses a greater quantity of self-forgetfulness, here in *Prince Caspian* Lewis gives us a glimpse at the process of transformation.

A Woodland Bonfire on Midsummer Night

The great victory at Beruna is followed by a great victory feast. As was the case with the Pevensies' coronation feast in the final chapter of *The Lion, the Witch and the Wardrobe*, Lewis's great meals are neither as memorable nor as moving as his more humble ones. Walter Hooper argues this point in *Past Watchful Dragons*, observing, "Sumptuous feasts very properly follow coronations and victories, but I suspect most of us are more vulnerable to the descriptions of the more ordinary Narnian fare" (82).

The events foretold, but not assured, in the great dance of Tarva and Alambil find their culmination here in a final dance, as Bacchus and Silenus lead a "magic dance of plenty" (211). Wherever their hands and feet touch, a great feast springs into existence. Lewis provides readers with one of the collage-style lists he used to great effect in the first book. We are told of "sides of roasted meat that filled the grove with delicious smell, and wheaten cakes and oaten cakes, honey and many-colored sugars and cream as thick as porridge and as smooth as still water, peaches, nectarines, pomegranates, pears, grapes, strawberries, raspberries—pyramids and cataracts of fruit." The feast is complemented with a variety of wines—"dark, thick ones like syrups of mulberry juice, and clear red ones like red jellies liquefied, and yellow wines and green wines and yellow-green and greenish-yellow"—which are served in "great wooden cups and bowls and mazers."

Perhaps because there is so much abundance, and much of it so extravagant, the feast Bacchus supplies here may not stay in our minds the way Mr. Tumnus's tea for Lucy does in *The Lion, the Witch and the Wardrobe*, with its "nice brown egg, lightly boiled, for each of them, and then sardines on toast, and then buttered toast, and then toast with honey, and then a sugar-topped cake" (15). The same could be said about the delightful and homey supper of "good freshwater fish" that the children shared with the Beavers, with its "great and gloriously sticky marmalade roll" (74) or, in this story, the dinner with Trumpkin of bear meat and apples.

Perhaps another factor is at work here as well. In *The Last Battle*, Jewel will tell Jill that in between the adventures recorded in the Chronicles, there were hundreds and thousands of years when "notable dances and feasts, or at most tournaments" are the only important events (100). These times of peace and plenty, these "good, ordinary times" as Jill calls them, do not make for particularly memorable tales, which is why Lewis sticks to writing about the times of conflict. Perhaps Lewis's lavish celebration feasts are less poignant than the more commonplace meals taken along the way because the journey has been more interesting than the arrival, at least in the first two books.

The victory banquet takes on a more special feeling near its end. The narrator reports, "Thus Aslan feasted the Narnians till long after the sunset had died away, and the stars had come out; and the great fire, now hotter but less noisy, shone like a beacon in the dark woods. . . . As the talk grew quieter and slower, one after another would begin to nod and finally drop off to sleep with feet toward the fire and good friends on either side" (212–13). Readers familiar with *The Four Loves* may be reminded of a similar passage where Lewis, drawing from his own experience with friends, states, "Those are the golden sessions; when four or five of us after a hard day's walking have come to our inn; . . . our feet spread out towards the blaze and our drinks at our elbows; when the whole world, and something beyond the world opens itself to our minds as we talk" (72). At moments like these, Lewis concludes, "Each member of the circle feels, in his secret heart, humbled before all the rest. Sometimes he wonders what he is doing there among his betters. He is lucky beyond desert to be in such company."

In this description of Caspian's forces gradually dozing off around the embers of the victory bonfire, we are shown perhaps more clearly than anywhere else in *Prince Caspian* what the War of Deliverance, as it will come to be called, was fought for. The wholesome, ordinary goodness that permeates this scene assures readers that here, at long last, wrong has been made right, what was lost has been restored, and Narnia is Narnia again. Back in chapter ten, Aslan promised Lucy that all Narnia would be renewed. And so, at last, it has been. As Thomas Howard comments, "It is a theme right at the center of all of Lewis's vision: simplicity, good fellowship, the goodness of creation, the sheer pleasure of good tastes and smells and textures. . . . What are all wars and all economics and all politics about? Do they not all come down in the end to the business of allowing people to return to their hearthsides and to family and friends and good fellowship?" (41).

The final volume of the Chronicles of Narnia, *The Last Battle*, will end with a great cast of characters in a long procession further up and further in to Aslan's Country. We are not told what kinds of experiences they go on to share, but surely this scene of fellowship around a fire's glowing coals must have been one they go on to repeat often.

Aslan Provides Another Home

The next day messengers are sent all over the country to the scattered Telmarines, informing them that "Caspian was now King" (213) and that Narnia would "henceforth" belong to the Old Narnians "quite as much as to the men" (214). It could be argued that Caspian will not technically assume his kingship until after his coronation, and that rather than "henceforth," Narnia "once again" will belong to all its residents, but Lewis is not concerned with strict accuracy here. His point is that the humans—and this includes the human rulers—will no longer have a privileged status above the other residents of Narnia.

Any of the Telmarines who so choose may stay in Narnia under these conditions. Aslan promises to provide "another home" for anyone who will not fully submit to the new order (214). Nikabrik demonstrated the problems caused by a lack of true allegiance, problems that never go away but only get worse. When Peter, Edmund, Susan, and Lucy assumed their thrones at the end of *The Lion, the Witch and the Wardrobe*, only "remnants" of the Witch's forces remained (183). Here readers are told that more than half of the Telmarines turn up to leave Narnia on the appointed day. Earlier it was noted that while he does not join in the fighting this time, Aslan has been busy in a number of ways, providing help in various forms. Here in the final chapter, Aslan undertakes yet one more task, one that only he can accomplish: the problem of what to do with the great number of Telmarines who refuse to live in a world where they cannot be in control.

Early in the novel when Caspian first learned how the Telmarines had silenced the trees and streams and driven the Old Narnians into hiding, his response was, "Oh, I do wish we hadn't" (51). Readers learned a significant fact in Doctor Cornelius's reply: "Many of your race wish that in secret" (52). Caspian's tutor has not been the only character forced to appear as something he was not. A portion of the Telmarines opposed Miraz's policies, although they were less open in their opposition, perhaps out of necessity. Here readers are told more about this Telmarine minority: "Some of them, chiefly the young ones, had, like Caspian, heard stories of the Old Days and were delighted that they had come back. They were already making friends with the creatures" (214). Aslan has liberated not just the Old Narnians; here the good Telmarines are also freed to return to their real selves.

With the emphasis in *Prince Caspian* on a later, more complicated period in life, entire groups of people, such as the Telmarines and the dwarfs, will not be painted with a broad brush, as either all good or all bad. When Lewis provides a detailed portrait of the Calormenes in *The Horse and His Boy*, he will again refuse to categorize a whole group in a single way.

The other Telmarines, many of them older men who had been important under Miraz, are not happy with either of Aslan's offers. They do not want to remain in Narnia but are distrustful of Aslan's pledge of a new home. Like the travelers Lewis depicts in *The Great Divorce* who are unhappy in both hell and heaven, nothing will satisfy them. Still clinging to their notions of superiority, the bitter Telmarines reject the prospect of living in Narnia with "a lot of blooming performing animals" and the spirits of the trees, whom they disdainfully label as "ghosts" (214). They complain about Aslan's proposal to give them a home elsewhere: "Take us off to his den and eat us one by one most likely" (215). The narrator points out that the more these sulky and suspicious Telmarines talk to one another, the "sulkier and more suspicious" they become. In *The Great Divorce*, the guide George MacDonald comments on this kind of attitude to the narrator: "Ye call it the Sulks. But in adult life it has a hundred fine names—Achilles' wrath and Coriolanus' grandeur, Revenge and Injured Merit and Self-Respect and Tragic Greatness and Proper Pride" (69).

After the children's return from Narnia at the end of *The Lion, the Witch and the Wardrobe*, the Professor told them they should not try to use the same route twice to get to Narnia. As a lesson in trust for the Pevensies and as a storytelling device for Lewis, each of the successive journeys between Narnia and England will be different in some way. Here in *Prince Caspian*, Aslan has caused a doorway to be set up. Made of two stakes of wood with a third bound across the top, it looks like a "doorway from nowhere into nowhere" (215).

As Paul Ford has noted, "Doors are a recurrent Narnian motif" (175). A brief listing of doors, doorlike structures, and doorways in the Chronicles shows their prominence. At the start of *The Lion, the Witch and the Wardrobe*, the children discovered an entire country behind the wardrobe door, and at the adventure's conclusion they found their own country still waiting on the door's other side. In *Prince Caspian*, the children will be returned to the British train platform by way of this strange doorway of stakes. In *The Voyage of the Dawn Treader*, Edmund, Lucy, and Eustace will return to England through Aslan's "door in the sky" (248). Jill and Eustace will travel through a real door in the stone wall of Experiment House in *The Silver Chair*. The Narnians in *The Last Battle* will pass out of their world through the door of a stable. Earlier in *Prince Caspian*, Aslan told Lucy, "Things never happen the same way twice" (143), and this becomes one of the messages Lewis communicates clearly through his very different doors between worlds.

Aslan tells the Telmarines, "I will send you all to your own country, which I know and you do not" (216). The lion then reveals that the Telmarines were originally pirates who came to Telmar from an island in Earth's South Sea. It is to this island, which Aslan states "is no bad place" (218), that they will be returned. After learning he was a descendant of shipwrecked pirates, some of whom were murderers and drunkards, Caspian admits to Aslan, "I was wishing that I came of a more honorable lineage" (218).

In his book *Not a Tame Lion*, Bruce Edwards has argued, "The dramatic climax of the story is not the victory over King Miraz in battle but the discovery of King Caspian's true lineage—he, too, is a son of Adam" (74). In a moving declaration that Paul Ford has called "one of the most important statements in the Chronicles about the dignity and humility of the human race" (66), Aslan addresses the boy king's discouragement, saying, "You come of the Lord Adam and the Lady Eve, and that is both honor enough to erect the head of the poorest beggar, and shame enough to bow the shoulders of the greatest emperor on earth. Be content" (218).

As if in support of Aslan's statement, which is as true for the rest of the Telmarines as it is for Caspian, "a burly, decent-looking fellow" among them becomes the first to accept Aslan's gift of transit (218). Aslan breathes on him, and readers are told, "A new look came into the man's eyes—startled, but not unhappy—as if he were trying to remember something" (219). Presumably what the man is trying to remember is the noble side of being human, the honor he seems to have misplaced or forgotten until now.

When the man walks boldly through the doorway and vanishes, the remaining Telmarines immediately "set up a wailing" (219), and Lewis takes this opportunity for a final look at the topic of seeing and believing. One of the "clever" Telmarines objects to Aslan, "We don't see any other world through those sticks. If you want us to believe in it, why doesn't one of *you* go? All your own friends are keeping well away from the sticks" (219–20). Reepicheep at once steps forward, volunteering to prove Aslan's good faith by stepping through the arch with his band of mice, but the lion has other plans.

Aslan tells Reepicheep that if he and his troupe were to use the doorway to travel to Earth, "They would do dreadful things to you in that world" (220), a statement suggesting that the majority of humans would be more like the Telmarines than the Pevensies. Aslan does not go into detail about what exactly these "dreadful things" might be. In his essay titled "Vivisection," Lewis expressed serious concerns about "the infliction of pain" upon animals in the name of science (225). Readers might imagine that in addition to making Reepicheep perform like a circus animal, the inhabitants of our world would do other, even crueler things to an unusually large, talking mouse.

Like his earlier explanation of the Telmarines' origins, Aslan's words here to Reepicheep make it clear that he has a knowledge of conditions beyond Narnia and that Narnia is not the only world he knows and visits.

Well! We *Have* Had a Time

Peter suddenly tells the others, "Come on, our time's up" (220). He reveals that Aslan has talked with him and Susan about their departure and about "other things" but states, "I can't tell it to you all. There were things he wanted to say to Su and me because we're not coming back to Narnia" (221). Readers might recall that in *The Lion, the Witch and the Wardrobe*, Edmund also had a private talk with Aslan, and the narrator also made a point about its privacy: "There is no need to tell you (and no one ever heard) what Aslan was saying, but it was a conversation which Edmund never forgot" (139). Paul Ford has suggested, "Respect for the privacy of 'one's own story' is important in Narnia. Lewis himself had an intense sense of privacy, and this theme is apparent in the Chronicles" (351).

So what were these "things" that Aslan wanted to say to Peter and Susan since they are leaving Narnia for good? We never find out. However, in *The Voyage of the* Dawn Treader we will be told Aslan's final words to Edmund and Lucy when they learn they will not return to Narnia. Aslan informs them that henceforth they will meet him in their own world, telling them, "There I have another name. You must learn to know me by that name. This was the very reason why you were brought to Narnia, that by knowing me here for a little, you may know me better there" (247). It might be expected that Aslan's final conversation with Peter and Susan here in *Prince Caspian* took a somewhat similar direction.

When the children tumbled out of the wardrobe at the end of the first book, they were magically dressed in their original clothes in a way never explained. Since *Prince Caspian* is a somewhat more realistic book, this time Lewis provides the mechanism for the exchange. Under the cover of trees, the four change back into their school clothes, which have been brought in bundles from Caspian's castle. After affectionate good-byes to "all their old friends" and a wonderful and terrible farewell to Aslan himself (222), they line up with Peter in front, the other three behind him, and the Telmarines behind them. As they march through the door, there is a moment when they can see "three things at once"—the Telmarines' island, the glade in Narnia, and the gray surface of the train platform. As the children look back on the glade, they see "the faces of Dwarfs and Beasts, the deep eyes of Aslan, and the white patches on the Badger's cheeks." This is the last image of Narnia Peter and Susan will have. The next moment, they all find themselves sitting on the train platform in the country station "as if they had never moved from it" (223).

At the end of *The Voyage of the* Dawn Treader, Lewis will have the narrator step in to give a final report on what happens in Narnia after Edmund, Lucy, and Eustace are gone. Readers find out that Caspian and his men get safely back to Narnia and that Caspian went on to marry Ramandu's daughter. Here in *Prince Caspian*, we never learn what Caspian's first days as king were like. We are not told whether his aunt Prunaprismia and his baby cousin were among the Telmarines who stayed in Narnia and, if so, whether they all got along or not. We never know if Glozelle was killed in battle after he murdered Miraz or if he ever stood trial for his crime. Back in chapter seven, Pattertwig was sent to Lantern Waste while Trumpkin went on the shorter journey to Cair Paravel. Readers can only assume that the resourceful squirrel made it back safely and was told the good news that help from Susan's horn did come, although in its own way and its own time. In the first book, Aslan "quietly slipped away" relatively soon after establishing the four kings and queens on their thrones (182). Aslan is still in Narnia at the end of *Prince Caspian*. Readers never learn how long he stays to help Caspian.

Here at the end of the second volume of the Chronicles of Narnia, we are not so naive to think that the Narnians the Pevensies leave behind will simply live happily ever after. We, like the four children themselves, have learned something and are a little more mature. Before Miraz there was the White Witch, and after him there will be other tyrants who will want to seize Narnia for their own and turn it aside from the course Aslan has set for it. But for now, Peter, Susan, Edmund, and Lucy have left their beloved Narnia in good hands. In *The Voyage of the* Dawn Treader, Caspian will report to Edmund that after three years of his reign, "it couldn't be better. There's no trouble at all now between Telmarines, Dwarfs, Talking Beasts, Fauns and the rest" (20).

Prince Caspian has all along been about a later stage in the four children's development. They are older in this book than the first. In fact, Peter and Susan are too old to return to Narnia again. Because the children are older, people, situations, and choices have a greater complexity. Aslan himself is not the same as before but appears bigger to them. Peter, who could be said to be speaking for all of them, concludes, "It's all rather different from what I thought" (221). And this is what growing up looks like: old expectations are overturned; new ways of seeing are introduced. One of the most significant changes is that instead of calling for help, the children *are* the help. This realization always comes as a surprise, but Lewis's point is that it makes sense when it does come. Just as the four Pevensies have depended on Aslan for help, he increasingly depends on them to serve as his agents in providing help. And Lewis would have us understand that this is as it should be.

On the final page of *Prince Caspian*, as the children sit on the gray, gravelly platform with their luggage piled around them, everything seems "a little flat and dreary" compared to what they have been through, but only for a moment (223). As has already been mentioned, Lewis does not want his readers to despise real woods because they have read of enchanted ones, and he does not want his protagonists to find their own world somehow diminished because they have been to Narnia. He wants the journey to cause all real things in the Pevensies' world to be a little enchanted. And so they are. After a moment, everything seems "unexpectedly nice in its own way" (223), and this nice feeling is meant to contrast with the "gloomy" mood that hung over the train platform as they waited in chapter one (4).

What exactly seems unexpectedly nice in its own way? We are meant to think perhaps everything does, but Lewis lists three ordinary elements in particular that take on this special flavor. The four children experience "the familiar railway smell," they see "the English sky," and they contemplate "the summer term before them" (223). In these three commonplace elements, we find what might be labeled a *sacramental ordinary*, a deeply rooted sense of enjoyment and appreciation of the commonplace that was an essential part of Lewis's life.

Lewis employed a similar celebration of the ordinary at the end of *Out of the Silent Planet*, where Ransom returns to England from his travels to a distant world. Lewis finishes the story this way:

> He contrived to get into a lane, then into a road, then into a village street. A lighted door was open. There were voices from within and they were speaking English. There was a familiar smell. He pushed his way in, regardless of the surprise he was creating, and walked to the bar.
>
> "A pint of bitter, please," said Ransom. (149)

Lewis's love for and delight in everyday things began during his youth and was encouraged by his boyhood friend Arthur Greeves. In his autobiography, *Surprised by Joy*, Lewis writes about the special appreciation of the "homely" that Greeves helped to instill in him:

> But for him I should never have known the beauty of the ordinary vegetables that we destine to the pot. "Drills," he used to say. "Just ordinary drills of cabbages—what can be better?" And he was right. Often he recalled my eyes from the horizon just to look through a hole in a hedge, to see nothing more than a farmyard in its mid-morning solitude, and perhaps a gray cat squeezing its way under a barn door,

or a bent old woman with a wrinkled, motherly face coming back with an empty bucket from the pigsty. (157)

George Sayer has written that "the most precious moments to Jack in his ordinary life" were those times when he "was aware of the spiritual quality of material things, of the infusion of the supernatural into the workaday world" (317). And it is just this element that Lewis gives us a taste of, and perhaps a taste for, here in *Prince Caspian*.

In his last words in the book, Peter concludes, "Well! We *have* had a time" (223). Given their last-second rescue of Trumpkin, the bear attack, their dangerous brush with the sentry outpost, the two beheadings, Peter's nearly fatal combat with Miraz, the destruction of the bridge, and the victorious battle, this is British understatement at its best. Edmund then declares, "Bother! I've left my new torch in Narnia." And this becomes the story's final sentence.

On one level, Edmund's declaration is Lewis's way of adding a button to this scene, his way to end the book with a laugh. Lewis used this same device at the end of *The Lion, the Witch and the Wardrobe*, where he had the Professor declare, "Bless me, what *do* they teach them at these schools?" (189). He will end *The Magician's Nephew* with a similar kind of tag as Uncle Andrew comments about Jadis, "She was a dem fine woman, sir, a dem fine woman" (202). But Edmund's announcement serves as more than just a lighthearted comment. It can also be seen as Lewis's way of giving a sense of unity and completeness to the novel. Since the children used the flashlight to search in the treasure chamber of Cair Paravel back in chapter two, mentioning it here helps to remind us of this beginning and of all that has taken place since then.

After the children returned in *The Lion, the Witch and the Wardrobe*, they had the problem of the Professor's missing coats to solve. In the process of tying up this loose end, Lewis was also able to have the children make an important connection with a wise grown-up. Here in *Prince Caspian*, the children do not discuss their adventure with anyone else, nor should they. Now experienced travelers themselves, they have no need for the kind of advice they received following the first trip. In addition, Edmund's flashlight is not a loose end in the way the missing coats were. Since we are never told he lost it, there is no reason why it cannot still be in his pocket. So why bring it up?

Back in chapter two, readers were told that Edmund's electric torch "had been a birthday present less than a week ago" (24). In addition to helping end the book on a light note and providing a feeling of completeness, Lewis uses Edmund's missing flashlight to say something about Edmund and, by extension, about all four children. If Edmund were a normal boy of eleven, if he had not made two journeys to Narnia, we might expect him to be quite upset at having lost a prized birthday present, particularly in 1941 when such gifts were harder to come by. Here Edmund is bothered by the loss—he is still a boy—but he is not *overly* bothered. Through their adventures in Narnia, he and his siblings have come to know what matters most—in any world. The loss of Edmund's torch cannot compare to all they have gained.

Conclusion

And so we come to the close of Lewis's second Chronicle of Narnia, with the children right back where they started—sitting on a bench on an empty train platform, their trunks and playboxes stacked around them. Lewis started writing his second Narnia tale about a boy named Digory who could understand the speech of trees, but he ended up with a story of how Aslan gave speech back to trees that had been silenced.

We leave Peter, Susan, Edmund, and Lucy here at the sleepy country station, waiting for the trains that will take them to their separate schools. They have taken the next step in their development and have experienced a more complex time of life, a time when people and circumstances are not as easily divided into good and evil, a time when decisions are more difficult. The difficulties they have faced have not just revealed their character; they have, in part, helped create that character. If readers glance at Pauline Baynes's illustration of the four children tumbling out of the wardrobe at the end of *The Lion, the Witch and the Wardrobe* and compare it to the picture of them here as they suddenly find themselves sitting on the train platform, it is clear that all four Pevensies are significantly older than when they came back the first time.

What the illustrations cannot show is that Peter, Susan, Edmund, and Lucy are also wiser. And so are we if, as we have traveled with them, we have been careful to learn the same lessons they have.

Discussion Questions

Gilbert Meilaender makes the following observations about the indirect way Lewis teaches moral lessons through the use of the Narnia stories: "Moral education which interests Lewis does not look much like teaching. One cannot have classes in it. It involves the inculcation of proper emotional response and is as much a 'knowing how' as a 'knowing that.' It cannot be taught by listening to a lecture or filling out a worksheet" (212). Meilaender maintains that Lewis, like Aristotle, believed that moral principles "are learned indirectly." He concludes, "This is also the clue to understanding the place of the Chronicles of Narnia within Lewis's thought. They are not just good stories. Neither are they primarily Christian allegories (in fact, they are not allegories at all). Rather, they serve to enhance moral education, to build character. They teach, albeit indirectly, and provide us with exemplars from whom we learn proper emotional responses" (212–13).

No one has read the Chronicles of Narnia and said, "I want to be like Edmund when he was betraying his brother and sisters" or "I want to be just like Miraz." We want to be courageous and compassionate like Lewis's protagonists, to share their loyalty, kindness, resilience, and resoluteness. Lewis's stories convince us we do not want to have the negative qualities of his antagonists, to be treacherous, cowardly, cruel, or selfish.

Earlier it was claimed that Lewis's insights about life are powerful and deeply moving *because*, not *despite*, the fact they occur in the make-believe world of Narnia, that we are able to see the truth of

Lewis's statements about the human condition with greater clarity and poignancy because they are conveyed in a fairy-tale land. Listed below the following questions are the themes and moral lessons that have been presented through the characters and events of *Prince Caspian*.

1. Are there other themes, or generalizations about life, presented in *Prince Caspian* that you would add to the list below?
2. Where do we see these themes in the other Chronicles?
3. Which of these themes seems to be most important in your life at the moment?

Themes Explored in *Prince Caspian*

1. Evil appears rarely as evil but typically under some other guise.
2. Help often comes in an unanticipated form, in a manner that is so unexpected and strange that it may be recognized as help only in looking back on it.
3. Real community is made up of different types of individuals with different gifts and different abilities.
4. Celebration, joy, and merriment are central to life, not elements reserved only for holidays or vacations.
5. The virtuous life is an adventure, one with hardship that must be taken seriously, but one not to be missed because it is the only path that leads to genuine happiness, real fulfillment, and true community.
6. A life without virtue is not glamorous, fun, or exciting but rather is petty, spiteful, dominating, and devouring.
7. In some ways, small, everyday suffering is harder to bear than the greater, more majestic kind.
8. Right ruling requires a proper stance toward not just the subjects but also the land being governed.
9. True freedom is freedom from the self, freedom to turn one's attention outward, toward the things that give purpose and meaning.

Works Cited

Ashliman, D. L. *Folk and Fairy Tales: A Handbook.* Westport, CT: Greenwood, 2004.

Carretero-Gonzalez, Margarita. "Sons of Adam, Daughters of Eve, and Children of Aslan: An Environmental Perspective on *The Chronicles of Narnia.*" In *C. S. Lewis: Life, Works, and Legacy.* Vol. 2. Westport, CT: Praeger, 2007.

Chesterton, G. K. "The Red Angel." In *Tremendous Trifles.* Middlesex, UK: The Echo Library, 2006.

Colbert, David. *The Magical Worlds of Narnia.* New York: Berkley, 2005.

Davis, Bill. "Extreme Makeover: Moral Education and the Encounter with Aslan." In *The Chronicles of Narnia and Philosophy.* Edited by Gregory Bassham, Jerry L. Walls, and William Irwin. Chicago: Open Court, 2005.

Dickens, Charles. *Little Dorrit.* New York: Penguin, 1998.

Downing, David. *Into the Region of Awe: Mysticism in C. S. Lewis.* Downers Grove, IL: InterVarsity Press, 2005.

Duriez, Colin. *A Field Guide to Narnia.* Downers Grove, IL: InterVarsity Press, 2004.

Edwards, Bruce. *Not a Tame Lion.* Wheaton, IL: Tyndale, 2005.

Filmer, Kath. *The Fiction of C. S. Lewis: Mask and Mirror.* New York: St. Martin's Press, 1993.

Focus on the Family Radio Theatre. *Prince Caspian: The Return to Narnia.* Wheaton, IL: Tyndale, 2000.

Ford, Paul F. *Companion to Narnia.* Rev. ed. New York: HarperSan-Francisco, 2005.

Gibson, Evan. C. S. *Lewis: Spinner of Tales.* Grand Rapids: Christian University Press, 1980.

Glover, Donald. C. S. *Lewis: The Art of Enchantment.* Athens, OH: Ohio University Press, 1981.

Green, Roger Lancelyn, and Walter Hooper. C. S. *Lewis: A Biography.* New York: Harvest, 2002.

Gresham, Douglas. *Jack's Life.* Nashville: Broadman & Holman, 2005.

Hinten, Marvin. *The Keys to the Chronicles.* Nashville: Broadman & Holman, 2005.

Hooper, Walter. C. S. *Lewis: A Companion and Guide.* New York: HarperCollins, 1996.

———. *Past Watchful Dragons: A Guide to C. S. Lewis's Chronicles of Narnia.* London: Fount, 1980.

Howard, Thomas. *The Achievement of C. S. Lewis.* Wheaton, IL: Harold Shaw, 1980.

Jacobs, Alan. *The Narnian: The Life and Imagination of C. S. Lewis.* New York: HarperSanFrancisco, 2005.

Kocher, Paul. *Master of Middle-Earth: The Fiction of J. R. R. Tolkien.* New York: Ballantine, 1972.

Lewis, C. S. *The Abolition of Man.* New York: Collier, 1955.

———. *The Collected Letters of C. S. Lewis: Narnia, Cambridge, and Joy 1950–1963.* Vol. 3. Edited by Walter Hooper. New York: HarperSanFrancisco, 2007.

———. *The Discarded Image.* Cambridge: Cambridge University Press, 2004.

———. *English Literature in the Sixteenth Century.* Oxford: Oxford University Press, 1954.

———. *The Four Loves.* New York: Harvest, 1988.

———. *The Great Divorce.* New York: Touchstone, 1974.

———. *A Grief Observed*. New York: HarperSanFrancisco, 1961.

———. "*The Hobbit*." In *On Stories and Other Essays on Literature*. Edited by Walter Hooper. New York: Harvest, 1982.

———. *The Horse and His Boy*. New York: Harper Trophy, 1994.

———. *The Last Battle*. New York: Harper Trophy, 1994.

———. *Letters of C. S. Lewis*. Edited by W. H. Lewis and Walter Hooper. New York: Harvest, 1993.

———. *Letters to an American Lady*. Grand Rapids: Eerdmans, 1971.

———. *Letters to Children*. Edited by Lyle W. Dorsett and Marjorie Lamp Mead. New York: Touchstone, 1995.

———. *Letters to Malcolm: Chiefly on Prayer*. New York: Harvest, 1992.

———. *The Lion, the Witch and the Wardrobe*. New York: Harper Trophy, 1994.

———. *The Magician's Nephew*. New York: Harper Trophy, 1994.

———. "Membership." In *The Weight of Glory and Other Addresses*. New York: HarperSanFrancisco, 2001.

———. *Mere Christianity*. New York: HarperSanFrancisco, 2001.

———. "Miracles." In *God in the Dock*. Grand Rapids: Eerdmans, 1996.

———. *Miracles*. New York: Touchstone, 1996.

———. "On Stories." In *On Stories and Other Essays on Literature*. Edited by Walter Hooper. New York: Harvest, 1982.

———. "On Three Ways of Writing for Children." In *On Stories and Other Essays on Literature*. Edited by Walter Hooper. New York: Harvest, 1982.

———. *Out of the Silent Planet*. New York: Scribner, 1996.

———. *Perelandra*. New York: Scribner, 2003.

———. *A Preface to Paradise Lost*. Oxford: Oxford University Press, 1961.

———. "Preface to the 1961 Edition." In *The Screwtape Letters*. New York: Macmillan, 1982.

———. *Prince Caspian*. New York: Harper Trophy, 1994.

———. *The Problem of Pain*. New York: Touchstone, 1996.

————. *The Screwtape Letters*. New York: Touchstone, 1996.

————. *The Silver Chair*. New York: Harper Trophy, 1994.

————. *Spirits in Bondage*. New York: Harvest, 1984.

————. *Surprised by Joy*. New York: Harvest, 1955.

————. *That Hideous Strength*. New York: Scribner, 2003.

————. "Vivisection." In *God in the Dock*. Grand Rapids: Eerdmans, 1996.

————. *The Voyage of the Dawn Treader*. New York: Harper Trophy, 1994.

————. "The Weight of Glory." In *The Weight of Glory and Other Addresses*. New York: HarperSanFrancisco, 2001.

Manlove, Colin. *C. S. Lewis: His Literary Achievement*. New York: St. Martin's Press, 1987.

Meilaender, Gilbert. *The Taste for the Other: The Social and Ethical Thought of C. S. Lewis*. Grand Rapids: Eerdmans, 1998.

Mills, David. "The Writer of Our Story: Divine Providence in *The Lord of the Rings*." *Touchstone* 15, January/February 2002, 22–28.

Myers, Doris T. *C. S. Lewis in Context*. Kent, OH: Kent State University Press, 1994.

Perrine, Laurence, and Thomas Arp. *Literature: Structure, Sound, and Sense*. 6th ed. New York: Harcourt Brace, 1993.

Plato. *The Republic*. Mineola, NY: Dover, 2000.

Rogers, Jonathan. *The World According to Narnia: Christian Meaning in C. S. Lewis's Beloved Chronicles*. New York: FaithWords, 2005.

Ryken, Leland, and Marjorie Lamp Mead. *A Reader's Guide Through the Wardrobe*. Downers Grove, IL: InterVarsity Press, 2005.

Sayer, George. *Jack: A Life of C. S. Lewis*. Wheaton: Crossway, 1994.

Schakel, Peter. *Reading with the Heart: The Way into Narnia*. Grand Rapids: Eerdmans, 1979.

————. *The Way into Narnia: A Reader's Guide*. Grand Rapids: Eerdmans, 2005.

Senor, Thomas. "Trusting Lucy: Believing the Incredible." In *The Chronicles of Narnia and Philosophy*. Edited by Gregory Bassham, Jerry L. Walls, and William Irwin. Chicago: Open Court, 2005.

Shakespeare, William. *Hamlet*. New York: Cambridge University Press, 2005.

———. *Henry IV, Part I*. New York: Cambridge University Press, 1998.

———. *Love's Labors Lost*. New York: Oxford University Press, 2002.

———. *Macbeth*. New York: Oxford University Press, 1998.

———. *A Midsummer Night's Dream*. New York: Cambridge University Press, 2002.

———. *The Tempest*. New York: Cambridge University Press, 2005.

Shippey, Tom. *J. R. R. Tolkien: Author of the Century*. New York: Houghton Mifflin, 2000.

Tolkien, J. R. R. "*Beowulf*: The Monsters and the Critics." In *The Monsters and the Critics and Other Essays*. Edited by Christopher Tolkien. Boston: Houghton Mifflin, 1984.

———. *The Fellowship of the Ring*. Boston: Houghton Mifflin, 1994.

———. "Foreword to the Second Edition." In *The Fellowship of the Ring*. Boston: Houghton Mifflin, 1994.

———. *The Letters of J. R. R. Tolkien*. Edited by Humphrey Carpenter. Boston: Houghton Mifflin, 2000.

———. *The Return of the King*. Boston: Houghton Mifflin, 1994.

———. *The Two Towers*. Boston: Houghton Mifflin, 1994.

Devin Brown is a Lilly Scholar and professor of English at Asbury College. His book *Inside Narnia: A Guide to Exploring The Lion, the Witch and the Wardrobe* is currently in its sixth printing. His novel for young people, *Not Exactly Normal*, was named as one of Bank Street College's best children's books of the year. Devin and his wife, Sharon, live in Lexington, Kentucky, with their fifteen-pound cat, Mr. Fluff. Devin is currently serving as visiting writer-in-residence at Transylvania University.

INSIDE NARNIA
A Guide to Exploring The Lion, the Witch and the Wardrobe

The Chronicles of Narnia series has sold over 85 million copies worldwide and has single-handedly introduced people of all ages to the central doctrines of Christianity. Coinciding with the Walden Media/Walt Disney Pictures film *The Lion, the Witch and the Wardrobe*, this book guides readers through the novel that started it all.

Inside Narnia offers a close reading of *The Lion, the Witch and the Wardrobe*. Tracing through the book chapter by chapter, Devin Brown explores the features of C. S. Lewis's writing, supplies supplemental information on Lewis's life and other books, offers comments and opinions from other Lewis scholars, and shows the work's rich meanings. Insightful and thorough, *Inside Narnia* will dig deeper into Lewis's magical world to reveal biblical truths that often go uncovered. Fans of C. S. Lewis and those who meet him through the film will want to read this book.

"A close literary analysis . . . in a scholarly yet accessible manner, centering arguments around the belief that most Narnia books are primarily devotional rather than literary. This book often reads like an engaging running commentary rather than a mere collection of essays. Highly recommended."

—*Library Journal*

BakerBooks
a division of Baker Publishing Group
www.bakerbooks.com